"It's hard enough to forge a path in today's world of work without the constant stream of misleading cultural messages about career decision-making. That's why *101 Career Myths Debunked* is such an important book. In it, Elizabeth Campbell helps readers test their assumptions with practical, evidence-based guidance that really works. This is a go-to resource for anyone navigating a career transition, because in career development, wise choices are informed choices. I strongly recommend it!"

Bryan J. Dik, *PhD, Professor of Psychology at Colorado State University, author of* Redeeming Work, *and co-inventor of the PathwayU career assessment platform*

"As I read this book, I felt as if I was talking with a career coach who was teaching me how to think clearly about my career and life. Engaging with Dr. Campbell and her workbook will help you to make better choices and take more effective actions as you build your career. This workbook provides excellent career education and coaching strategies to help readers avoid common misconceptions that can stall career decision making and reduce job satisfaction."

Mark L. Savickas, *PhD, Professor of Career Counseling and author of* Career Adaptability

"Dr. Campbell empowers the reader to challenge their own limiting beliefs and gives them a template to bust through the career barriers that hold many of us back. If you feel trapped by your own flawed thinking and outdated programming, this well-researched and well-referenced book is the solution you need to guide you to your own authentic work-life journey."

Brock Armstrong, *movement coach and CBT practitioner at BrockArmstrong.com*

"An extremely helpful and insightful book! Campbell's sage advice and well-designed workbook will boost your motivation, brighten your mindset, and guide you through doable action steps to achieve your dreams. I've ordered several as graduation gifts, and the book would be just as useful for mid-life career changes. I would recommend it to anyone working on creating a rewarding career—and life."

Monica Reinagel, *author, coach, and co-host of the* Change Academy *podcast*

"I found myself nodding in agreement as I read *101 Career Myths Debunked*. It resonated closely with my own career journey and my identity as a lifelong learner. Dr. Campbell seamlessly articulates the thought processes and beliefs that so many who have achieved success acquired along the way. If you are looking for a roadmap to discovering what you are uniquely created to do and how to get there, this book is the perfect guide!"

Lisa Woodruff, *founder and CEO of Organize 365®*

"This workbook is a must read and must DO for anyone who wants to approach their career building with confidence! Whether you are brand new to the workforce, are switching careers, or simply want to get promoted in your current field, this book is full of simple but powerful ideas that will get you where you want to be."

Jill Angie, *life coach and CEO of Not Your Average Runner*

"*101 Career Myths Debunked* is a thought-provoking career planning workbook that dispels myths, provides facts, and inspires productivity. This workbook will help you manage your mindset, find your direction, and take action so you can achieve career success."

Marie Smith, *master trainer and instructor for the National Career Development Association*

101 Career Myths Debunked

What if everything you know about careers is false? Bombarded by toxic misinformation about unemployment and failing career prospects, job hunters are often halted by fear. *101 Career Myths Debunked* is essential reading for college students, job hunters, and career changers to discover the myths holding them back and reveal the surprising truths and practical steps that will set them on the path to career success.

Written by a counseling psychologist and career psychology expert, *101 Career Myths Debunked* is your personal career coach and ultimate planning guide. This easy-to-use workbook will show you how to boost your confidence and build a life you love. It walks you through the entire career development process and helps you deal successfully with everything you need to consider. You'll learn practical new ways to move forward from your present uncertainty into a promising future.

Elizabeth L. Campbell, PhD, a counseling psychologist specializing in career development, has over a decade of experience counseling, researching, and teaching about careers and the helping professions.

101 Career Myths Debunked

The Ultimate Career Planning Workbook

Elizabeth L. Campbell

Routledge
Taylor & Francis Group

NEW YORK AND LONDON

Cover image: Getty Images

First published 2023
by Routledge
605 Third Avenue, New York, NY 10158

and by Routledge
4 Park Square, Milton Park, Abingdon, Oxon, OX14 4RN

Routledge is an imprint of the Taylor & Francis Group, an informa business

Library of Congress Cataloging-in-Publication Data
Names: Campbell, Elizabeth L. (Psychologist), author.
Title: 101 career myths debunked : the ultimate career
planning workbook / Elizabeth L. Campbell.
Other titles: One hundred one career myths debunked
Description: New York, NY : Routledge, 2023. |
Includes bibliographical references and index. |
Identifiers: LCCN 2022001621 (print) |
LCCN 2022001622 (ebook) | ISBN 9780367195113 (hbk) |
ISBN 9780367195120 (pbk) | ISBN 9780429261770 (ebk)
Subjects: LCSH: Career development. |
Vocational guidance. | Job hunting.
Classification: LCC HF5381 .C2545 2022 (print) |
LCC HF5381 (ebook) | DDC 650.1–dc23/eng/20220404
LC record available at https://lccn.loc.gov/2022001621
LC ebook record available at https://lccn.loc.gov/2022001622

ISBN: 978-0-367-19511-3 (hbk)
ISBN: 978-0-367-19512-0 (pbk)
ISBN: 978-0-429-26177-0 (ebk)

DOI: 10.4324/9780429261770

Typeset in Palatino
by Newgen Publishing UK

Dedication

To my Mom and Dad, who made my career possible.

◼ Contents

■ List of Myths

Decision-Making Myths

Education Myths

Job-Hunting Myths

Working Myths

■ List of Actions

Decision-Making Actions

Education Actions

Job-Hunting Actions

Working Actions

■ Acknowledgments

Many thanks to all whose efforts helped me write this book. I'd like to express my heartfelt gratitude to everyone who contributed to the success of this project, including my students, clients, and supervisees. Further appreciation goes to the many research participants who responded to surveys, those of you who shared your experiences and stories, and those who took the time to offer feedback and recommend my work to others.

A big thanks to my research assistants and teaching assistants for their contributions, encouragement, useful critiques, and the gift of their time. Thank you to Kenzie Davidson and Spencer Davidson for their collaboration and writing on the initial career myth project. A special thanks to Jacob Floyd for his input and editing for the book, and for his illustration for the PALMS criteria—your ongoing support means the world. I'm especially indebted to Christopher Reichert—I can't tell you how much I value your input and appreciate you as my editor and friend.

Thank you to Routledge for helping me bring this book into the world and for your ongoing support of my work.

Finally, as I have expressed before and surely will again, I am forever grateful to Casey Pettitt, my loving family, and my wonderful cats for their constant love and support. Thank you for making all this possible.

You are all loved and appreciated!

Bethy

Chapter 1

Introduction

What if everything you know about careers is false? Career advice is everywhere. Whether you're a student, a first-time job hunter, or a mid-career changer, you have a lot to consider in your search. Information and resources are widely available, and everyone seems to know a lot about the subject. Some advice reflects valuable truths and helpful tidbits to move you toward a rewarding career choice, but much of the information we encounter is out-of-date, exaggerated, and outright nonsense that will scare you and hold you back. We have all heard the doom and gloom news associated with the job market and career prospects. But the truth is hardly as bad as it seems, and the likelihood of success is far more hopeful than much of the chatter would lead you to believe. The truth about careers is surprisingly motivating and will set you on the path to success.

If achieving your career goals is a journey, view this workbook as your map and me as your guide. I'm Elizabeth Campbell, a psychology professor and therapist specializing in career and vocational psychology. I have over a decade of experience counseling, researching, and teaching about careers and have worked with thousands of students and clients to help them cultivate a career and life they truly enjoy. I've learned the basic principles to career success and I'm eager to share them with you. If you want to learn the truth about career choices and planning with easy-to-follow guidance, this is the book for you! Thank you for the opportunity to accompany you on your career journey.

So – What is This Book Anyway?

Ideally, we would all have our own personal career counselor to support us at key moments of our careers. Unfortunately, this isn't realistic; career counseling may not be practical or available to everyone. That's why I wrote this workbook! My aim is to make career coaching accessible for anyone who wants to proactively manage their career. With this book, we can develop a very personal coaching relationship, and, as with all relationships, you'll get out of this what you put into it. I hope you choose to be an active participant with me, and not just a reader. No matter where you currently find yourself in your career journey, this workbook breaks down the path to success into manageable steps. Together we will explore the entire

DOI: 10.4324/9780429261770-1

career development process, learn to successfully navigate difficult choices, and implement practical new ways to move forward from your present uncertainty to a promising future.

To do that, we need to start with a confident and accurate mindset. Self-efficacy is the term for having a strong belief in your ability to be successful, and it's a foundational prerequisite to career development (Choi et al., 2012; Lent et al., 2002). You must believe to achieve. Self-efficacy is not simply positive thinking—it also necessitates accurate awareness of your capacity to manage the realities of the process (Choi et al., 2012). Through both a realistic understanding of the process and a genuinely positive mindset about your ability to be successful, you're ready to take the steps to achieve your dreams.

High self-efficacy prompts us to take action to achieve our goals. Unfortunately, most of the students and clients I work with begin with low self-efficacy, preventing them from acting on their plans. Research corroborates that low self-efficacy halts action toward career goal achievement (Paivandy et al., 2008). Plagued with misinformation about career development and beaten down by hopeless thinking, their self-confidence and beliefs in a bright future grow dim. As you turn to this workbook for help, you might find yourself with similarly low self-efficacy. As someone who's been there myself and supported others in hopeless spaces, my heart goes out to you. Please know you aren't lazy or broken, and success is still possible. You might be scared and confused, which is understandable given the career development process isn't well understood by most people and carries seemingly daunting consequences.

This is precisely why this book is different. More than just a compilation of action steps to follow, this workbook is grounded first in your mindset. Together we'll confront the career myths that bring down your self-efficacy through a process called cognitive restructuring (Beck, 2011), in which we reframe dysfunctional thoughts to more functional ones by challenging them with accurate information. Throughout this workbook, we'll identify dysfunctional thinking and learn the accurate and encouraging truths to refute them. In this way, this workbook will directly speak into your fears and alleviate them, bolstering your self-efficacy and equipping you for action. The combination of cognitive restructuring paired with clear action steps is suggested by research to be the best method for successful career development (Beck, 2011). Through addressing your thoughts and your actions, this workbook will provide you with the steps to follow and the motivation to complete them.

Background and Important Concepts

In my research, I've discovered that career confusion pervades even the very definition of the concept. The term *career* once signified a singular, short-term occupation. Now the terms *job* and *occupation* are used to denote single instances of paid employment, while *career* is a broad term synonymous with *vocation*, *mission*, and *calling*, representing a lifelong journey through a range of aspects of life, learning, and work (NCDA, 2017). Comprised of all the roles you assume throughout your lifespan, your career includes education and training, paid and unpaid work, volunteering, time with family and friends, leisure and hobby activities, and more.

Another concept we frequently use is *career development*, which is a lifelong process of understanding yourself and how you contribute to the larger world through these many different roles (Super, 1957). Your career development begins at birth as you create your self-concept and continues throughout life in your many social and occupational interactions. Within career development is a great deal of preparation and planning. As you select a particular path to pursue, countless *career choices* will emerge throughout your life (Holland, 1959). Each of these decision points represents an opportunity for planning and consideration, but also leaves you vulnerable to being stymied in your decision making by career myths.

Career myths are the falsehoods and bogus claims made about careers and the career development process (Pinkney & Ramirez, 1985). They represent dysfunctional thinking and lead to dissatisfaction and feelings of powerlessness (Otu & Omeje, 2021). Career myths are usually held as negative or self-defeating thoughts about ourselves and the world of work, and they do nothing but make us feel bad. For example, the dysfunctional thought, *there are no jobs for me*, is a myth that does not inspire much hope or motivation to engage in career planning. Believing that no jobs are available may keep you unemployed or in a job you hate out of fear that no other possibilities exist.

Career myths can present in different ways, but they are all sabotaging beliefs that hold you back from your goals. Despite their negative consequences, career myths most often present as pessimistic, such as, *I won't be accepted at my job for being different*; however, they can sometimes present as optimistic, such as, *I can avoid making mistakes*. Optimistic statements may seem motivating but will ultimately set you up for failure if they're unrealistic. In both cases, such self-statements ultimately promote a negative attitude that halts career development progress. With this kind of thinking, our ability to make sound and informed career decisions becomes seriously impaired, preventing positive changes to our current situation (Paivandy et al., 2008).

The career myths contained in this book are the result of several different sources: some career myths derive from fears that have been propagated and widely believed but debunked by new research studies. Others represent information that was once true but no longer accurately reflects the current job climate. And most career myths are simply exaggerations or misinformation that are presented as true and factual. They manifest our fears and supposed worst-case scenarios. Although career myths represent beliefs—some even long and widely held beliefs—they are completely false.

So what? The problem with these career myths is that they can interfere with your career journey, which is one of the most important aspects of your life. You can get seriously stuck. Research studies have demonstrated career myths' dangerous impact. One such study examined the relationship between career myths and career development difficulties of college students (Larson et al., 1988). The researchers found that career myths were related to career indecision, meaning that students who believed in career myths were less likely to make career choices. Career myths can paralyze us from moving forward in our career journey and finding true success.

In addition to halting progress toward goals, career myths are associated with a multitude of other detrimental effects including low self-esteem, high anxiety, career indecision, and poor overall performance (Paivandy et al., 2008). For example, the thought, *work cannot be enjoyable*, is a career myth. It primes a job seeker to expect work to be miserable and accept a job that confirms low expectations. The truth is that a great deal of satisfaction and enjoyment can and does come from work roles (Bolles, 2020). With some planning and preparation, you can maximize the possibility of finding work you love. But you cannot do it without first challenging the myth of inevitable discontent. This is essential because people tend to trust the messages they tell themselves. Our expectations affect our behaviors so considerably that it often causes our expectations to be fulfilled (Lent et al., 2002). Career myths hurt our career development and must be overturned to attain success.

Chances are you have already fallen victim to bad advice. Many have realized the danger of career myths and have taken steps to correct the problem. University career centers across the country have tried to combat the problem by developing their own fact sheets of common career myths and responses to help college students in their career journeys (e.g., Lock Haven University, n.d.). Online websites and blogs have attempted to do the same (e.g., Crosby, 2005). While I applaud their independent efforts, these resources are insufficient. Most sources present only a few myths; yet, taken together, it becomes clear there are many common career myths. Each resource targets a small audience and often requires membership to access the information, such as university career centers. Perhaps most importantly is the question of accuracy: although these myth/fact resources claim to present correct information, some of them replace common myths with new inaccuracies. The problem of widespread career myths remained, until now. This book aims to set the record straight.

How to Use This Book

This book is meant for all those who want to know the truth and plan ahead at all career stages. You might complete this workbook on your own, in counseling, or as part of a class or other group program. Depending on your needs and requirements, you may choose to complete or be assigned only parts or sections of the book. Work at your own pace and complete as much or as little as you need.

Return to this book often as it will grow with you as you progress in your career. Each chapter represents a different stage of the career development process. The book is divided into the following categories, organizing career myths about:

◆ career decision making and choosing a career in Chapter 2;
◆ education and preparing for a career in Chapter 3;
◆ job hunting and finding a career in Chapter 4; and
◆ working, building success, and changing careers in Chapter 5.

I recommend starting by choosing the chapter that best represents your current needs, then work through the myths of that chapter in order, without leaving any out, since each action builds on the previous one within each chapter. If you're not sure about where to start, begin with Chapter 2 and work through the book in order.

This book is divided into four primary sections, each covering a different stage of your career journey. But don't take this to mean that only one specific chapter can apply to you at any given time. Career journeys are rarely strict, linear progressions; you may go back and repeat steps—sometimes you may even skip one! No matter where you are in your voyage, this book is at your disposal in its entirety. Here there are no spoilers.

As the career development process is cyclical, all the activities contained in this book are relevant and useful to revisit throughout your career. Go through the chapters as needed for your current circumstances and return to them as new questions and circumstances arise. For instance, Chapter 2 helps you decide what career you want to pursue and is useful to review whenever you find yourself questioning or wanting to refine your career goals. Chapter 3 offers guidance for college students and includes helpful reappraisals of past college experience or future returns to school. Chapter 4 helps you on the job hunt, where you'll likely find yourself multiple times as you advance in your career. Chapter 5 offers guidance in working, building success, and considering possible changes. This can be valuable to periodically review in an ongoing process of refinement throughout our working lives.

As you complete each chapter, you'll notice that each is similarly structured. Within each subsequent chapter is several related career myths. Each *Myth* is numbered and stated in quotes as a truism (even though we know they're filthy lies!) For example, your first myth is listed as, "Myth 1: Choosing a career is easy." A *Fact* section immediately follows, providing you accurate information to dispel the myth and boost your motivation and confidence. Lastly, an *Action* section provides an activity to complete before moving to the next myth. Together, each action builds on the previous one to move you one step at a time through the career planning process. You may have heard the saying, "How do you eat an elephant? One bite at a time." Just like our elephant, each action in this workbook takes the big, complex tasks of career development and breaks them up into small, achievable bites.

Some actions are easier to complete than others, but every one of them is worth doing. Don't try to breeze through this workbook in a weekend. Action exercises introduce you to a variety of free online resources, guide you through outside activities, and prompt you for written reflections, so give yourself time to complete them. The actions work best when you can immerse yourself in deep reflection and research in a quiet and undisturbed space. Sometimes action steps will prompt you to talk to other people, but know that you can always ask those you trust for their input on any of the actions. Other people can provide ideas when you're uncertain how to answer or offer useful new perspectives and insights you may not have considered. Your response is always going to be very individual to you. If an exercise is unclear or merits adjustments for your situation, feel free to do so in a way that yields the best results for your planning and self-discovery. Focus on progress, not perfection.

Before you jump in, bookmark the workbook links available on my website. Several of the activities incorporate valuable free online resources, which you'll need to utilize to move forward in the workbook. A shortened URL of bit.ly/careermythlinks is included throughout the book but having the links already available saves you time and makes them much easier to access. I'll also update activities and replace any broken links on my website to maximize your workbook experience. You'll find the workbook links to all the free resources and my latest updates at:

elizabethlcampbell.com/careermythlinks

I wrote this book to provide you a simple and straightforward guide to successful career planning, with a collection of career myths, facts, and actions in one verified anthology. By the end, you'll understand things about career development that most people will never know. Most importantly, you'll put what you learn into practice to meet your goals and achieve career success. Wherever you are in your journey, I'm eager to walk with you and hope this book helps you take the next step. Let's get started!

Reach Out to Your Coach

You can find me online at elizabethlcampbell.com and I welcome you to reach out to me directly. If you have questions or would like to share your story of how this book helped you, I'd love to hear from you!

References

Beck, J. S. (2011). *Cognitive therapy: Basics and beyond* (2nd ed.). Guilford Press.

Bolles, R. N. (2020). *What color is your parachute? Job-hunter's workbook* (2020 ed.). Ten Speed Press.

Carr, D. L. (2004). *The effect of a workbook intervention on college students' reframes of dysfunctional career thoughts: Technical report 37.* https://career.fsu.edu/sites/g/files/imported/storage/original/application/5375846722108caedc58e8a9130a0249.doc

Choi, B. Y., Park, H., Yang, E., Lee, S. K., Lee, Y., & Lee, S. M. (2012). Understanding career decision self-efficacy: A meta-analytic approach. *Journal of Career Development, 39*(5), 443–460. https://doi.org/10.1177/0894845311398042

Crosby, O. (2005). Career myths and how to debunk them. *Occupational Outlook Quarterly.* www.bls.gov/careeroutlook/2005/fall/art01.pdf

Holland, J. L. (1959). A theory of vocational choice. *Journal of Counseling Psychology, 6*(1), 35–45. https://doi.org/10.1037/h0040767

Larson, L. M., Heppner, P. P., Ham, T., & Dugan, K. (1988). Investigating multiple subtypes of career indecision through cluster analysis. *Journal of Counseling Psychology, 35*(4), 439–446. https://doi.org/10.1037/0022-0167.35.4.439

Lent, R. W., Brown, S. D., Talleyrand, R., McPartland, E. B., Davis, T., Chopra, S. B., Alexander, M. S., Suthakaran, V., & Chai, C. M. (2002). Career choice barriers, supports, and coping strategies: College students' experiences. *Journal of Vocational Behavior, 60*(1), 61–72. https://doi.org/10.1006/jvbe.2001.1814

Lock Haven University Center for Career and Professional Development. (n.d.). *Top 10 career myths.* https://community.lhup.edu/careerservices/files/10CareerMyths.pdf

National Career Development Association (NCDA). (2017). *National Career Development Guidelines (NCDG) framework.* https://associationdatabase.com/aws/NCDA/asset_manager/get_file/3384?ver=3306476

Otu, M. S., & Omeje, J. C. (2021). The effect of rational emotive career coaching on dysfunctional career beliefs in recent university graduates. *Journal of Rational-Emotive & Cognitive-Behavior Therapy, 39,* 555–577. https://doi.org/10.1007/s10942-020-00383-y.

Paivandy, S., Bullock, E. E., Reardon, R. C., & Kelly, F. D. (2008). The effects of decision-making style and cognitive thought patterns on negative career thoughts. *Journal of Career Assessment, 16*(4), 474–488. https://doi.org/10.1177/1069072708318904

Pinkney, J. W., & Ramirez, M. (1985). Career planning myths of Chicano students. *Journal of College Student Personnel, 26*(4), 300–305.

Super, D. E. (1957). *The psychology of careers: An introduction to vocational development.* Harper & Bros.

Chapter 2

Decision Making

In this chapter, we break down decision-making myths, including "the right job will use all of my gifts and talents" and "career tests will tell me what I should do." We'll look at the facts and explore some actions you can take to boost your decision making. Actions will walk you through the process of selecting a career direction by evaluating and putting together factors of importance to you. If you're trying to decide what to pursue for a career, or just feel uncertain and want to refine your goals, start here!

Myth 1

"Choosing a career is easy."

Fact

Choosing a career is an involved process, and can be very challenging (Crosby, 2005), in some cases so challenging that progress slows or comes to a halt altogether. For example, avoidance of—or even complete withdrawal from—career planning is common, and can result in defaulting or blindly drifting into a career. The false belief that career choices are easy fails to acknowledge the inevitable challenges you'll face along the way and, when unanticipated hardships strike, will leave you vulnerable to the self-blame that commonly results and halts progress toward career goals (Germer, 2009).

If you're struggling to make career decisions, you're not alone. Surveys by the Rockport Institute show these challenges are widespread among people at all levels of career development. One survey found that 64% of college seniors had serious doubts as to whether they chose the right major, while 70% of successful professionals reported that they didn't know how to go about making competent decisions and could have done a much better job making life choices (Lore, 2011). In fact, most people put more energy into buying a car or scheduling a vacation than they do into career planning (Lore, 2011). If you find yourself stuck and struggling with career indecision, you're in the majority.

Refuse to let these struggles hold you back by facing them directly. This is an involved process for most everyone and it is normal to struggle, but don't let that stop you. Understand the investment is well worth it; deliberate and intentional career planning and decision making is linked with reduced future difficulties and increased long-term satisfaction and success (Weitzman & Fitzgerald, 1996).

DOI: 10.4324/9780429261770-2

The first step in embracing the challenge is to understand it. Choosing a career isn't easy because it isn't a singular choice but rather a series of experiences and choices over an extended period. Career development is a lifelong process of understanding yourself and how you contribute to the world through many different roles (Super, 1957). It begins at birth as you start to develop your self-concept, and continues throughout life in your many social and occupational interactions. In this way, we are always developing. Life experiences and choices such as the school you attend, the classes you take, the friends you hang around with, every paid or unpaid job or activity you engage in—all of these represent steps in your career development journey. You've taken many steps already and now you're preparing to take your next.

Within intentional career development is also a great deal of preparation and planning. Throughout their life and various career choices, each person faces countless decisions when selecting a particular career path (Holland, 1959). Each of these decision points represents an opportunity for planning and consideration, but also leaves you vulnerable to facing uncertainty, challenges, and of course, harmful career myths.

Despite these challenges, career development is actually a simple process that has remained largely unchanged since it was originally proposed in 1908 by the founder of vocational guidance, Frank Parsons. Parsons (1909) articulated the process this way:

> In the wise choice of a vocation there are three broad factors: (1) a clear understanding of yourself, your aptitudes, abilities, interests, ambitions, resources, limitations and their causes; (2) a knowledge of requirements and conditions of success, advantages and disadvantages, compensation, opportunities, and prospects in different lines of work; (3) true reasoning on the relations of these two groups of facts
>
> (Parsons, 1909, p. 5)

Put more simply, Parsons' three-step career development process can be boiled down to the following: 1) learning and developing a clear and comprehensive awareness about yourself; 2) understanding and gathering an extensive knowledge base about relevant aspects of the world of work; and 3) finding a synergistic fit between a) your wants and needs and b) what the work world wants and needs. The three-step career development process is represented in Figure 2.1.

Figure 2.1 Career Development Process

These three simple steps can help you find a fulfilling career and cultivate a meaningful life. Don't let the simplicity of the steps imply they're fast and easy; they're not! You need to gear up and devote significant time and commitment to wrestle with big questions. But the good news is we'll wrestle through it together. In the coming pages you will learn a lot and engage in persistent soul-searching to find and maintain your ultimate career fit.

Action 1 – Goal Setting

Intentional career development starts with goals. According to author and career coach Gary Ryan Blair (2009), "The best opportunities in life are the ones we create. Goal setting provides for you the opportunity to create an extraordinary life" (p. 57). Together, we're embarking on a journey of self-discovery to get you where you most want to be. So, where do you want to be at the end of this workbook? Goals provide direction, help us measure progress, and nurture our motivation to keep going (Lore, 2011). We need to start by setting specific, measurable goals to help articulate what you want to get out of this process.

Your goals for this workbook are unique to you and where you find yourself in your career development journey. Perhaps you want to learn more about yourself for the fun of it. Or maybe you're trying to make a major decision in your life such as choosing your college major, entering the job market for the first time, considering a career change, or contemplating retirement. You might be at a crisis point and have no idea what to do next. Perhaps you've already made some initial decisions about your future and are seeking confirmation for your choices. Or maybe you're in a class that requires you to engage in this process and haven't yet considered what you want out of it.

Whether you are completing this workbook as part of a class, counseling, or on your own, it is helpful to set goals for what you want to gain from this process. Set your goals for completing this workbook by responding to the following questions:

What do you want to achieve from this workbook? Remember, the more specific you are with your goals, the more you will get out of this workbook.

_____

_____

_____

_____

_____

Why are these things important to you?

_____

_____

_____

_____

_____

Myth 2

"This book won't work for me."

Fact

This workbook is all about approaching career development with a healthy mindset. Unlike the other myths we'll confront, the truthfulness of this myth depends on you. You will get out of this book what you put into it. If you shift your mindset to believing this book will work for you, it likely will. This is due to what sociologist Robert Merton (1948) called self-fulfilling prophecies—beliefs that bring about their own fulfillment. Self-fulfilling prophecies are incredibly strong and can predict positive or negative outcomes. For example, ineffective drugs can sometimes improve a person's health if they believe they will, a phenomenon known as the placebo effect (Tennen & Affleck, 1987). While the power of believing can be healing, it can also produce powerfully detrimental results. Numerous studies on stereotype threat demonstrate that apprehension of negative evaluation produces poorer performance (Steele et al., 2002). For example, with all other factors being equal, students believing to be at risk for failing perform worse in school (Steele, 1997).

Career development struggles can result in a downward spiral of negative self-fulfilling prophecies. In my work as a career counselor, many of my clients seek help with self-belief after being battered repeatedly by career hardships. If you're in that same dark place, your feelings are understandable. The difficulties you've witnessed or endured, the fear and avoidance of the process, and the times you've been stuck can bring anyone down. Combined with career myths, the amount of false information and bad advice circulating around makes it is easy to fall into self-degrading thinking traps and believe that the job market is hopeless. You must never lose faith that you can prevail through difficulty and reach your desired goals.

Negative thinking as a self-fulfilling prophecy is dangerous because it can produce painful emotions and ineffective behaviors (Campbell, 2020). For example, after losing a job, negative thoughts, such as "I'm a failure" and "No one will hire me again," can result in emotions such as hopelessness and depression. Behaviors such as avoiding another job search can lead to even more negative thoughts. Alternatively, constructive thoughts, such as "I still have value" and "This is my chance to try a new job," can reinforce job-seeking behaviors while promoting feelings of hope and anticipation. For this reason, positive thinking about careers has emerged as a key factor for successful career development (Savickas, 2005).

As we work through this book together, you can begin to develop a healthier mindset by embracing hope. Doing so shifts the self-fulfilling prophecy phenomenon to work in your favor by heightening your mood and encouraging effective behaviors (Campbell et al., 2017). Positive mindset requires you to reframe negative thoughts by developing a new, more positive perspective of yourself and your career development (Campbell, 2020). As a counselor, I help my clients reframe their beliefs to be more productive as initial motivation for our work. With that being said, I don't encourage unrealistically positive "psychospeak" ("I'm the best and everyone will want to hire me!") but rather balanced, hopeful realism ("With effort, I can achieve my goals.")

When it comes to working through this book together, let's reframe to a hopeful, balanced mindset. Instead of "This won't work for me," shift to a more productive curiosity of *"How* can this work for me?" (Forleo, 2019). Contained within these pages are the best of what I've learned about career development from over a decade of researching, teaching, and counseling people on the subject. Rather than shutting down ideas as unhelpful or irrelevant, seek out ways they can apply to you. Throughout this book, you may stumble upon familiar information that is designed to help you experience the material in a new constructive way. The information can be useful to anyone regardless of what stage of career development they are currently in. I myself regularly engage in many of these activities for continued self-growth and satisfaction. Remain humble and open to the possibility that no matter what your current situation is, your journey to fulfillment starts here.

So how can this book work for you? There are two strategies to consider when feeling uncertain. First, try reconsidering the information you're presented. Let's try by reexamining information we've learned so far about the career development process.

Figure 2.2 Career Development Process

```
   ┌─────────┐        ┌──────────┐        ┌──────────┐
   │  Learn  │        │Understand│        │          │
   │  About  │  ══▷    │  World   │  ══▷    │Find a Fit│
   │Yourself │        │ of Work  │        │          │
   └─────────┘        └──────────┘        └──────────┘
```

The process seems so simple and intuitive: Step 1 says to learn about yourself. Is that how most people choose a career? No – people usually skip Step 1 in favor of Steps 2 and 3 by only looking at the world of work and searching for a fit. The thought process goes something like this: "What do I want to do for work? Maybe a teacher? No. A musician? No. A doctor? No…" and so on. With the millions of job choices out there, this type of trial-and-error hunting is wildly inefficient and ineffective, leading people to become overwhelmed before eventually stopping altogether.

This is precisely why the process needs to start with learning about yourself. By taking stock of who you are, you're better able to take a targeted dive into the world of work by only considering jobs that match well with who you are. The first step of learning about yourself allows you to drastically narrow down the field to jobs that actually suit you.

Reconsidering this three-step process in detail illuminated the importance of the first step. We did that by breaking down seemingly basic information into details and examining how we can benefit from the information. When we remain curious and resist the urge to dismiss simple information as unhelpful, our analysis can yield critical takeaways.

A second suggestion for getting the most out of this workbook is to be willing to try different tactics. There is intentionally a lot of repetition in this book to help you gather essential information and take necessary steps forward in your career development. We need to fight the bad advice you've been given and replace it with helpful truth. When learning new material, it can be helpful to repeat content in multiple ways. For example, you *hear* a lecture, and *see* your professor's slides, while *writing* your notes; later on you may *speak* key words to yourself as you go over flashcards. In a similar way, the action strategies we cover in this book will also employ a variety of methods, including reflecting, reading, writing, listening, talking, watching, doing, etc. Some of these activities may be more helpful than others, but all of them will help combat the career myths that sabotage your efforts. Stay open to innovation and trying new things. You never know what will lead to your next breakthrough!

Action 2 – Visualization Drawing

Let's try an unconventional tactic to reframe opportunities for growth, embrace different strategies, and expand our willingness to try new things by visualizing the future and drawing what comes to mind. Visualizations and drawing exercises can be helpful in bringing information that may be hidden or unexpressed into our conscious awareness; it can also help you create your future (Mills, 2017).

To begin this ten-minute exercise, give yourself five minutes to imagine and visualize a perfect day at work. Are you with others or by yourself? What are you wearing? What are your surroundings like? Once finished, use the remaining five minutes to draw the most important aspects of your perfect day at work in the space provided below. Include as much detail as you can in your drawing.

What do you think are the most important elements of your drawing and why?

_____

_____

_____

_____

_____

Myth 3

"I already know what I need to do."

Fact

Well, actually there *is* some truth to this myth: you probably do know what you need to do *at some level*. As with the previous myth, the facts surrounding this one are common sense. Believing you already know what to do is harmful toward your efforts because you're more prone to breezing past familiar information that still needs a closer analysis to be fully understood. Our aim is deep processing at a very conscious and intentional level. Read carefully and process deeply.

So far, we've learned that the three-step career development process begins with learning about yourself. Most people don't skip this step because they believe self-knowledge is unimportant, but rather because they genuinely think they already know themselves. They check off the first step and hurriedly rush on to learning about the world of work without having a foundational understanding of themselves. This is a mistake. Even for my most insightful and self-aware students and clients, we start with learning (or re-learning) who they are. While it may be true that you understand your identity and character, you may not be focused on the aspects of yourself most relevant in making career decisions. Learning about yourself as part of the career development process requires discovering key criteria to prime you for a targeted exploration of the work world.

A variation of this myth I often hear is, "I've already learned what I need to know about myself." This is used as another justification to tiptoe around self-exploration and move into learning about the world of work. This is problematic for career development because knowing yourself is more than merely discovering who you are consistently. Instead, it is about knowing who you are right now, *at this point in time* (Holland, 1997). Choosing your next career step shouldn't be based on who you were five years ago. We need the most up-to-date snapshot of who you are to ensure we honor what fits you best in this present moment.

So, what specifically do you need to know about yourself? It comes down to five criteria: 1) personality, 2) abilities, 3) likes and dislikes, 4) meaning and values, and 5) supplemental factors (Campbell, 2014). You can remember these five criteria using the acronym PALMS, as shown in Figure 2.2. Everything you need to know about yourself is contained in your PALMS!

Figure 2.2 PALMS

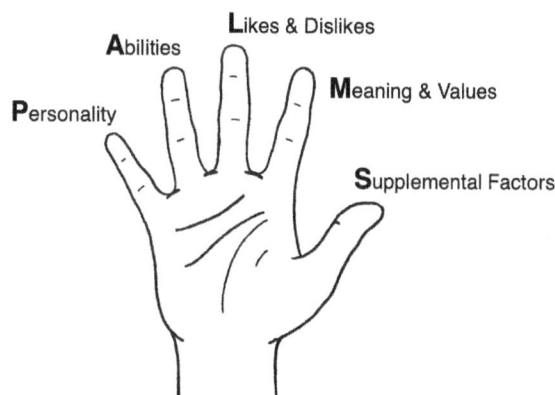

Personality is the combination of qualities that inform behaviors (Schultz & Schultz, 2017). Research has shown that successful career development occurs when people have the personality characteristics required to be successful in the areas they choose (Brown & Lent, 2013). Examples of personality characteristics that impact career choices are outgoingness, conscientiousness, and courage.

Abilities describe our strengths, skills, gifts, and talents—what we can accomplish and are good at doing (Bolles, 2020). The earliest career placement tests focused on measuring abilities, and remain an important factor for career success (Brown & Lent, 2013). Examples of these abilities include teaching, driving, writing, and playing an instrument.

Likes and Dislikes refer to our interests or preferences for certain activities (Brown & Brooks, 1996). Research shows that personal interests play a key role in career decisions (Holland, 1997). An example of likes and dislikes would be a preference for artistic activities over athletic ones.

Meaning and Values refers to the moral principles and purpose that guide your life, as well as your most important values in a career. These encapsulate what you care about and want to contribute to the world through your work. Richard Bolles (2020), author of the job-hunting book, *What Color is Your Parachute?* stated that your meaning and values answer the question, "What kind of footprint do you want to leave on this earth, after your journey here is done?" (p. 68). Creativity, helping others, security, and freedom are all examples of meaning and values.

Supplemental Factors refers to the unique set of additional aspects that influence career decision making. Considered a catch-all category, supplemental factors acknowledge and encourage us to pause and consider the unique circumstances that might influence our career development. These factors can be both internal and external. Factors such as identity awareness and decision-making readiness are examples of internal ones. Culture and family commitments are examples of external factors.

Now that we understand what we need to know about ourselves, we're ready to dive in and learn about who we are and how this informs the next steps of our career development process. Using the PALMS framework, we'll use the next several activities to learn more about ourselves and reflect on what we can gain from the information.

Action 3 – Career Development Review

Take a moment to reflect on what you've learned so far about career development. We've covered two foundational concepts that define career development and will guide us through the rest of this workbook:

1. The career development process, as shown in Figure 2.3.

Figure 2.3 Career Development Process

2. Learn about yourself using PALMS criteria, as depicted in Figure 2.4.

Figure 2.4 PALMS

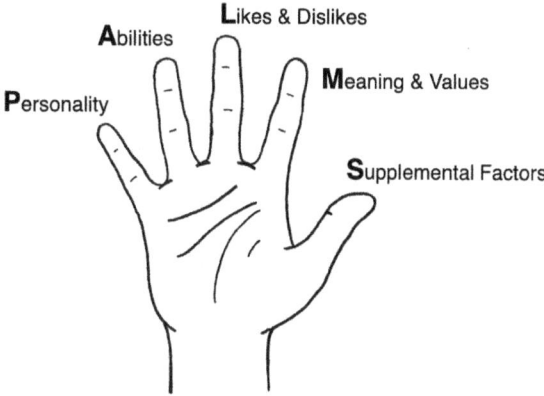

Reflect on these concepts as you answer the following questions:

What are the most significant insights, reminders, or ideas you've gained from reading this chapter so far?

_____

_____

_____

_____

_____

How can this information be helpful for you?

_____

_____

_____

_____

_____

Myth 4

"Career tests will tell me what I should do."

Fact

A healthy dose of optimism is helpful, but believing that a career test can make career decisions for you is a myth. People are often told that taking a test will tell them what to do, but many are surprised and disappointed when they learn that no test can envision exactly what your career should be. That said, despite their inability to predict the future, career tests *can* help you learn helpful information about yourself (Jordan & Marinaccio, 2017) and research has shown them to be effective when used this way (Brown & Ryan Krane, 2000).

Career tests must be approached realistically in order to be effective. Counter to the "test 'em and tell 'em stereotype" of merely taking a test and passively receiving declarations of who you are (Brown & Lent, 2013), career tests should be used to hunt for clues and suggestions about who you *might* be. These tests suggest how your attributes might be categorized into certain groups. For example, a career test won't tell you that you'll be an artist; instead, it might suggest that you fall into a category of people that tend to be inclined toward artistic activities. As a unique individual, you are the ultimate expert on yourself, and *you* must grapple with test feedback to decide whether you agree or disagree (Bolles, 2020). The value of career tests comes from gaining information that you can respond to, rather than inventing answers out of thin air. For example, the question, "What do you like to do?" is harder to answer than, "The test suggested you like to cook. Is that true?" In this way, the National Career Development Association (NCDA) describes career testing as a process and not just a product (Jordan & Marinaccio, 2017). You will benefit most from this process by reflecting on your test results and comparing them with your current understanding of yourself. By doing so, you can learn more about yourself and broaden your possibilities.

Hold on—did that just say *broaden?* Yes, you read that right. This may come as a surprise since many people wrongly assume that the career development process focuses primarily on narrowing down options. A prominent misconception is that career choices should begin with a broad range of information that is then narrowed down, following the path of an upside-down triangle, as shown in Figure 2.5.

Figure 2.5 Career Choice Triangle

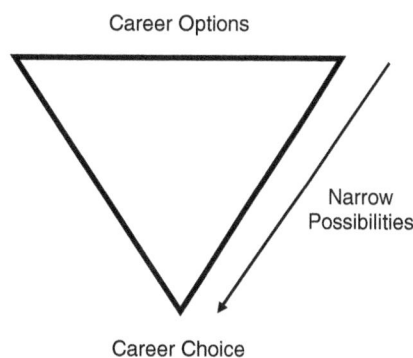

While narrowing is the ultimate goal, career choices should instead follow the path of a diamond, as depicted in Figure 2.6.

Figure 2.6 Career Choice Diamond

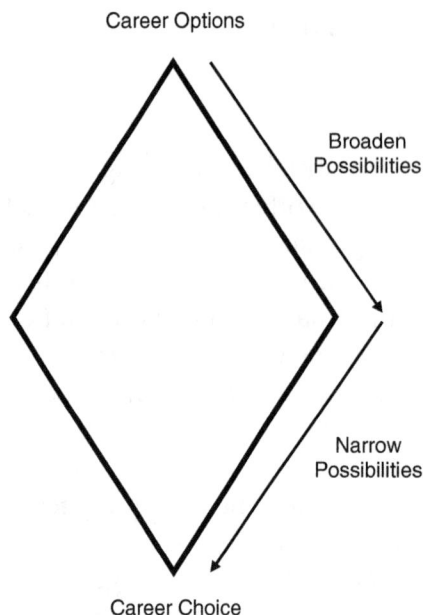

Since most people don't begin with a wide range of information, their understanding first needs to be broadened to include all available information and possibilities; only then is it appropriate to narrow down the options to find a true and informed fit. With this in mind, expect that career tests will aid in your process by showing you new possibilities about yourself before we begin to narrow them again (Bolles, 2020).

A number of career tests are available from a variety of sources (and price points) that can provide valuable information about your attributes. However, career tests do not need to be formal psychometric measures in order to gather helpful information (Pope et al., 2011). For our purposes, you'll receive guided instruction on how to effectively utilize free online inventories to gather information, consider their accuracy, and learn more about yourself. These tests will provide general information about how you might best operate in the work world, in addition to specific suggestions for careers that may be well suited for you. Remember they are not telling you what you should do; we are considering information and searching for clues.

Using the PALMS criteria as our guide, we'll begin by learning more about your personality. As stated earlier, personality is the consistent aspects of a person's character that influence behavior (Schultz & Schultz, 2017). Successful career development necessitates that a person possesses the personality characteristics required to be successful in the areas they choose (Brown & Lent, 2013).

Action 4 – Personality Assessment

Learn more about your personality by taking the 16 Personalities test (NERIS Analytics Limited, 2011) available at bit.ly/careermythlinks. Read your results carefully, particularly the overview, strengths and weaknesses, career paths, and workplace habits sections.

    Write your personality type, code type, and careers of highest interest below. Personality Type is located at the top of your results on the Introduction page (e.g., Advocate Personality). Code type is located in parentheses after personality type (e.g., INFJ-T). A list of potential careers is provided in the Career Paths section of your results. Select at least two careers from this list that are the highest interest to you (e.g., Counselor).

Personality Type:

_____

Personality Code Type:

_____

Careers of Highest Interest:

_____

_____

_____

_____

Myth 5

"I'm not qualified to do anything."

Fact

You took a personality test and it suggested that a career as a surgeon might be a good fit for you. But you don't know how to perform surgery—you don't even have steady hands—and you have no interest in spending the next decade in school trying to become one. You think, *What a waste of time! Career tests won't help because I'm not qualified for their suggestions.* Next thing you know, negative thinking takes over and prevents you from taking any more tests.

This kind of thinking represents a misunderstanding about career tests that measure a specific criterion, such as personality. Personality represents your tendencies and temperament (Schultz & Schultz, 2017), and personality tests answer questions such as, "In what kinds of environments are you most comfortable? Are you a people person, or are you more comfortable with projects and tasks?" (Miller, 2010, p. 76).

As we can see from the PALMS acronym, personality isn't the same as likes and dislikes, or abilities. For example, if your personality reveals a tendency to be detail oriented, it might suggest conducting research as a well-suited career. However, you might not possess the skills needed for research or even be interested in it. Still, having a detail-oriented personality type fits well with a diverse range of career activities, such as overhauling an engine, auditing financial statements, tailoring an evening gown, or debugging a piece of code. With this in mind, avoid prematurely dismissing certain aspects of your personality simply because you noted a mismatch between other PALMS criteria.

Reflecting on personality and the other PALMS criteria is valuable because of their unique significance toward positive life outcomes. Collectively, these criteria serve an important role as no single aspect is a determining factor. As such, it is important to avoid prematurely judging results before investigating all criteria individually.

Remember that you are trying to broaden, not narrow, your prospects, so avoid eliminating entire categories of possibilities based on one mismatch. For example, hastily applying likes and dislikes to personality test results by rejecting all outdoor jobs and refusing to consider any outside job from paramedic to athletics coach can rob us of valuable personality cues. When looking at personality alone, an emerging pattern shows that all the above jobs coincide with a personality style of extraversion and outgoingness. Although the jobs themselves might not be an ideal fit, the knowledge that you may prefer a job where you can be outgoing opens a whole new category of possibilities. For this reason, the current focus should be primarily on looking for patterns and gathering cues about personality alone. We can set aside the other criteria for the time being, as we will be inspecting and integrating them in later activities when it is time to begin the narrowing process.

Personality is an important factor in decision making and career development. It facilitates a person's ability to find their niche in the world of work and is related to a variety of positive career outcomes (Roberts et al., 2007). Lore (2011) notes that, "Making sure your personality matches your work is one of the most important things you can do to guarantee that your career will be highly satisfying and stay that way for years to come" (p. 183). Interestingly, the benefit goes both ways: matching personality with work improves long-term career satisfaction and encourages advantageous personality development (Brown & Lent, 2013). By engaging in satisfying work, personality characteristics become more stable, open, thorough, and robust, leading to an overall more fulfilling life.

Action 5 – Personality Reflection

Keeping your focus on personality, take a moment to reflect on your 16 Personalities test results from the previous activity.

Ask yourself: Are your personality results accurate or not? If there are aspects that don't seem to fit you, look at the other personalities listed and see if others fit you better. For results that seem excessively wrong, consider retaking the test. Once you are reasonably satisfied with your results and somewhat confident that you have identified what your traits are, answer the following questions.

In what ways do my personality results seem accurate?

_____

_____

_____

_____

_____

In what ways do they seem inaccurate? How would I describe myself instead?

_____

_____

_____

_____

_____

Summarize what you learned about your personality by completing the following sentence.

My personality can be described as…

_____

_____

_____

_____

_____

Myth 6

"My career should be based on what I'm best at doing."

Fact

Beware of any career myths containing the word "should." Why *should* your career be determined by what you're best at? The problem with "should" is that it puts pressure on us to be or do something based on what we think we're supposed to be or do, rather than on who we are and what we want (Schultz & Schultz, 2017). If we honestly desired to communicate what we wanted, we'd likely say, "I want my career to be based on what I'm best at doing." But that's not what most people say. In fact, my clients often tell me the exact opposite! They frequently lament that they defaulted into their despised careers because they were good at them. For instance, one unhappy economist said she pursued her career simply because she had an aptitude for math. Other clients worry that they'd feel guilty leaving a career that they are highly gifted in, such as the opera singer who was reluctant to leave the theater out of fear for "wasting" her singing talent. The most important principle to take from these examples is that abilities alone should not dictate your career choices. While your many abilities are an important consideration in your career choices, they are not the most important, or singular determining factor.

Abilities are often differentiated from skills as distinct concepts (Segal, 2017; Snow, 1996). Abilities are physical or mental capacities that come easily or naturally to someone (Segal, 2017), whereas skills are derived from our abilities and are more specific and job-related, as they are concrete proficiencies gained through practice (Snow, 1996). For example, culinary chefs often have the ability of manual dexterity and develop a skill for using knives. In order to expand career possibilities, we're going to focus on the wider concept of abilities before discussing skills. We'll explore what you could theoretically do with training and experience, not what you are already trained in doing.

Abilities are an important component in career decision making but, as we have discovered, they aren't everything and need to be considered as one factor among the rest of the PALMS factors. Research has found that abilities predict occupational performance, and substandard work performance tends to be partially due to lack of related abilities (Swanson & Schneider, 2013). These findings suggest that considering your abilities during the decision-making process is an important part of finding a well-suited career.

Don't fall prey to the trap of believing that abilities are everything. Other PALMS factors are still vitally important. While abilities may be good at predicting how good you are at your job, they are a poor predictor of how satisfied you are by your job (Metz & Jones, 2013). For now, we'll keep our focus on abilities with the understanding that they are just one important component of career decision making.

Action 6 – Abilities Assessment

Learn more about your career-related abilities by taking the Virginia Education Wizard Skill Assessment (2008) available at bit.ly/careermythlinks. Note that this test uses the term "skills" differently than we have, and more closely resembles the broader category of abilities. After taking the test, read your results carefully; they can be found under "Skills Assessment" by clicking "Explain Results."

Once completed, write your results for top abilities below. Abilities are located under "Skills Assessment" by clicking "Show Career Clusters" and then "Show Careers." "Abilities" as we define them will be listed as "Career Clusters" (e.g., Education and Training). A list of potential careers is also provided. Select at least two careers from this list that are of the highest interest to you. Be sure to investigate all careers based on "Required Education" (e.g., four-year degree) to discover all possibilities for your abilities. Select at least two careers from this list that most align with your abilities.

Abilities:

1. _____

2. _____

3. _____

Careers of Highest Interest:

_____

_____

_____

_____

Myth 7

"The right job will use all my gifts and talents."

Fact

You have many strengths, and it is unlikely that one job will effectively make use of all of them. Fortunately, a career doesn't need to be all-consuming; you can utilize your other gifts, such as your hobbies, leisure activities, family time, and volunteer work in different areas of your life (Super, 1990). Utilizing all your strengths or even the strongest one isn't necessary—simply having the ability to do a job well is enough to prompt good performance outcomes.

Abilities are important to consider because they predict occupational performance and success (Metz & Jones, 2013). In order to choose a career that effectively utilizes at least some of your abilities, you need to identify what ones you possess. Abilities can be divided into two types, both of which are important to consider: normative and ipsative. Normative abilities are identified by comparing yourself with other people (Colman, 2015). They represent aspects that make you uniquely more capable than most others. For example, even if math was your weakest subject in school, having successfully completed an advanced-level math course may put your mathematical reasoning abilities ahead of the general population (Wahlstrom & Williams, 2003). In this way, although you may not ordinarily list math as one of your personal strengths, it is valuable to recognize it as a normative ability.

Normative abilities are important and helpful in landing a job. When employers consider strengths, they are often comparing applicants based on normative abilities (Bolles, 2020). For instance, an employer searching for a typist would likely select an applicant who typed 80 words per minute over one who typed 60 when deciding between two otherwise equally qualified applicants. Despite the importance of normative abilities, they are easy to overlook because they aren't necessarily ipsative.

Ipsative abilities are your areas of highest strength when compared with yourself (Colman, 2015). For example, the typist discussed above might be more adept at running than typing, making running their ipsative ability. When considering all your strengths, your ipsative abilities are the ones you consider to be your greatest assets. However, your greatest assets are relative to yourself and don't compare to those of others. This is why your ipsative personal best could be a normative weakness when compared to the general population. Don't let this discourage you; remind yourself that everyone has their own strengths, weaknesses, struggles, and capabilities. You are the only person who can compare yourself with who you used to be, and no one can do that better than you.

Ipsative abilities are important because they shape our understanding of our own abilities. When asked, "What are your areas of greatest strength?" the response is usually our ipsative abilities. Identifying areas of personal strength gives us confidence and increases well-being, which aids in job hunting by helping us to promote ourselves to employers (Miller, 2010).

Both normative and ipsative abilities are important to recognize and embrace as personal strengths. While they are both valuable, normative abilities are easily forgotten since ipsative abilities come to mind more regularly than normative ones. This is especially true if you regularly spend time around people with similar skill sets. For example, if you work in a sales job surrounded by proficient salespeople, it's easy to overlook your normative abilities in verbal communication and persuasion. Your environment can tint your perception by falsely convincing you that "everyone" has your same skillset, despite the rarity of such abilities outside your immediate surroundings.

Similarly, career ability tests usually highlight normative abilities but often fail to identify ipsative abilities. The ability test you took in the last activity, the Virginia Education Wizard Skill Assessment, highlights areas of strength compared to others. The rank order of your top three abilities are the only ipsative component (Virginia Education Wizard, 2008). For example, even if you don't rank your teaching ability as a personal best, "Education and Training" might emerge as one of your normative strengths. For this reason, reflecting on your career ability test results in addition to your personal strengths is essential to identifying your potential normative and ipsative abilities.

Action 7 – Abilities Reflection

Reflect on your Virginia Education Wizard Skill Assessment results from the previous activity. Remember that the skill assessment focuses on clues about your normative abilities. Be sure to consider and reflect on both your normative and ipsative abilities in your response.

Ask yourself: Do your results accurately reflect your abilities? Are there other abilities you believe to be your best that aren't represented in your results? For results that seem excessively wrong, consider retaking the test. Once you are reasonably satisfied with your results and somewhat confident that you have identified your abilities, answer the following questions.

In what ways do my ability results seem accurate?

_____

_____

_____

_____

_____

In what ways do they seem inaccurate or incomplete? How would I describe myself instead or in addition?

_____

_____

_____

_____

_____

Summarize what you learned about your abilities by completing the following sentence, including both normative and ipsative ability in your response.

My abilities are:

_____

_____

_____

_____

_____

Myth 8

"None of the things I like to do are career related."

Fact

As we continue to learn about ourselves using the PALMS criteria depicted in Figure 2.7, we've arrived at L, which stands for likes and dislikes. At this point you may not be able to list any career paths that you like or dislike—or have the opposite struggle of everything sounding potentially interesting. Both situations are problematic and challenging but both necessitate a deeper investigation of your interests.

Figure 2.7 PALMS

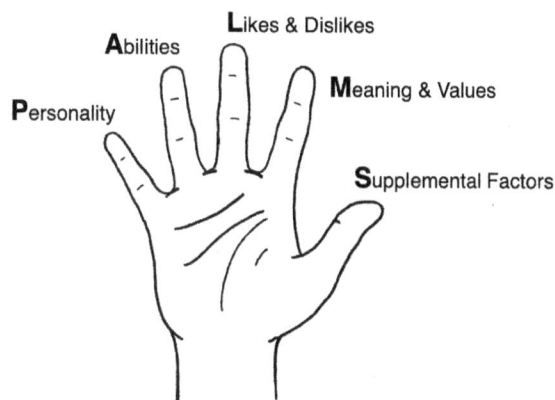

Recall the career development process as depicted in Figure 2.8. We're using the PALMS criteria to learn about ourselves prior to understanding the world of work. At this point, your task is to think about all the activities you like and dislike. Our interests can lead to many different professions. For example, someone who likes music might enjoy a career as a performer, but also as a music teacher, promotor, producer, choir director, disc jockey, or music retailer (Taylor & Hardy, 2004). Later, we'll make connections with your interests and careers when we move into understanding the world of work.

Figure 2.8 Career Development Process

Likes and dislikes refer to our interests or preference for certain activities (Brown & Brooks, 1996). It answers the questions: what are you passionate about? What energizes you? What activities or subjects engage you for long spans of time? Research shows that interests largely contribute to career decisions (Holland, 1997).

It's important to consider likes and dislikes in career decisions because they increase career satisfaction for both the worker and their organization (Hansen, 2013), meaning, people who pair their interests with their careers tend to be happier and please their bosses more. Knowing your interests can help you reach these goals.

Action 8 – Likes and Dislikes Assessment

Learn more about your likes and dislikes by taking the O*NET Interests Profiler (My Next Move, 2021) available at bit.ly/careermythlinks. Read your results carefully, including your results, job zones, and careers.

Note the three interest categories you scored highest in (e.g., Social, Investigative, Artistic) and the careers you find most interesting. Read about the different job zones and choose the one most applicable to you; for example, choose job zone 4 if you already have or might want to earn a bachelor's degree. You can return to the job zones page as many times as you'd like to view the different careers for each job zone. Once you choose a job zone, a list of corresponding careers will appear. Select at least two careers from these lists.

Interests:

1. _____

2. _____

3. _____

Careers of Highest Interest:

_____

_____

_____

_____

Myth 9

"My life will consist of one career."

Fact

Your life will likely consist of many careers. Just like every aspect of life, career planning is unpredictable and is prone to unforeseen changes. Your dream job changes over the years; it likely has already if you compare your current dream career with that of your childhood. Similarly, job shifts are also common: on average, people change jobs less than every five years and at least twelve times throughout their lives (BLS, 2021).

Career change is both a normality and a necessity. By moving jobs, workers benefit financially from salary increases that are higher than their current employer (Miller, 2018). Additionally, remaining in the same place long term shows little reward in terms of ongoing job security. Explained by Bolles (2020), "To have only one plan, one option, in any situation, is a sure recipe for despair" (p. 236). Since career change is likely, let go of the vision of a single career. Do not permanently shackle yourself into a miserable career by forcing an unalterable decision. Instead, be flexible and prepared for a dynamic and diverse career future.

This may sound intimidating at first glance, but don't let that sour your vision. Preparing for a diverse assortment of future careers can be an exciting, meaningful, and valuable process. People change and grow throughout their whole lives, and you can have a vibrant career life that changes with you. Every job and experience you have—good, bad, or otherwise—shapes you into who you are. Collectively, they comprise your life, what vocational theorist Donald Super deemed, "the grand narrative" (Super et al., 1996). Your career is not a motionless pond, to leap into blindly and stagnate in for decades, but a flowing river of progressive experiences that collectively cultivate fulfillment and enrich your life.

Additionally, preparing for multiple careers allows you to make simpler and more informed decisions now. Recognizing that there is no singular career destiny awaiting you removes the pressure to make a perfect choice. As you can't currently determine every future career move, your focus shifts to taking the next best step. Framing your career choices as individual steps that lead you in a continually evolving path toward your goals acts as a reminder that there are multiple avenues to success (Super, 1957).

Right now, focus on the present moment while remaining open to change. Avoid the trap of believing there's only one career for you—there are always multiple possibilities, and you can always change. Don't focus on what you're going to do forever, but instead on what you're going to do next.

Currently, we're focusing on the present by learning about ourselves through the PALMS criteria and considering our likes and dislikes. Our current step focuses on collecting information about the things you enjoy as clues for what careers might fit you. Furthermore, exploring interests has an added value of increased career exploration (Randahl et al., 1993). Research suggests that engaging with your likes and dislikes goes beyond the benefits of self-exploration by also strengthening your career development process moving forward.

Action 9 – Likes and Dislikes Reflection

Consider your interests and reflect on your O*NET Interests Profiler from the previous activity. Ask yourself: Are your results for your likes and dislikes accurate or not? If there are aspects that don't seem to fit you, review the other interest categories listed and see if others fit you better. For results that seem excessively wrong, consider retaking the test. Once you are reasonably satisfied with your results and somewhat confident that you have identified your top interest categories, answer the following questions.

In what ways do my results about my likes and dislikes seem accurate?

_____

_____

_____

_____

_____

In what ways do they seem inaccurate? How would I describe my likes and dislikes instead?

_____

_____

_____

_____

_____

Summarize what you learned about your likes and dislikes by completing the following sentence.

My interests are…

_____

_____

_____

_____

_____

Myth 10

"People work because they have to."

Fact

While it is true that most adults need to work as a means of survival, believing that to be the only incentive to work is both inaccurate and harmful to your career development. Work does fulfill basic financial needs by putting food on the table and a roof over our heads, but this is a vast oversimplification. As stated by leadership expert John C. Maxwell (2013), "We were created for meaningful work, and one of life's greatest pleasures is the satisfaction of a job well done" (p. 1).

Work satisfies a variety of other wants and needs beyond a stable income. For example, it often denotes public identity in the United States. Notice how often people say, "What do you do?" implying the question, "What is your occupation?" or "What do you want to be?" instead of, "What occupation do you aspire to have?" Use of the words *do* and *be* demonstrate that a person's occupation is viewed as a central part of identity (Brown & Lent, 2013). Furthermore, we often define our personal identity through our jobs. Donald Super explained that work is the means through which people implement a self-concept by living out who they believe themselves to be (Super et al., 1996). Work also satisfies existential needs and psychological well-being by structuring our time and adding meaning to our lives. Bolles (2020) said work answers the question, "What kind of footprint do you want to leave on this earth, after your journey here is done?" (p. 114). In positive psychology, a state of "flow" refers to the complete absorption within an activity (Csikszentmihalyi, 1990). Commonly referred to as "in the zone," a flow state creates an intense immersion that results in altering one's own self-awareness and passage of time. Of course, not everyone is fortunate enough to obtain these additional benefits from their jobs, but striving for them is a worthwhile aspiration as they represent the meaning and values we ascribe to work.

Meaning and values refer to your life purpose, the moral principles that guide your life, and what you value most in a career. Meaning and values encapsulate what you want to contribute to the world through your work by answering the questions, what does work mean to you and what do you value about it? As we've discussed, there are common meanings and values that most people ascribe to work. Ranging from basic survival needs to satisfying existential aspirations, meaning and values are a highly individualized and widely diverse aspect of the career planning process. Some people desire a career as a helper, some crave a space to be creative, while others yearn for status and prestige.

What do you most want out of your career? The meanings and values you identify while answering this question are important because they provide benefits beyond an income. Believing your career can connect to deeper meaning puts you on the path to *making* it mean more.

Look beyond the mere paycheck and recognize all the additional benefits work can provide you with. Author L. P. Jacks (1932) offers this inspiration:

A master in the art of living draws no sharp distinction between his work and his play, his labour and his leisure, his mind and his body, his education and his recreation. He hardly knows which is which. He simply pursues his vision of excellence through whatever he is doing and leaves others to determine whether he is working or playing. To himself he always seems to be doing both.

(pp. 1–2)

By pursuing what you value, you can cultivate a life you love.

Action 10 – Meaning and Values Assessment

Learn more about your meaning and values by taking the California Career Zone Work Importance Profiler (California Career Resource Network, 2020) available at bit.ly/careermythlinks. Read your results carefully, including your work values results and occupations.

The results are your three highest work values. The test highlights your top two but examine your top three. View occupations and select at least two careers from this list that are of the highest interest to you (e.g., Pump Operator). Write all of these below.

Work Values:

1. _____

2. _____

3. _____

Careers of Highest Interest:

_____

_____

_____

_____

Myth 11

"I can rely on 'Best Career' lists."

Fact

Right now, all the career myths you've internalized might be screaming at you to ditch learning more about yourself. Who cares what your preferences are? Maybe you just need to be flexible and adjust to a truly awesome career. I recall times in my own life when I needed a job and falsely bought into this myth. I searched outside sources for the best job and unsuccessfully attempted to mold myself to fit. Similarly, clients will often request information on the current "hot" careers and insist they can learn to enjoy them. Although this often seems plausible to us, the research strongly says otherwise (Brown & Lent, 2013). Your PALMS criteria are notably stable over time, and conscious efforts to change or mold them rarely work (Brown & Hirschi, 2013). Regardless of how marvelous an advertised career appears, it's bad for you if it's not a good fit.

Furthermore, a "Best Career" list is rarely the most accurate or helpful source for guidance and development. While there isn't any harm in scanning a career list to identify any jobs of interest, these lists should not be used as a main determinant for your career path. Many online and magazine articles written by self-dubbed "experts" identify which jobs are the most advantageous for people to seek in today's market. These articles might have legitimate data to support their conclusions, but our world is in constant motion—today's job market may not resemble tomorrow's job market, meaning that these lists quickly become inaccurate (Smith & Van Genderen, 2018).

With this understanding, it is wiser to proceed with the career development process of first learning about yourself through the PALMS criteria. Currently, we're learning about your meaning and values. The current outlook on today's job market is not as valuable as the unique set of values you want to derive from your work (Rounds & Jin, 2013).

Meaning and values are particularly important within career selection. Finding a career that fits your values is related to overall satisfaction, better job performance, organizational commitment, and job stability (Rounds & Jin, 2013). In other words, when you care deeply about the work you're doing, you'll not only feel happier, but also invest more into your work and increase loyalty toward it over time.

Action 11 – Meaning and Values Reflection

Consider your values and the meaning you derive from work, and reflect on your California Career Zone Work Importance Profiler results from the previous activity. Ask yourself: Are your results for your work values accurate or not? If there are aspects that don't seem to fit you, return to the test and see if others fit you better. For results that seem excessively wrong, consider retaking the test. Once you are reasonably satisfied with your results and somewhat confident that you have identified your top work values, answer the following questions.

In what ways do my results about my work values seem accurate?

_____

_____

_____

_____

_____

In what ways do they seem inaccurate? How would I describe my work values instead?

_____

_____

_____

_____

_____

Summarize what you learned about your work values by completing the following sentence.

My meaning and values are…

_____

_____

_____

_____

_____

Myth 12

"Learning how to choose a career will prompt me to choose one."

Fact

Unfortunately, it's not that simple. However, you've already taken a great first step by working through this book to learn the most effective ways to choose a career. As you've already discovered, learning new information is only part of the process—you must act as well. If you neglect the action steps provided in this book, you may learn about career development, but you won't achieve your career development goals. For that, your goals need action.

Although learning and doing are distinct steps, they are both important components of the process. Mental activities such as learning new information represent an earlier phase of the process than behavioral change. This process is called the Stages of Change or Transtheoretical Model (Prochaska et al., 2005).

As shown in Figure 2.9, the Stages of Change Model consists of five stages: precontemplation, contemplation, preparation, action, and maintenance (Prochaska et al., 2005). The precontemplation stage is when you are unaware or unwilling to change. In this case, that might mean saying, "I can't make a career decision." The contemplation stage represents considering change: "I may make a career decision." The preparation stage involves planning and taking steps toward that change, as in, "I'm learning how to make a career decision." The action stage refers to modifying behavior: "I'm engaging in decision-making activities." The maintenance stage comprises sustaining modifications: "I continue to monitor my career development." Recognize that learning about career development lies within the preparation stage, whereas engaging in career decision making falls into the action stage. In this way, both learning and action play an important role in finding a career fit.

Figure 2.9 Stages of Change

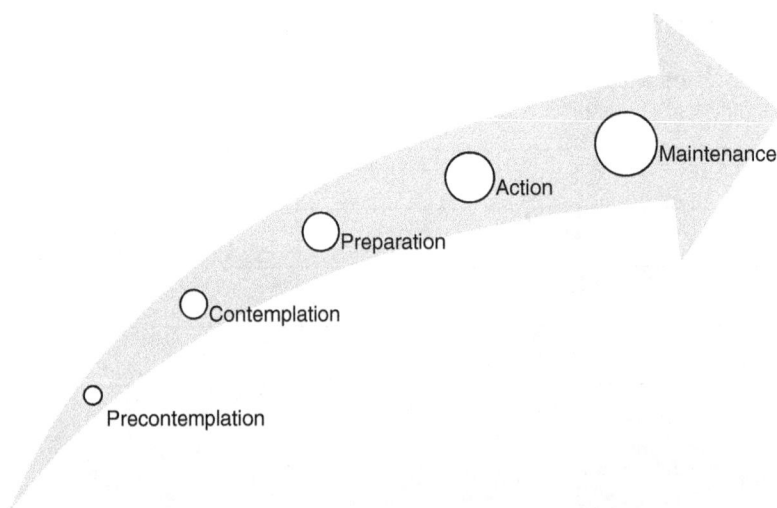

To review, we've learned that collecting information about yourself is an essential first step within career development. As we approach the end of our PALMS criteria, we'll shift our focus to S, which stands for supplemental factors. Supplemental factors are the unique extra aspects of a person or their situation that influence their career decision making. Considered a catch-all category, supplemental factors encourage us to pause and consider all the individual circumstances that may influence our career development. Supplemental factors can include internal considerations such as identity awareness and decision-making readiness, as well as external ones, like culture and family commitments.

*

Action 12 – Supplemental Factors Assessment

Supplemental factors can include a vast array of considerations as they are highly individualized for each person. Right now, we're going to focus specifically on decision-making readiness because of its importance to our later action strategies. To learn about your decision-making readiness, take the Career Decision-Making Difficulties Questionnaire (Gati et al., 1996) available at bit.ly/careermythlinks. The purpose of this questionnaire is to identify difficulties you might experience while choosing a career. Read your results carefully, including areas of significant or moderate difficulty and recommendations to address difficulties.

Write your three highest areas of difficulty below. Read recommendations for all difficulties and select at least two recommendations from this list that interest you.

Highest Areas of Career Decision-Making Difficulty:

1. _____

2. _____

3. _____

Recommendations of Highest Interest:

_____

_____

_____

_____

Myth 13

"I can choose a career all on my own."

Fact

Although you're responsible for your career choices, it's impossible not to be influenced by your context. Your career isn't secluded; it continually shapes and is shaped by other components of your life and self. There are many factors to consider before making a career choice.

Our PALMS criteria include S, the catch-all category for supplemental factors. This is where we consider contextual extras that may impact our decisions. Below are a few examples to get you started. Remember, there are countless other supplemental factors and yours may differ from what is listed below.

Decision-making readiness. Decision-making readiness is a supplemental factor that refers to how prepared you are to make a career decision (Super et al., 1996). The test you took in Myth 12, the Career Decision-Making Difficulties Questionnaire, measured decision-making readiness (Gati et al., 1996). Contemplate if difficulties such as lack of information, belief in sabotaging career myths, low motivation, or lack of self-awareness might interfere with your ability to make career choices. Your Career Decision-Making Difficulties Questionnaire results will help you determine this supplemental factor.

Relationships. Relationships are another supplemental factor that may be worth considering while making career decisions. Relationships, particularly family, impact work choices and need to be considered for effective life decision making (Burnett & Evans, 2016; Campbell et al., 2015). For instance, your spouse or romantic partner may have a say in your decision making. Perhaps you need a job that keeps you nearby to care for your aging parents. Ask yourself, who is impacted by your career decisions? Who is in your life and what role do they play in your career choices?

Life roles and lifestyle. It is impossible to make an informed career choice without factoring in role and lifestyle considerations (Campbell et al., 2015). Life roles typically include domains such as a worker, family member, volunteer, and hobbyist. Together, these domains comprise the grand design of your overall lifestyle (Hartung, 2013). Ask yourself, what might affect your choices besides work? For example, you may be considering a part-time career, but your primary role is as a full-time parent. On the other hand, you might be an avid surfer who wants a job with flexible hours that allow you to catch some summer waves. Carefully reflect on the roles you want in your lifestyle.

Identity and culture. The ways we understand ourselves and the groups we belong to are vital considerations during career selection. Identity refers to our self-definition, which can consist of a variety of characteristics such as race, ethnicity, gender identity, sexual orientation, language, spiritual orientation, age, physical abilities, and many others (Campbell, 2020). Culture includes the traditions, values, and norms of the societies or groups we belong to (Colman, 2015). What are important identity and culture considerations for your career choices? For example, for one person a career that affirms LGBT identity is important, whereas another might seek a job that includes Sundays off to observe religious practices. What aspects of your identity and culture are most important in your career choices?

Action 13 – Supplemental Factors Reflection

Previously, we investigated the possible supplemental factor of decision-making readiness by taking the Career Decision-Making Difficulties Questionnaire. To reflect more on your supplemental factors ask yourself: Are your results for this questionnaire accurate or not? If there are aspects that don't seem to fit you, return to the test and see if others fit you better. For results that seem excessively wrong, consider retaking the test. Once you are reasonably satisfied with your results and somewhat confident that you have identified what your primary difficulties are, answer the following questions.

In what ways do my results about my decision-making difficulties seem accurate?

_____

_____

_____

_____

_____

In what ways do they seem inaccurate? How would I describe my potential decision-making difficulties instead?

_____

_____

_____

_____

_____

What other supplemental factors come to mind that might impact your career choices? Review the factors described (relationships, life roles and lifestyle, identity and culture), as well as any other factors that spontaneously occur to you. These factors don't need to be final or exhaustive—just make note of considerations that strike you at this point.

_____

_____

_____

_____

_____

Summarize what you learned about your supplemental factors by completing the following sentence.

Supplemental factors I want to keep in mind are…

_____

_____

_____

_____

_____

Myth 14

"I should know exactly what I'm doing before I pursue it."

Fact

Career development begins by broadening our understanding of self and the world of work before narrowing down toward a decision. Believing you need to identify your final target before making progress leads to another sabotaging career myth.

Truth be told, you'll never know exactly what you're doing or have all of the information before you start. As one of my mentors told me, "Most decisions in life are made with insufficient information, and all you can do is make the best decision with the information available at the time." This is especially true while making career decisions. With the understanding that you can continue to assess and make judgments as you move forward, you gather information and make the best decisions you can (Segal, 2017).

We have now finished collecting information about ourselves and are ready to move on to the next step. Let's review the career development process, as shown in Figure 2.10.

Figure 2.10 Career Development Process

Learn About Yourself → Understand World of Work → Find a Fit

You learned about yourself by exploring the PALMS criteria. It's now time to summarize and reflect on what you've learned. This will prepare us for upcoming myths where we transition to the second step of the career development process: understanding the world of work.

Action 14 – PALMS Summary

As preparation for the second step of the career development process, it's time to read your PALMS! In other words, review all the information you've learned about yourself from the PALMS criteria. To do so, return to and review your responses for each of the following myths:

> Myth 2 Action – Visualization Drawing
> Myth 5 Action – Personality Reflection
> Myth 7 Action – Abilities Reflection
> Myth 9 Action – Likes and Dislikes Reflection
> Myth 11 Action – Meaning and Values Reflection
> Myth 13 Action – Supplemental Factors Reflection

Look for similarities and differences across your responses. What patterns emerge? What seems inconsistent? For example, one of your likes might have been "Social," and you may have identified relationships as a work value, but your visualization exercise might have yielded a drawing of you working alone. Attempt to explain or reconcile these differences. Perhaps you might like a career that balances time working with others and working alone. Or perhaps you may need to relook. If you can't reconcile them, try reevaluating. Perhaps this reveals that other people are more important to your career than you thought, and you might change your vision. Note your conclusions by answering the questions below.

What patterns emerged from your responses? What inconsistencies did you discover?

_____

_____

_____

_____

_____

How do you make sense of these patterns and inconsistencies? What can you take from this information that might be helpful for you?

_____

_____

_____

_____

_____

Note remaining insights and understandings that emerged from this exercise and summarize what you learned here. Throughout the PALMS reflections, what are the most significant reminders, insights, or ideas you've gained about yourself?

_____

_____

_____

_____

_____

Myth 15

"My career path will be conventional."

Fact

Planning for a conventional career path is like buying oceanfront property in Tucson, Arizona – it's an imaginary idea that will set you up for difficulty and disappointment. Many people falsely view their career path as a perfect linear trajectory of preparatory occupations leading to a predestined career goal, as depicted in Figure 2.11.

Figure 2.11 Conventional Career Path

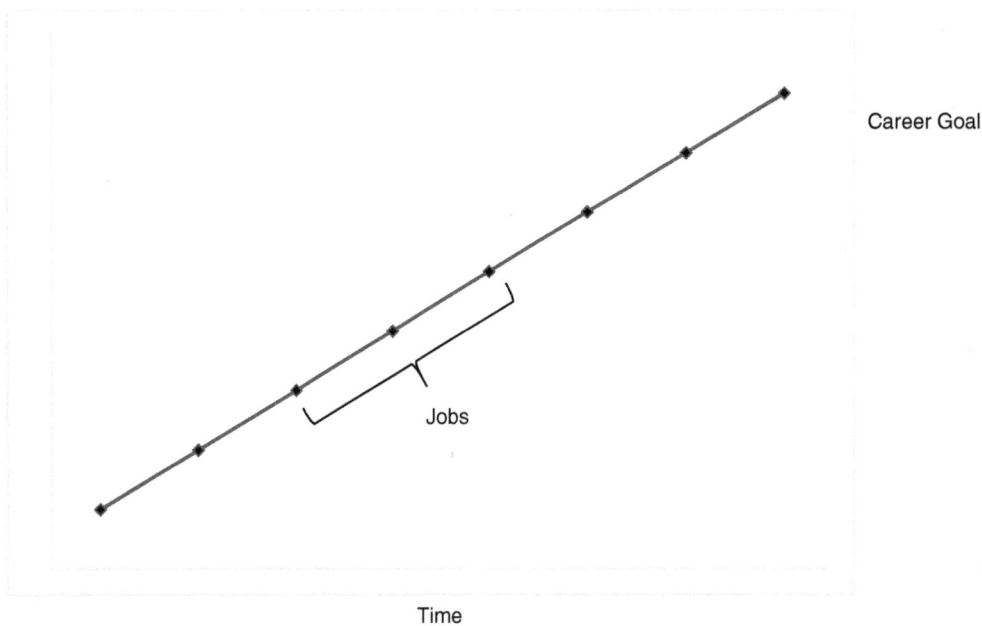

Career Goal

Jobs

Time

A career path is rarely conventional; instead it's an evolving process of trying different jobs and changing course based on what you learn (Super et al., 1996). Furthermore, occupations may satisfy shifting wants and needs that may seem unrelated to your long-term goals. For example, you may need to temporarily prioritize a well-paying job or schedule flexibility while attending school. Although there are more twists and turns than expected, you are still on your career path the entire time.

You're encouraged not to view this as discouraging—we want those twists and turns because they provide us with experiences that shape our direction. We don't set out on our career path knowing exactly where we're going to land. If we did, we'd all be working in the field that we imagined as children. (We can't all be Bob the Builder and Doc McStuffins!) Additionally, a career path is nonlinear because the end point is always changing. As a person learns through experience, their ideal career continually evolves in accordance. Every role and experience serves as a pivot point to adjust your sights toward a moving target (Campbell et al., 2015). Ideally, you will enjoy your work, but your career path won't end there. You'll continue to form new dreams and shift toward them.

Given its dynamic nature, it's difficult to discern your career path at any given point along the route. Many believe they are completely lost and abandon their path entirely rather than recognize they've been on the same path the whole time. Avoid this mistake by recognizing career paths are unconventional and have nonlinear points, shifting goals, and undefined endings, as shown in Figure 2.12.

Figure 2.12 Unconventional Career Path

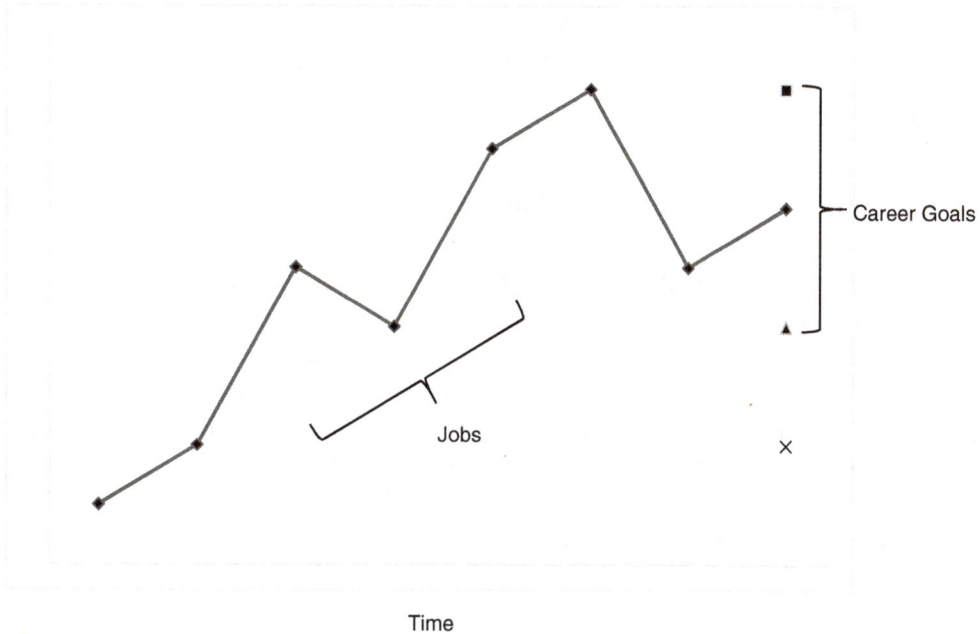

Time

The only way a career path can be understood is by looking backward and connecting the dots. Search for patterns and trends while expecting the unknown. The path will shape itself; your task is to focus on the next step.

Action 15 – Career Patterns

Take your next step by transitioning into understanding the world of work. Return to your career test results and review your responses for each of the following myths:

Myth 4 Action – Personality Assessment
Myth 6 Action – Abilities Assessment
Myth 8 Action – Likes and Dislikes Assessment
Myth 10 Action – Meaning and Values Assessment

For each of these tests, you identified at least two occupations that emerged as potentially good fits for you. You may have the same or different careers listed over multiple tests.

Look for similarities across your chosen occupations. Do any patterns emerge among the types of occupations you selected? How might you group multiple careers into categories? For example, you might notice a pattern of teaching or education-related jobs like professor, librarian, or school counselor. You may discover some seemingly loose or tangential associations, such as various occupations like mechanic and electrician involving working with your hands. Note your reflections by answering the questions below.

What patterns emerged from your chosen occupations?

_____

_____

_____

_____

_____

What clues do these patterns provide about you? What helpful information can you take from this?

_____

_____

_____

_____

_____

Review your occupation choices and narrow your list to your top five careers of interest. These do not represent your final five choices for a career; they are simply the five that we will use for our next action. There isn't a risk in narrowing your list now as additional choices may arise later, and you can always change your mind.

List your top five careers of interest:

1. _____

2. _____

3. _____

4. _____

5. _____

Myth 16

"I won't know if I like a career until I'm in it."

Fact

When buying a car, you'd be foolish to randomly point to one and say, "that one!" Instead, you research options, ask advice, weigh preferences, and even take a test drive before committing to a purchase. The thoughtful research and consideration that goes into car buying also needs to be applied in career selection (Lent & Brown, 2013). Careers are a serious commitment, and picking one blindly is unwise.

Continue to follow the career development process as depicted in Figure 2.13, which involves 1) learning and developing a clear and comprehensive awareness about yourself; 2) understanding and gathering an extensive knowledge base about relevant aspects of the world of work; and 3) finding a synergistic fit between a) your wants and needs and b) what the work world wants and needs.

Figure 2.13 Career Development Process

Understanding the world of work involves reviewing and collecting valuable information on an assortment of available jobs. Gathering and learning information about different careers can help you filter your options before ever trying them out (Hartung, 2013).

However, people often don't know where to gather accurate and comprehensive information about careers (Jordan & Marinaccio, 2017). They often rely on generic online search engines that provide unhelpful trendy "hot job" lists. Fortunately for us, there are free and accessible online databanks of available careers. Although they are trickier to navigate than an over-hyped job list, they provide helpful data-driven information that we will walk through together.

Action 16 – Career Research

One of my favorite career search sites is the Occupational Information Network (O*NET, 2021), available at bit.ly/careermythlinks. O*NET is a database of occupations that includes detailed information on job tasks, tools and technology, knowledge, skills, ability, education, interests, work styles, wages, and employment information. You may recognize we already used this site to explore your likes and dislikes, but we are returning to gather more information from it.

Using the list of at least five careers from the previous myth, enter each career name into the search bar labeled, "Occupation Quick Search." You'll repeat this process for each of your five careers. From the available list, choose the best option for your interests. For example, you might search "sales" and choose "retail salesperson" from a list of related options. Don't hesitate to explore several related titles if you're uncertain which one to select.

A summary report for your chosen occupation is then presented. Read the entire summary report and note aspects you like and dislike about each occupation. These reports are long and can become easily overwhelming, so take breaks if needed. If they are too exhausting, stick to the job summaries and "Tasks" at the top of the page. For more information about what each of the categories on the summary report mean (e.g., Tasks, Knowledge, Skills), visit O*NET's Online Help description of summary reports available at bit.ly/careermythlinks.

On the summary report, note that clicking the + icon next to an item reveals a list of related occupations. Use this feature whenever you encounter something of particular interest. For example, you might get excited at the prospect of the work task, "greet customers and ascertain their wants and needs" (O*NET, 2021). Clicking on this task reveals other careers with similar tasks for your consideration such as Hotel Clerks and Insurance Agents.

Confirm that you're still interested in your five careers after reading about them. If you aren't, return to your test results from earlier myths or select related occupations using the + icon. Continue this process until you have a list of five careers of continued interest.

Make sure that you understand each of your chosen occupations well enough to explain what the occupation is and why you like it. Record this information below.

Career #1:

Occupation Title: _____

Description: _____

_____

_____

_____

_____

What interests me: _____

_____

_____

_____

_____

Career #2:

Occupation Title: _____

Description: _____

_____

_____

_____

_____

What interests me: _____

_____

_____

_____

_____

Career #3:

Occupation Title: _____

Description: _____

_____

_____

_____

_____

What interests me: _____

_____

_____

_____

_____

Career #4:

Occupation Title: _____

Description: _____

_____

_____

_____

_____

What interests me: _____

_____

_____

_____

_____

Career #5:

Occupation Title: _____

Description: _____

_____

_____

_____

_____

What interests me: _____

_____

_____

_____

_____

Myth 17

"I should pick what I want and accept no substitutes."

Fact

Although it may be tempting to reject all substitutes, remember that successful career development requires flexibility. Recall our career development process of 1) learning about yourself, 2) understanding the world of work, and 3) finding a fit. This second step of understanding the world of work is intended to encourage and welcome alternatives. This is when "teaser" content designed to entice you is appropriate and even desired! Go ahead and get lost in career-related headlines just as you would with online ads and videos. At this point it is helpful to investigate and consider all kinds of substitutes instead of shackling yourself to a single option.

The reason for this is illustrated by our career choice diamond, as shown in Figure 2.14.

Figure 2.14 Career Choice Diamond

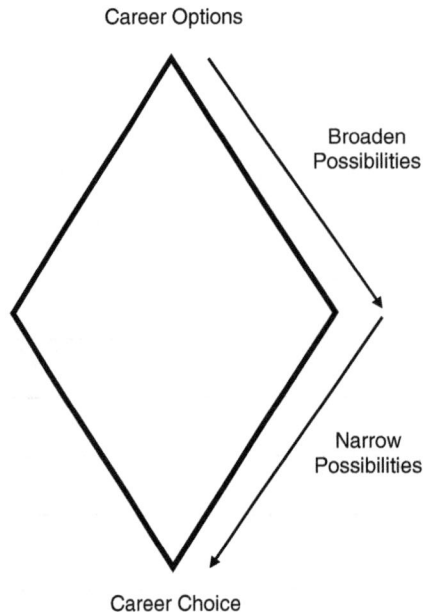

Effective career decision making begins by broadening our options to include all available information and possibilities, followed by narrowing down the options to find a true and informed fit (Bolles, 2020). Although we have already tightened our search by reviewing a handful of personality matching careers, we will not be confined by them. Shackling yourself to a singular option is counterproductive because you'll be left with no available alternatives if things don't unfold seamlessly. Our current focus is to expand our knowledge of available careers by finding new options or confirming ones we've already discovered. We want to encourage and consider alternatives now, so that we can better commit to a single option later.

Action 17 – Related Careers

Explore related careers using online occupational databases. We've already learned how to research careers using O*NET using the + icon. Review the previous myth's action step for instructions.

Another one of my favorite sources is the Occupational Outlook Handbook (OOH, 2021), available at bit.ly/careermythlinks. My clients generally find this site to be more user-friendly than O*NET. Although it doesn't offer as much information about individual occupations, OOH includes introductions to a broader range of occupational titles. I recommend using both sites for their unique benefits in the career development process. If one site has incomplete or confusing information about a given occupation, you can supplement it by searching the other one.

Try using OOH for this search, but feel free to supplement with O*NET if needed or desired. Using the list of five careers from the previous myth, enter the name of each career into the OOH search bar labeled, "Search Handbook." You'll repeat this process one by one for each of your five careers. From the available list, choose the best option for your interests. For example, you might search "detective" and choose "police and detectives" from a list of related options. Don't hesitate to search and explore several related titles if you're uncertain which one to choose.

A summary for your chosen occupation will be presented along with tabs along the top of the report for different sections (e.g., What They Do, Work Environment, How to Become One). Read the tabs for your chosen occupations and note aspects you like and dislike about each occupation. These reports are long and can become easily overwhelming, so take breaks if needed and if they are too much to take in, stick to the summary tab. Many of the occupations include a short video introducing the occupation, which can be an informative and entertaining addition to your search.

Next, click the "Similar Occupations" tab on the top right of the report. This tab shows a table of occupations that share several similar characteristics to the one you searched. Given their shared characteristics, these related occupations are also likely to be a good fit for you (Taylor & Hardy, 2004).

Thoughtfully consider each of these options by selecting occupations that sound interesting and reading the summary about unfamiliar ones. Take time to read the entire report if you're especially fascinated by a specific occupation.

This is where you can use the clickbait approach to rapidly educate yourself about careers: start by setting a timer for 20 minutes and allow yourself to fall into a targeted rabbit hole of similar occupations. Continue by searching and reading about an occupation of interest, then search similar occupations and repeat the process until the timer is complete. If you reach a point where no new occupations of interest emerge, search another job from your list and repeat the process. By the end of this exercise you'll have been introduced to several occupations in your areas of interest.

Once you've completed this exercise, write about your search experience by recording your answers below.

List five occupational titles you researched that emerged from your similar occupations search. Choose the five that were the most interesting to you:

1. _____

2. _____

3. _____

4. _____

5. _____

You've researched options and considered alternatives, and now it is time to narrow your choices down to your top four careers. These can be the same as your previous choices or new ones from your research. Consider bookmarking or even printing the OOH pages for these careers so you can easily refer to them later.

Record the occupational titles for the top four careers that are of most interest for you now:

1. _____

2. _____

3. _____

4. _____

Myth 18

"Someone else can make my career decisions for me."

Fact

As you begin to narrow options, you may be tempted to recruit others to guide your decisions. However, making career choices is a personal responsibility, and imposing this duty upon others is ineffective (Campbell, 2020). Besides, blindly taking someone else's advice without using your own judgment is likely to disappoint and frustrate. Even following good advice can foster dependency and reinforce an inability to make life choices for yourself. Regard decision making as a muscle that requires frequent conditioning to prevent atrophy. The more you make decisions for yourself, the better you become at making them. Although there are many helpful resources to take advantage of, it is still in your best interest to make your own decisions.

This doesn't mean you should refuse all assistance and go it alone. In fact, appropriately utilizing support is especially helpful in the career development process (Mills, 2017). People who support you and know you well can help by offering useful feedback. Having a third party to regularly dialogue with can provide you with an objective perspective in addition to added support and encouragement. Now is a golden opportunity to identify the people who can help inform your choices as we continue to approach finding a potential career fit. Remember to keep your ears open and attentive to their perspective while retaining ownership of your decisions.

Action 18 – Support People

Write down two people who support you and who you believe will be influential in your career decision making. These may be friends, family members, religious leaders, mentors, teachers, fellow students, supervisors, coworkers—the list goes on. Who do you usually go to for support or advice? Try to identify at least two, but feel free to include more if desired.

My support people:

1. Name: _____

2. Name: _____

Ask them the following questions:

- How would you describe me?
- What career can you envision me doing?
- Share your top four careers from the previous myth that you are currently exploring. What is your response to these choices? Any feedback about these careers or which to choose?
- What advice do you have for me as I continue to develop my career?

Compile their responses and summarize what you learned from them by answering the questions below.

What did you learn from talking with your support people?

_____

_____

_____

_____

_____

How can this information be helpful for you? What do you want to keep in mind moving forward?

_____

_____

_____

_____

_____

Myth 19

"Career counseling is a waste of time."

Fact

Career counseling can help you progress throughout your career development journey. In fact, research has repeatedly demonstrated that the benefits of career counseling can rival and even exceed the positive effects of traditional mental health counseling (Brown & Ryan Krane, 2000; Whiston & James, 2013). This is because careers play a substantial role in an individual's life, and career counseling provides the same benefits of increased wellness in addition to focusing on specific career goals (Brown & Lent, 2013).

Those who overlook career counseling often don't know what it is, or its purpose. When used properly, career counseling provides guidance and support through the decision-making process. The primary role of a career counselor is to help guide you through career-related decisions, handle life transitions, negotiate work–life balance, and achieve overall life satisfaction and wellness (Jordan & Marinaccio, 2017). Through the use of talk therapy and individualized assessments, career counselors help you learn more about yourself and more clearly determine your next steps. Counselors often advise clients about education, training programs, careers, and even financial support. Additionally, counselors may help with preparations including resume writing, interviewing, and networking. Regardless of where you currently stand, career counseling can help you attain your desired future (Bolles, 2020).

Action 19 – Career Counseling

If you aren't already working with someone, consider if career counseling may be beneficial for you. As discussed, working with a counselor offers increased support, guidance, and accountability. Review your previous workbook responses and ask yourself whether professional guidance is desired or needed in order to complete the instructed activities. Specifically, take a closer look at your results concerning the Career Decision-Making Difficulties Questionnaire you completed in Myth 12. If you struggle making decisions, your results likely suggested considering a career counselor. Even if you don't see a need for career counseling, a mere interest is enough reason to give it a try.

Whether you are unsure about moving forward, or want more support in doing so, career counseling can aid in the process. Keep in mind that most colleges offer career counseling at their career center, and these services are often extended to alumni. For those not associated with a university, career counselors and assessments are also available to the community.

One strategy for finding a career counselor is conducting an Internet search for career counselors in your area. You can visit a site such as Psychology Today, available at bit.ly/careermythlinks, enter your location, and search. Since most counselors on this site are licensed mental health professionals who provide general personal counseling, filter your results so that you can easily identify those who specialize in career counseling. This filter can be found on the left side under "Issues" by clicking "Career Counseling.".

Check your counselor's credentials to verify that they are a National Certified Career Counselor who is licensed to practice counseling in your state and have received the necessary training (National Career Development Association, 2017). Visit the National Career Development Association (NCDA) website available at bit.ly/careermythlinks and enter your location under the search bar "Need Help?" to find NCDA credentialed members in your area. Look for the credential "Certified Career Counselor" for professionals that are licensed in mental health counseling in addition to career issues.

Even if you do not plan to pursue career counseling now, it can be helpful to gather the names of potential counselors for the future. Click on the names of the career counselors you find to read their bios. Select three career counselors who you might be interested in working with. Include their names and information below to contact now or possibly use later. Not everyone wants or needs career counseling but it's helpful to know additional help is available if ever needed.

1. Name: _____

   Phone Number: _____

   Website: _____

   What interests me about working with them: _____

   _____

   _____

   _____

   _____

2. Name: _____

   Phone Number: _____

   Website: _____

   What interests me about working with them: _____

   _____

   _____

   _____

   _____

3. Name: _____

   Phone Number: _____

   Website: _____

   What interests me about working with them: _____

   _____

   _____

   _____

   _____

Myth 20

"My career will make me feel legitimate to everyone else."

Fact

The work we do is viewed as a crucial part of our public identity (Brown & Lent, 2013). This is especially true in western culture where individual identity is emphasized. As we continue to discuss the role of others in the career development journey, we need to protect ourselves from inappropriately folding to outside pressure and public opinion.

While discussing your career path, expect to dislike and even disagree with some of the feedback you receive from others. Keep in mind that some disagreement can be helpful as it illustrates honest communication and encourages us to think deeply about our plans. I recall times in my own life when well-meaning loved ones responded to my aspirations of becoming a psychologist with disappointment and skepticism. Furthermore, when you interact with someone whose initial opinions don't match your own carefully constructed plans, don't be afraid of proceeding with your own self-knowledge. When this happens, simply thank the advice giver kindly (Miller, 2010). Avoid being a people pleaser that tries to hopelessly charm everyone and instead recall the reasons for your choice, consider feedback, and avoid tying your self-worth into the initial impressions of others.

Remember that regardless of what anyone says or does, you always retain the ability to make your own career decisions in the best way you see fit. It is not possible to please everyone, nor is it your obligation to do so (Germer, 2009). Keep in mind that those who have expectations for your professional future are usually well intentioned and want to aid in your success. Unfortunately, despite their good intentions, their guidance might not always be helpful in the present moment. Given that you know yourself better than anyone else and will be most affected by your decisions, your evaluations carry the most weight.

Action 20 – Informational Interviews

We'll continue to include others in appropriate ways in our career development process. To do this, you'll conduct informational interviews with people who work in three of your careers of interest. Informational interviews are simply conversations with professionals to find out if you might like their job (Bolles, 2020). These interviews allow you to form contacts with people in your fields of interest, learn more about the jobs themselves, and gather additional feedback to support your decision making.

Begin by reading the step-by-step instructions on informational interviewing provided by the career coaching website Campus Career Coach (Grad Leaders, 2016), available at bit.ly/careermythlinks. This brief and comprehensive guide discusses the benefits of interviewing, how to find interviewees, arrange a meeting, and what to say throughout the interview. While in-person interviews are best, keep in mind that interviews can be done by phone, video conferencing, email, etc.

Next, plan your strategy. Narrow your careers of interest down to your top three choices. Find one person to interview for each of your three choices. Using the tools you gathered from the provided instructions, answer the following questions:

What strategies will you implement to find interviewees? Review the provided suggestions in addition to considering referrals from family and friends, using social media, and contacting organizations directly with requests.

_____

_____

_____

_____

_____

What five questions will you ask your interviewees? Feel free to develop your own or use the provided questions from the instructions.

1. _____

2. _____

3. _____

4. _____

5. _____

Contact your three interviewees and conduct your informational interviews. Be sure to request continued contact and send a thank you note as outlined in the instructions. Summarize what you learned from each informational interview below. Include notes on whether you're still interested in each career and why.

Interview #1:

_____

_____

_____

_____

_____

Interview #2:

_____

_____

_____

_____

_____

Interview #3:

_____

_____

_____

_____

_____

Myth 21

"I will like this job because I know other people who enjoy it."

Fact

Spending time with someone who loves their work can be an uplifting experience. Chances are you experienced this firsthand while completing the previous action. Although these experiences can be influential, they can also feed into the myth of believing that you will enjoy a specific job just because someone else does.

Several times I have been an interviewee in informational interviews where I have enthusiastically expressed my heartfelt love of my work. Most interviewers are understandably attracted to this joyfulness, but do not pursue my line of work after learning what it entails. The takeaway is that to properly discern your compatibility with a job, you must separate the facts you gathered from the emotions that your interviewee felt for their job.

Although talking is helpful, its benefits are limited. Experience is crucial to gathering additional information about the world of work (Campbell, 2013). But don't think this means you need to shackle yourself to a job before knowing whether it is a good fit. On the contrary, you can try out a career in the form of job shadowing. In fact, spending just a few hours experiencing a typical workday in a given career can help you know whether it's something worth continued pursuit.

Action 21 – Job Shadowing

To learn more about the world of work and further refine your choices, we'll now turn toward gathering real-world experience. You'll engage in a few brief job shadowing exercises with people working in two of your careers of interest.

Begin by reading an overview of job shadowing, complete with instructions on how to set up and conduct a job shadow, provided by another career coaching website, Live Career (Hansen, 2020), available at bit.ly/careermythlinks.

Next, plan your strategy. Narrow your careers of interest down to your top two choices. Find one person for each of your choices to shadow. Use the same methods from the previous myth in addition to information you learned from the linked article above to find professionals to shadow. Before you shadow anyone, answer the following questions:

What information could you gather from job shadowing that couldn't be obtained from reading about a job or talking about it?

_____

_____

_____

_____

_____

Contact and conduct your two job shadows. Be sure to request continued contact and send a thank you note. Summarize what you learned from each job shadow below. Include notes on whether you're still interested in each career and why or why not.

Job Shadow #1:

_____

_____

_____

_____

_____

Job Shadow #2:

_____

_____

_____

_____

_____

Myth 22

"My career will find me."

Fact

You are unlikely to randomly stumble upon your career choice. While it is seductive to fantasize about a Career Prince Charming guiding you toward a happily ever after, this sort of thinking will leave you frustrated and stuck forever. Don't make the mistake of anxiously waiting; rather, you must be the hero of your own story by actively bearing the responsibility of making decisions that bring you closer toward your goals.

The fact is that good-fitting careers rarely present themselves in an obvious fashion. For example, in one study, only 17% of working adults agreed with the statement, "I was drawn by something beyond myself to pursue my current line of work" (Dik & Duffy, 2012, p. 48). This would suggest that the remaining 83% of people had to make challenging decisions to find a well-fitting career.

There is no need to cringe at the thought of making career decisions. Even if you're in the minority and feel an external pull toward a certain career, I'd still encourage you to work through the decision-making process. By doing so, you might realize that you prematurely committed to a specific job. Additionally, by practicing your decision-making skills, you will be better prepared for the future (Lore, 2011). Studies show that the ability to make career decisions is strongly associated with greater confidence and emotional stability, decreased choice and commitment anxiety, higher goal directivity, and healthy relationships (Brown et al., 2011). Actively practicing your decision-making abilities is a straightforward strategy to improve your overall well-being.

To improve our career decision-making abilities, we have been following the three-step career process, as shown in Figure 2.15. So far, you've increased your awareness about yourself and gathered an extensive knowledge base about relevant aspects of the world of work. Now it is time to turn our focus to finding a synergistic fit between your wants and needs with what the work world wants and needs.

Figure 2.15 Career Development Process

The third step involves matching the information you gathered about yourself with careers of interest. To keep anxiety at bay, remind yourself that career decisions are not permanent. You'll be guided through the decision-making process in this workbook, but you can always revise your choices later. If a certain career loses its appeal, you can easily look elsewhere. Altering your aim is a normal part of the process and should be expected.

In this third step, the goal is to narrow down choices to a single career. Keep in mind that this is not evidence that you'll only acquire one lifelong job. As discussed in previous myths, you'll likely occupy multiple careers throughout your life. Personally, I currently hold multiple careers simultaneously, including a university professor and private practice counselor. To narrow down your choices simply, we will reduce them in succession. Remember that this is not a definite decision but rather a tentative step. You can always return for alternative choices.

Action 22 – Decision Making

To find a fit, we need to consider what "fit" means for you. Are you a multipotentialite—that is, a jack of all trades—or a specialist? By identifying your decision-making type, you can improve your self-awareness and reduce lurking anxieties. Watch the following TED Talk, "Why Some of Us Don't Have One True Calling," from career coach Emilie Wapnick to learn more, available at bit.ly/careermythlinks.

Do you consider yourself a multipotentialite or specialist? Why?

_____

_____

_____

_____

_____

How might that impact your career decisions? What might you want to keep in mind moving forward?

_____

_____

_____

_____

_____

Myth 23

"I can expect a career epiphany."

Fact

Career development is an ongoing journey, not a spontaneous epiphany or random flash of inspiration. Many people mistakenly believe that some revelation will come to them out of the blue, leading them to carve their unique path with crystal-clarity (Dik & Duffy, 2012). As you can probably guess by now, this thinking is misguided. Most decisions are made without sufficient information, and this is especially true in the career decision process. Even if you do experience a rare career epiphany, you will need to make many more decisions without such a vision (Rogue Recruiter, 2013). It is wiser to anticipate your career path will require the courage to take reasonable risks based on the best information you have at the time.

This isn't to say that inspiration can't strike, merely that it comes in the form of muted whispers, not blaring foghorns. Consulting these quiet intuitions is helpful when making a career decision (NERIS Analytics Limited, 2011). Rather than looking to the sky for thunderous feedback, listen carefully for hunches that provide modest feedback in the form of a gut sensation or impulse. Monitor these internal signals and rate the sensations that emerge when you make a decision. Bear in mind, it is a common error to confuse lingering uncertainty with the belief you dislike (or like) something. When practiced, you'll likely find that even your positive reactions are subtler than you might expect (Landrum, 2009). Once understood, you can skillfully apply these internal signals to career information you've collected to improve the decision-making process.

Action 23 – Mind Mapping

In continuing the process of finding a fit, you'll learn to consult your intuition using a mind map exercise. A mind map encourages intuition and uses both sides of the brain by combining drawing (right side) with the free association of words (left side). Mind mapping is a visual method intended to be performed rapidly. This method bypasses your logical and verbal censors and taps into your unfiltered intuitive reactions (Burnett & Evans, 2016).

Complete a mind map using your top two careers of interest. The purpose is to bypass your logic (we'll consult logic later) to access your intuitive preferences.

To create a mind map, select one of your top two careers of interest. Write it in the center of the space provided below and draw a circle around it. Around the circle, list six reactions to your career, jotting down the first things that come to mind. Anything is acceptable. Your words may include descriptors (e.g., "fun"), feelings (e.g., "nervous"), related ideas or concerns (e.g., "money"), or seemingly random words (e.g., "orange")—there are no limitations to your mind map. Once complete, create a ring around your career circle by drawing a larger circle around your reaction words.

Repeat this reaction step by writing down words in a second ring that are related to the first. Feel free to write down more reactions to the central career as well. Let whatever feelings you have emerge unfiltered on the page without judgment. Keep going until you have at least three rings of six-word associations on each ring. An example mind map is provided in Figure 2.16.

Figure 2.16 Example Mind Map

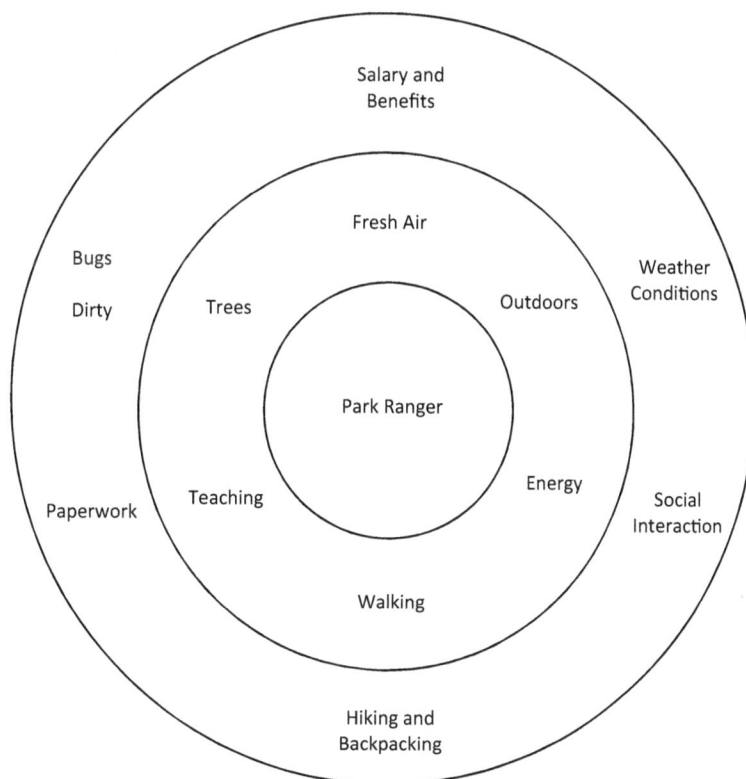

Repeat the entire process to create a mind map for your other selected career. Review your mind maps and answer the questions below.

Career #1: Draw your mind map below.

Career #2: Draw your mind map below.

Review your mind maps and highlight reactions that are particularly interesting or stand out. What are three reactions from each map that catch your eye?

Career #1:

1. _____

2. _____

3. _____

Career #2:

1. _____

2. _____

3. _____

How might those reactions impact your career choice? What might you want to keep in mind when making a choice?

_____

_____

_____

_____

_____

Myth 24

"My career is something I can plan out step-by-step."

Fact

Regardless of how carefully you plan, it's nearly impossible that your career will fall in line with your pre-determined steps. Life is unpredictable and rarely caters to a neatly formulated timeline. Having goals that reflect a general direction is helpful, but stringently planning each step of your career development is highly impractical (Bolles, 2020). Consequentially, attempting to fully control every aspect of your career journey is maladaptive because it blinds you to other opportunities. Our plans will best serve us if they remain flexible and resilient in the face of an unpredictable life (Robbins, 2008).

Scrap rigid step-by-step plans by tweaking the way you view your career choice. If your vision consists of strict rules and unbending goals, then reframe your choices as *hypotheses* or *best guesses* regarding the overall direction of your path. For example, replace the thought, "I need to become the head chef of my favorite restaurant," with, "I'm thinking of heading in the direction of becoming a chef, but will remain open to other possibilities along the way." We want to avoid the sabotaging effects of being overly exact with our long-term goals (Bolles, 2020). Keep in mind, however, that the specificity of our goals should appropriately correspond with how distant they are into the future. Instead of rigidly outlining *every* future step, focus on short-term steps that move you closer to a more generalized long-term direction (Campbell, 2008).

Action 24 – Pro/Con List

Although you can't plan out your career step-by-step, you can review the data to see what is currently the most reasonable. In the last myth, we consulted with intuition to find a career fit. Now, by making a list of positives and negatives, we'll use reasoning and analysis to continue finding a fit and make a decision (Mills, 2017).

To make a pro/con list, begin by returning to your previous myth actions and collecting everything you've learned so far. Take special note of your responses to the following myth actions:

- Myth 14 Action – Summary of what you learned about yourself
- Myths 15–17 Actions – Independent research on the world of work
- Myths 18–21 Actions – Collaborative exploration on the world of work
- Myth 23 Action – Consulting intuition to find a fit

Career #1: Pro/Con List
Create two pro/con lists, one for each of your top two careers of interest. Select one career and list as many positive aspects as you can about selecting this career over the other. For example, it could be more in line with your values, offers a flexible work schedule, etc. Try to list at least ten positives for the career:

1. _____
2. _____
3. _____
4. _____
5. _____
6. _____
7. _____
8. _____
9. _____
10. _____

Now list the cons or drawbacks of selecting this career over your other choice. For example, the need to relocate, having a gut feeling against it, etc. Try to list at least ten cons for this career:

1. _____
2. _____
3. _____
4. _____
5. _____
6. _____
7. _____
8. _____
9. _____
10. _____

Career #2: Pro/Con List
Now repeat the process and create a new pro/con list for your other career of interest. List at least ten positive aspects of choosing this career over the previous:

1. _____
2. _____
3. _____
4. _____
5. _____
6. _____
7. _____
8. _____
9. _____
10. _____

List at least ten drawbacks of choosing this career:

1. _____

2. _____

3. _____

4. _____

5. _____

6. _____

7. _____

8. _____

9. _____

10. _____

Now you'll review your lists and make a choice. Although intimidating, remember that this choice is not final and can be revised at any time. It is simply your current hypothesis that we will use to continue moving forward. Write your choice below and say aloud, "I choose this one."

Your (tentative best guess) career choice: _____

Congratulations on choosing a career to pursue!

Myth 25

"I can avoid making mistakes."

Fact

Making mistakes is an inevitable part of the process that cannot be avoided. For many, their difficulty making decisions is rooted in the fear of feeling like a personal failure if they make the wrong choice. This thinking is misguided; errors are a normal part of the process, not evidence of failure. A more accurate predictor of failure, in addition to success, is your resilience to adapt to a situation. As the proverb says, "the bamboo that bends is stronger than the oak that resists." Mistakes are inevitable; it is your response to these obstacles that matters most. Research has shown that successful individuals are highly skilled at adapting to their situations, favorable or otherwise (Brown & Hirschi, 2013). Instead of automatically degrading yourself when you stumble, challenge your initial impressions and have a calm and collected conversation with yourself. Is the story you tell unnecessarily tainted with pessimism? Were circumstances outside of your control? Search for reflective feedback and readjust your sights accordingly. Although the journey might have a lot more hindrances than you'd like, you never have to stop completely.

Authors Bill Burnett and Dave Evans (2016) refer to the ability to reframe mistakes into growth opportunities as *failure immunity*. To develop your failure immunity, you can note insights gained rather than blaming yourself for any deemed failures. For example, after further research, you may feel your career choice was a mistake. However, changing course is not evidence of failure. On the contrary, selecting a career can provide new information that was not previously apparent. By making a choice, you can further your understanding and proceed with critical insights that were not readily available before the decision.

Note that the process of finding a career fit persists well beyond a singular job choice. By acting on a career decision, you can gain more insights and information. Remember, you can always revisit the career development process to adjust your aims.

The three-step career development process is not a one-time activity, but should be reevaluated multiple times. Regardless of your current whereabouts, you're always somewhere in the three-step process of learning about yourself, understanding the world of work, and finding a fit. You may find yourself needing to revisit a single step or reconsider all three. I've worked with many clients who've spotted gaps in their self-awareness and need to reassess the first step. Others have needed to reexamine the second step to explore alternative career options. Revisiting these steps is a normal, helpful, and expected part of the process. I regularly reassess these steps and recommend you do the same to improve your overall career vitality.

Action 25 – Reframing Mistakes

Fear of making mistakes can make it difficult to proceed with a career choice. By combating this unproductive rumination, you can identify positive outcomes that have resulted from seemingly "poor" decisions in the past. For purpose of illustration, perhaps you are upset for not taking a gap year before attending college. Instead of ruminating on this irreversible blunder, you can focus on the positive outcomes that would not have otherwise emerged. This simple change in perspective helps redirect your focus on present actions that can positively influence your future (Greenberger & Padesky, 2016).

To improve your failure immunity, let's start by rethinking past "mistakes" as growth opportunities. Then, we'll plan for the high probability of revising your decision later. With failure immunity, "failure is just the raw material for success" (Burnett & Evans, 2016, p. 113).

Relabeling past mistakes as growth opportunities. Identify five "mistakes" you remember making in the last year. They can be in any area of life. In Table 2.1, briefly describe each one in the left-hand column. Using the right-hand column, describe a benefit that came from the deemed "mistake." This could be an insight you gained, something learned, an improved relationship, or any other unexpected perk that resulted from the error. Use this tool as a reminder to search for the stars when you feel lost in the darkening sky.

Table 2.1 Mistakes and Benefits

Mistake	Benefit
1.	1.
2.	2.
3.	3.
4.	4.
5.	5.

Expect to revise. The next step is to continue acting on your career choice through educational preparation or job hunting. These topics will be covered in Chapters 3 and 4, respectively. If you're uncertain whether education or job hunting is your next step, return to previous myth activities. Specifically, identify what type of preparation is necessary for your desired career. Use the following resources to determine whether you need additional education or can begin job hunting:

- Myth 16 Action – O*Net online database (in career summary report, see "Education")
- Myth 17 Action – OOH online database (see "How to Become One" tab)
- Myth 19 Action – Career counseling
- Myth 20 Action – Informational interviews
- Myth 21 Action – Job shadowing

Based on what you've learned, what is your next step in acting on your choice (exploring additional education or job hunting)? Why is that your next step?

_____

_____

_____

_____

_____

When acting on your choice, you may feel that your chosen career no longer seems to be a fit. In this situation, these activities can aid you:

- Myth 14 Action – PALMS summary of what you learned about yourself
- Myths 15–17 Actions – Independent research on the world of work
- Myths 18–21 Actions – Collaborative exploration on the world of work
- Myth 23–24 Actions – Consulting intuition and logic to find a fit
- Myth 25 Action – Reframing mistakes as growth opportunities

If you find yourself questioning your career choice, what section in this workbook do you believe will be the most helpful to return to? Why?

_____

_____

_____

_____

_____

References

Blair, G. R. (2009). *Everything counts: 52 remarkable ways to inspire excellence and drive results.* Wiley.

Bolles, R. N. (2020). *What color is your parachute? Job-hunter's workbook* (2020 ed.). Ten Speed Press.

Brown, D., & Brooks, L. (1996). *Career choice and development* (3rd ed.). Jossey-Bass Publishers.

Brown, S. D., Hacker, J., Abrams, M., Carr, A., Rector, C., Lamp, K., & Siena, A. (2011). Validation of a four-factor model of career indecision. *Journal of Career Assessment, 20*(1), 3–21. https://doi.org/10.1177/1069072711417154

Brown, S. D., & Hirschi, A. (2013). Personality, career development, and occupational attainment. In S. Brown & R. W. Lent (Eds.), *Career development and counseling: Putting theory and research to work* (2nd ed., pp. 299–328). Wiley.

Brown, S. D., & Lent, R. W. (Eds.). (2013). *Career development and counseling: Putting theory and research to work* (2nd ed.). Wiley.

Brown, S. D., & Ryan Krane, N. E. (2000). Four (or five) sessions and a cloud of dust: Old assumptions and new observations about career counseling. In S. D. Brown & R. W. Lent (Eds.), *Handbook of counseling psychology* (3rd ed., pp. 740–766). Wiley.

Bureau of Labor Statistics (BLS). (2021, August 31). *Number of jobs, labor market experience, and earnings growth: Results from a national longitudinal survey* [Press release]. www.bls.gov/news.release/pdf/nlsoy.pdf

Burnett, B., & Evans, D. (2016). *Designing your life: How to build a well-lived, joyful life.* Knopf.

California Career Resource Network. (2020). *Welcome to the Work Importance Profiler.* California Career Zone. www.cacareerzone.org/wip/

Campbell, E. L. (2008). *Anticipating work & family: A conflict of interests?* [Unpublished master's thesis]. University of North Texas, Denton.

Campbell, E. L. (2013). Anticipating work & family: Experience, conflict, & planning in the transition to adulthood. *Dissertation Abstracts International: Section B. Sciences & Engineering, 73*(8).

Campbell, E. L. (2014). *Career fearfest: Don't fear your career!* Lecture presented to Whitworth University psychology students, Spokane, Washington.

Campbell, E. L. (2020). *Helping skills training for nonprofessional counselors: The LifeRAFT model—providing relief through actions, feelings, and thoughts.* Routledge. https://doi.org/10.4324/9780429031380

Campbell, E. L., Campbell, V. L., & Watkins, E. (2015). Construct validity of anticipated work-family conflict & barriers measures. *Journal of Career Development, 42*(5), 370–380. https://doi.org/10.1177/0894845315571413

Campbell, E. L., Davidson, M., & Davidson, S. M. (2017). Effectiveness of LifeRAFT undergraduate helping skills model. *Psychology Teaching Review, 23*(2), 32–41.

Colman, A. M. (2015). *A dictionary of psychology* (4th ed.). Oxford University Press.

Crosby, O. (2005). Career myths and how to debunk them. *Occupational Outlook Quarterly.* www.bls.gov/careeroutlook/2005/fall/art01.pdf

Csikszentmihalyi, M. (1990). *Flow: The psychology of optimal experience.* HarperCollins.

Dik, B. J., & Duffy, R. D. (2012). *Make your job a calling: How the psychology of vocation can change your life at work.* Templeton Press.

Forleo, M. (2019). *Everything is figureoutable.* Portfolio/Penguin.

Gati, I., Krausz, M., & Osipow, S. H. (1996). A taxonomy of difficulties in career decision making. *Journal of Counseling Psychology, 43*(4), 510–526. https://doi.org/10.1037/0022-0167.43.4.510

Germer, C. K. (2009). *The mindful path to self-compassion: Freeing yourself from destructive thoughts and emotions*. The Guilford Press.

Grad Leaders. (2016). *Informational interviewing*. The Campus Career Coach. http://thecampuscareercoach.com/wp-content/themes/campus-career-coach/guides/informational_interviewing.pdf

Greenberger, D., & Padesky, C. A. (2016). *Mind over mood: Change how you feel by changing the way you think* (2nd ed.). The Guilford Press.

Hansen, J. C. (2013). Nature, importance, and assessment of interests. In S. D. Brown & R. W. Lent (Eds.), *Career development and counseling: Putting theory and research to work* (2nd ed., pp. 387–416). Wiley.

Hansen, K. (2020). *Researching companies and careers through job shadowing*. Live Career. www.livecareer.com/resources/jobs/search/job-shadowing

Hartung, P. J. (2013). The life-span, life-space theory of careers. In S. Brown & R. Lent (Eds.), *Career development and counseling: Putting theory and research to work* (2nd ed., pp. 83–113). Wiley.

Holland, J. L. (1959). A theory of vocational choice. *Journal of Counseling Psychology, 6*(1), 35–45. https://doi.org/10.1037/h0040767

Holland, J. L. (1997). *Making vocational choices: A theory of vocational personalities and work environments* (3rd ed.). Psychological Assessment Resources.

Jacks, L. P. (1932). *Education through recreation*. Harper and Brothers.

Jordan, L. A., & Marinaccio, J. N. (Eds.). (2017). *Facilitating career development* (4th ed.). National Career Development Association.

Landrum, R. E. (2009). *Finding jobs with a psychology bachelor's degree: Expert advice for launching your career*. American Psychological Association.

Lore, N. (2011). *The Pathfinder: How to choose or change your career for a lifetime of satisfaction and success*. Touchstone.

Maxwell, J. C. (2013). *How to love your work: The ABCs of loving your job*. Motivation and Success Strategies. www.getmotivation.com/motivationblog/2013/09/how-to-love-your-work-the-abcs-of-loving-your-job-by-john-c-maxwell/

Merton, R. K. (1948). The self-fulfilling prophecy. *Antioch Review, 8*(2), 193–210.

Metz, A. J., & Jones, J. E. (2013). Ability and aptitude assessment in career counseling. In S. Brown & R. Lent (Eds.), *Career development and counseling: Putting theory and research to work* (2nd ed., pp. 449–476). Wiley.

Miller, D. (2010). *48 days to the work you love* (2nd ed.). B&H Publishing.

Miller, S. (2018). *2019 salary budgets inch upward ever so slightly*. Society for Human Resources Management. www.shrm.org/resourcesandtools/hr-topics/compensation/pages/2019-salary-budgets-inch-upward.aspx

Mills, C. (2017). *Career coach: How to plan your career and land your perfect job* (2nd ed.). Crimson Publishing.

My Next Move. (2021). *O*NET Interest Profiler*. www.mynextmove.org/explore/ip

National Career Development Association. (2017). *Introduction to credentialing*. https://ncda.org/aws/NCDA/pt/sp/credentialing_intro

NERIS Analytics Limited. (2011). *16 Personalities*. www.16personalities.com

O*NET (2021). *O*NET OnLine*. www.onetonline.org

Occupational Outlook Handbook (OOH). (2021). www.bls.gov/ooh/

Parsons, F. (1909). *Choosing a vocation.* Houghton Mifflin and Company.

Pope, M., Minor, C. W., & Lara, T. M. (2011). *Experiential activities for teaching career development classes and facilitating career groups* (3rd ed.). National Career Development Association.

Prochaska, J. O., Norcross, J. C., & DiClemente, C. C. (2005). Stages of change: Prescriptive guidelines. In G. P. Koocher, J. C. Norcross, & S. S. Hill (Eds.), *Psychologists' desk reference* (2nd ed., pp. 226–231). Oxford University Press.

Randahl, G. J., Hansen, J. C., & Haverkamp, B. E. (1993). Instrumental behaviors following test administration and interpretation: Exploration validity of the Strong Interest Inventory. *Journal of Counseling and Development*, 71(4), 435–439. https://doi.org/10.1002/j.1556-6676.1993.tb02661.x

Robbins, S. (2008). *Ten great cultural career lies.* Stever Robbins, Inc. www.steverrobbins.com/articles/ten-career-lies/

Roberts, B. W., Kuncel, N. R., Shiner, R., Caspi, A., & Goldberg, L. R. (2007). The power of personality: The comparative validity of personality traits, socioeconomic status, and cognitive ability for predicting important life outcomes. *Perspectives on Psychological Science*, 2(4), 313–345. https://doi.org/10.1111/j.1745-6916.2007.00047.x

Rogue Recruiter. (2013, August 28). *10 career change myths.* Guerrilla Marketing for Job Hunters. www.gm4jh.com/10-career-change-myths/

Rounds, J., & Jin, J. (2013). Nature, importance, and assessment of needs and values. In S. Brown & R. Lent (Eds.), *Career development and counseling: Putting theory and research to work* (2nd ed., pp. 417–447). Wiley.

Savickas, M. L. (2005). The theory and practice of career construction. In S. Brown & R. Lent (Eds.), *Career development and counseling: Putting theory and research to work* (pp. 42–70). John Wiley & Sons, Inc.

Schultz, D. P., & Schultz, S. E. (2017). *Theories of personality* (11th ed.). Wadsworth Publishers.

Segal, A. M. (2017). *Know yourself, grow your career: The personal value proposition workbook.* Self-published.

Smith, L., & van Genderen, J. (2018). *Kick start your career: Successful strategies and winning techniques.* Routledge.

Snow, R. E. (1996). Aptitude development and education. *Psychology, Public Policy, and Law*, 2(3–4), 536–560. https://doi.org/10.1037/1076-8971.2.3-4.536

Steele, C. M. (1997). A threat in the air: How stereotypes shape intellectual identity and performance. *American Psychologist Journal*, 52(6), 613–629. https://doi.org/10.1037/0003-066X.52.6.613

Steele, C. M., Spencer, S. J., & Aronson, J. (2002). Contending with group image: The psychology of stereotype and social identity threat. *Advances in Experimental Social Psychology*, 34, 379–440. https://doi.org/10.1016/S0065-2601(02)80009-0

Super, D. E. (1957). *The psychology of careers: An introduction to vocational development.* Harper & Bros.

Super, D. E. (1990). A life-span, life-space approach to career development. In D. Brown & L. Brooks (Eds.), *Convergence in theories of career choice and development: Implications for science and practice* (pp. 63–74). Jossey-Bass.

Super, D. E., Savickas, M. L., & Super, C. M. (1996). The life-span, life-space approach to careers. In D. Brown & L. Brooks (Eds.), *Career choice and development: Applying contemporary theories to practice* (3rd ed., pp. 121–178). Jossey-Bass.

Swanson, J. L., & Schneider, M. (2013). Minnesota theory of work adjustment. In S. Brown & R. Lent (Eds.), *Career development and counseling: Putting theory and research to work* (2nd ed., pp. 29–53). Wiley.

Taylor, J., & Hardy, D. (2004). *Monster careers: How to land the job of your life.* Penguin Group.

Tennen, H., & Affleck, G. (1987). The costs and benefits of optimistic explanations and dispositional optimism. *Journal of Personality, 55*(2), 377–393. https://doi.org/10.1111/j.1467-6494.1987.tb00443.x

Virginia Education Wizard. (2008). *Skill assessment.* www.vawizard.org/wizard/skill-assess

Wahlstrom, C., & Williams, B. K. (2003). *College to career: Your road to personal success.* South-Western Educational Publishing.

Weitzman, L. M., & Fitzgerald, L. F. (1996). The development and initial validation of scales to assess attitudes toward multiple role planning. *Journal of Career Assessment, 4*(3), 269–284. https://doi.org/10.1177/106907279600400303

Whiston, S. C., & James, B. N. (2013). Promotion of career choices. In S. Brown & R. Lent (Eds.), *Career development and counseling: Putting theory and research to work* (2nd ed., pp. 565–594). Wiley.

Education

In this chapter, we'll look at your past, current, or future college experience in a new way. We'll debunk college career myths, including, "I can't afford college" and "certain college majors are unemployable." Instead, we'll look at the facts and identify actions you can take to make the most of your education in preparation for your future. Whether you're considering higher education for the first time, planning to return to school, or simply looking to reappraise your past college experiences, Chapter 3 has the information you need.

Myth 26

"I can't afford college."

Fact

If you've determined that your best-suited career choices require a college degree, then consider the thought that you may be unable to afford the costs of *not* going to college.

College pays, and you can pay it off. Cutting costs and living on a budget is a great place to start. For more information on creating a budget and managing finances, I recommend Dave Ramsey's (2003) book, *Financial Peace University*. Personally, I've followed the strategies outlined in this book to pay off debt and attain financial stability. Additional financial strategies such as living off campus and holding a part-time job can also ease financial burdens (Lobosco, 2017).

Furthermore, most students can receive grants and low-rate education loans that help them pay for college. Typically, education loans don't have to be paid back until the student is finished with school. Keep in mind, the average loan debt of an undergraduate education in 2020 is roughly $37,000 (Chamber of Commerce, 2020). Although substantial, this number is surprisingly less than the average car loan for a new vehicle at $39,721 (Jones, 2022). The point being, an investment in education can provide lifelong dividends, whereas a new car only provides short-term perks until it needs to be replaced.

It can also be helpful to consider the lesser-known benefits of college. For instance, workers with a bachelor's degree have lower unemployment rates and earn significantly more than those without a postsecondary education (BLS, 2020). For these reasons, attending college is a good financial investment even if you change your career later down the road. The advantages of a college education have a long-term, compounding effect. It's worth familiarizing yourself with these benefits before committing to a degree.

DOI: 10.4324/9780429261770-3

Action 26 – College Considerations

Follow the link to read an article summarizing the benefits that college provides: bit.ly/careermythlinks.

List and explain your three most compelling reasons for attending college below.

1. _____

_____

_____

2. _____

_____

_____

3. _____

_____

_____

Myth 27

"I have to go to college if I want a good job."

Fact

Although college degrees may be necessary for some jobs, they remain unnecessary for many good jobs. In fact, of the 20 jobs projected to grow at the fastest rate over the next decade in the United States, only ten require more than a high school diploma, according to the Bureau of Labor Statistics (2021). If you're looking for a job with good pay and high demand, you have many options without a degree.

Deciding whether to pursue more education or start working depends on individual factors. Practical needs are certainly an important consideration. We learned in the previous myth that jobs with a higher education degree tend to have a greater income; however, this isn't the case for all careers. College also requires delaying your opportunity to earn income (Indiviglio, 2010). The time spent studying in college translates to opportunity cost, which you can't afford if your life situation requires that you need immediate funds.

Another individual factor of important consideration is likes and dislikes and learning environment preference. We learned in Chapter 2 how important interests are for careers. The same goes for education: college students who find interest and enjoyment in their studies tend to persevere through school and perform better than those that don't (Wahlstrom & Williams, 2004). If you have little interest in academic pursuits, save yourself the misery and choose another path. Learning environment preferences are also important. Some people prefer academic learning environments and others prefer more practically oriented, hands-on learning situations (Harmon et al., 1994). Hands-on learners would benefit from working through on-the-job training opportunities rather than the college environment.

For those who decide they are better suited to enter the work world rather than college at this point in their career development, several options are available. Some possibilities include apprenticeships, military, and trade careers (Gross & Marcus, 2018). Apprenticeships are on-the-job training opportunities that often include a formalized certification program intended to prepare a worker for a specific job. Apprenticeships sometimes require only hands-on learning and others incorporate some accompanying study, such as readings and lectures. The United States military service offers a wide variety of job opportunities, including those specific to national defense, such as fighter pilots and infantry, while many others work in occupations equivalent to civilian occupations, such as electrical technicians, nurses, and photographers. Trade careers are manual labor jobs that require a specific skill set or training, and often include an apprenticeship. Currently in very high demand, trade careers offer job security and a comfortable salary. Skilled trades are available in a variety of industries and specific occupations: building trades, such as carpenters and electricians; mechanical trades, including machinists and locksmiths; industrial trades, such as stream engineers and ironworkers; and medical trades, including dental assistants and paramedics (Meier, 2018). The United States is in desperate need of these skilled workers (Gross & Marcus, 2018).

Action 27 – College Alternatives

Consider whether alternatives to college are a fit for you by reading an article and answering questions. Learn more about these possibilities available here: bit.ly/careermythlinks. The article is available in text or audio formats. Based on what you read, answer the following questions:

What are your reasons for why college is best for you at this point in your career development?

_____

_____

_____

_____

_____

What are your reasons for why work is best for you?

_____

_____

_____

_____

_____

What conclusions do you draw about what option is best for you?

_____

_____

_____

_____

_____

Myth 28

"I have to attend a four-year university."

Fact

Just as you can be successful without attending college at all, so too can you find success and satisfaction by attending a community college. Community colleges, also referred to as junior colleges or two-year colleges, offer courses that lead to certificates, licenses, and associate's degrees. Apprenticeships and skilled trade careers discussed in the previous myth sometimes join forces with community colleges for course training components. Community college coursework or an associate's degree is also preferred or required for certain skilled trades, such as air traffic controllers. Universities, also referred to as four-year colleges, offer courses that lead to bachelor's degrees, which are preferred or required for many types of careers in a variety of industries. Some people attend either a community college or a university and others start at a community college and transfer to a university to complete their bachelor's degree (Carignan, 2021).

Much like the decision of whether to attend college or enter the work world, the choice between a two-year and four-year college is not a one-size-fits-all answer. For most, cost is a primary factor (Carignan, 2021) since community colleges tend to be more affordable than universities. Interest and preference should also be considered as well, especially what learning environment best suits you and how you might want to use your degree. For example, if after visiting community colleges and universities you find yourself more drawn to the community college environment, that's an important consideration to factor in. If you already know what career you want and it requires an associate's degree or certification only offered at a community college, that would be equally important. Regardless of your choice of college, consider your options and make an informed choice that best fits your needs.

Action 28 – Community College or University

Explore whether attending a community college or university best meets your needs at this time by reading about your options and completing a decision-making activity, available here: bit.ly/careermythlinks. Read the article and follow the instructions under the heading "Decision Time" to complete an adapted version of the "SWOT Graph," which stands for Strengths, Weaknesses, Opportunities, and Threats. For our purposes, we'll just focus on the first two categories of strengths and weaknesses. Indicate strengths and weaknesses in Table 3.1 for both community colleges and universities, and then answer the question below.

Table 3.1 Community College or University

Community College		University	
Strengths	Weaknesses	Strengths	Weaknesses

What conclusions do you draw about what option is best for you?

_____

_____

_____

_____

_____

Myth 29

"Thinking about my career future can wait until I get to college."

Fact

Even if you're college-bound, it's never too early to start considering your career future. Career development is a lifelong process of learning about yourself as an individual and how you can positively contribute to the larger world. Although final career decisions are made in adulthood, the seeds of those decisions are planted long beforehand. This is why the years preceding college are a great time to explore additional job opportunities that improve your ability to make career-related decisions. Generally, people are only aware of the small number of occupations that immediately surround them during childhood. By exploring additional job opportunities, people can better understand the range of alternatives (Beggs et al., 2008). In short, don't hesitate to think about your career future before attending college. Not doing so unnecessarily crams many important decisions within a short period of time.

Adding to the challenge, the developmental stage of most undergraduates tends to conflict with the expectations placed upon them. Consequentially, you may feel pressure in college to immediately declare a major, thereby further emphasizing the need to think about your career ahead of time. Nevertheless, it's not as simple as making final choices prior to entering college, since important decisions also take place during college (Freedman, 2013). Although it can't all be figured out before college, you'll strongly benefit from starting your decision-making process earlier rather than later.

Action 29 – Time to Explore

Read the following article by coach and educator Liz Freedman (2013) in the college journal, *The Mentor*, available at bit.ly/careermythlinks. It offers additional explanation about the disconnect between the developmental stage of most incoming students and the challenges they face when they are undecided with their college major and career goals.

How does this alter or inform your views about your career future prior to college?

_____

_____

_____

_____

_____

What is one thing you can do now to move forward in your decision-making process?

_____

_____

_____

_____

_____

Myth 30

"College should wait until I know what I want to do."

Fact

Contrary to the previous myth, of delaying career exploration until college, an opposite but equally faulty suggestion is to postpone college until making a final career decision. As we've learned, college is highly advantageous and offers developmentally appropriate and structured guidance for finding a career fit. Trying to figure everything out by yourself is an inefficient use of time and resources. However, there is often pressure to make decisions before entering college. So then, if both college and decisions shouldn't wait, how do we move forward?

Once again, we'll proceed by making *tentative* decisions. To do so, let's intentionally make early decisions while remaining open and committed to the career decision-making process. Recall the three-step career development process from Chapter 2, as shown in Figure 3.1, of 1) learning about yourself, 2) understanding the world of work, and 3) finding a fit. Remember that this process should be dynamic and cyclical, meaning, it should be performed repeatedly throughout life, especially during college (Jordan & Marinaccio, 2017).

Figure 3.1 Career Development Process

College is like a trip to the career candy store—the ultimate treasure trove of career development opportunities. Your college years represent the ideal time to open your eyes, heart, and mind to all existing careers and even those not yet created (Vogt, 2007). Regard your career choices as hypotheses to be tested through the knowledge and experience you gain at college, expecting alterations and refinements throughout your education. Take advantage of this time by continually engaging in reflection and exploration activities to inform your decision making.

Unfortunately, college students often underutilize available resources because they don't know what opportunities are available, or why they're valuable (Auter & Marken, 2016). The benefits of college extend far beyond attending classes, especially when it comes to finding a career fit (Bruni, 2018). Your first step is to learn about the wealth of valuable activities available during school.

Action 30 – Investigating the Extras

Discover some of the available "extras" beyond coursework that college provides by reading the *Business Insider* article by Cutrone and Stanger (2012), "14 Ways Students Can Get More Out of College," available here: bit.ly/careermythlinks. The article references several ways to maximize your college experience and subsequently refine your career choices.

Make a list below of all the college "extras" mentioned in the article. Include additional extras you think of as well. List at least a total of ten extra opportunities that may be available to you in college.

1. _____

2. _____

3. _____

4. _____

5. _____

6. _____

7. _____

8. _____

9. _____

10. _____

Myth 31

"Going to a prestigious college will make me more successful."

Fact

Attending a prestigious college does not guarantee future success. Plans are not promises; no single decision will secure your future. Your life and career are a dynamic culmination of preceding events both within and beyond your control. The best you can do is make the most reasoned choice with the information available at the time. Attending a prestigious school might offer networking contacts and possibly a higher salary, but long-term career success is determined by your performance (Eide et al., 2016). The greatest predictor of your success is you, not the college you choose.

The effort you put into college is an important factor for success. A good-fitting school is one that you can see yourself succeeding at and offers the types of opportunities you think might interest or benefit you, such as academic and extracurricular offerings. Consider factors such as location, size, cost, college majors, amenities, and learning environment. People have different preferences for their learning environment, so make a list of qualities that are important to you. For some students, prestigious schools will naturally emerge as the best choice because of the priorities for what the schools offer; however, prestige will not rank as a top priority for the majority of students (Daugherty, 2020). Instead of seeking the *best* college, focus on finding the best college *for you*.

Action 31 – Planning the Extras

The best college for you is the place where you're most willing and able to actively engage in opportunities beyond the classroom. Accordingly, we need to identify what opportunities are most important to you. Review the list of college "extras" you made from the previous action and answer the following questions.

Which extras are most important to you and why? List your top three choices with a brief explanation about why they matter to you.

1. _____

_____

_____

2. _____

_____

_____

3. _____

_____

_____

Which three extras might pose the biggest challenge for you and why?

1. _____

_____

_____

2. _____

_____

_____

3. _____

_____

_____

Considering your priorities and challenges, what are you willing to commit to? Make a list of three specific goals you want to accomplish for your extras during college.

1. _____

2. _____

3. _____

Myth 32

"Students enter college knowing their academic major and career goals."

Fact

Most people are undecided about their academic major and career goals when they enter college. National statistics vary, but most report that the majority of entering college students are undecided about their majors. Even those who begin with a specific major or career in mind rarely continue with their original goals. In fact, the average student who enters college with a declared major ends up changing it three to five times! On the other hand, the average student that enters college undeclared only changes their major one to two times (NCES, 2017). Although it's beneficial to start thinking about your career early, avoid feeling pressured to make final decisions until after you enter college.

People often wrongly conclude that the actions of a vocal minority are representative of the entire group. If you are curious about the average college student, there is plenty of survey information readily available, such as that published online by the National Center for Education Statistics (NCES, 2017). It can be frightening and shaming to believe you're behind and that everyone else has their future pre-planned. Ironically, most students feel alone in this, but they're not—and neither are you (Vogt, 2007).

We've learned that while it's helpful to plan ahead, most students don't. It is best to proceed by making tentative decisions and postponing certain others, especially choosing a major, until college. As with career decisions, choosing a college major follows our same three-step process, although this time, we'll shift the process slightly to reflect our current goal of selecting a college major, as shown in Figure 3.2.

Figure 3.2 Choosing a College Major

The three-step college major decision process involves: 1) learning about yourself, 2) understanding college majors, and 3) finding a fit. The same strategies used in Chapter 2 for navigating the traditional career development process can similarly guide you through this process.

Action 32 – College Major Assessment

Taking career assessments specifically designed to help you learn about yourself and understand college majors can help you find a fit. Just as the career tests you took in Chapter 2 identified jobs that matched your personal characteristics, college major tests identify majors that match you.

Take a college major test to learn more about yourself and how you may best fit with available options. Complete the Career Clusters Interest Survey (Primé & Tracey, 2010), available at bit.ly/careermythlinks. This test is based on your likes and dislikes and offers broad categories of majors that may fit you best.

List your top three career clusters of interest below:

1. _____

2. _____

3. _____

Myth 33

"My college major determines my career path."

Fact

Your college major does not write your career path in stone. In fact, research indicates that your college major is not an accurate forecast of your future careers, and that most college graduates enter jobs that are unrelated to their prior field of study (Gelhaus, 2007).

Keep in mind that a bachelor's degree is broadly beneficial to your future success even if your major is in a specific field. Rather than anchor you to a specific domain, an undergraduate education provides a foundation of transferable skills in critical thinking and communication that are advantageous to any career (Vogt, 2007). One singular major can pave multiple different career paths. Consider that most hiring managers care more about a job candidate's skills than a specific college major (NCES, 2019).

Interestingly, although most people pursue careers that are unrelated to their college majors, they still express satisfaction with the preparation that their college education provided (Gelhaus, 2007). This is because obtaining a college degree is a significant undertaking, and in the process, you will necessarily develop transferable skills that are highly advantageous in a vast array of careers. Nevertheless, be sure to select a major that captivates your interest as you will consequentially spend a lot of time studying your selected major.

Action 33 – College Major Choice

Recall that our three-step decision process involves: 1) learning about yourself, 2) understanding college majors, and 3) finding a fit. In the previous action, you completed a test to learn more about yourself and how your interests might align with certain college majors. Our second step is understanding college majors.

Review a list of possible college majors by visiting the following link: bit.ly/careermythlinks. Consider your top three areas of interest identified in the previous myth action, as well as other majors that catch your eye.

What is emerging as your top college major of interest and why?

_____

_____

_____

_____

_____

Myth 34

"Certain college majors are required for admission into professional and graduate schools."

Fact

Although some professional schools desire certain academic prerequisites, a specific major is not required for most schools. In most cases, programs seek broad skills, such as the ability to speak and write well. For example, even though most students who plan to apply for medical school choose to major in biological sciences, these majors do not have higher acceptance rates than others (AAMC, 2021). Interestingly, math and humanities majors have the highest average acceptance rates for medical school. Keep this in mind, as you may want to seek broader fields of study for your undergraduate degree.

While most professional schools aren't limited by college major, they often require and prefer specific coursework (Hettich & Landrum, 2014). For example, medical school applications often require coursework in biology paired with volunteer experience within medical settings. Instead of exclusively focusing on a major, turn your attention toward the prerequisites that the professional schools favor. By taking a variety of courses connected to your interests, you can complete the preparatory coursework for a field that you are likely to pursue.

As an additional bonus, taking a variety of classes beyond your college major can boost your cognitive flexibility, critical thinking skills, and grants you new perspectives (Petrie et al., 2002). Finally, experience is a prerequisite for effective future planning (Campbell, 2013). Without experience, knowing what you want to pursue is simply a guess.

Once more, your college major does not condemn you to one distinct field forever. The importance is not the subject itself, but your ability to deeply explore a topic and complete your degree. The classes and experiences you pursue during college make all the difference.

Action 34 – Course Selection

To recognize the importance of taking certain courses while planning your college degree, take the time to explore specific classes across majors that interest you. Choose those that you care about, in addition to those that spark your curiosity.

Review your university's course catalog. Read course titles and descriptions. List your top ten classes you're most interested in taking below.

1. _____
2. _____
3. _____
4. _____
5. _____
6. _____
7. _____
8. _____
9. _____
10. _____

Myth 35

"I cannot change my major."

Fact

Odds are you will change your major during your college career. According to the National Center for Education Statistics (NCES, 2017), approximately 80% of college students in the United States change their major at least once, while the average student changes their major at least three times.

Keep in mind, the path you forge will change with your personal growth and increased self-awareness. Don't let this scare you either. Your preferences and self-awareness *should* evolve throughout the process. Rather than something to fear and avoid, recognize alterations for what they are—progress.

Once you have decided on your major, it's important to have a flexible plan that leaves room for self-development. Common mistakes tend to lie within the extremes. These include having no plans, or over-planning to the point of becoming rigid. Both errors can ultimately keep you from attaining your goals and should be avoided (Malnig & Malnig, 1984). The better option is to intentionally create a plan that has room for flexibility. This can take the form of creating a backup plan and providing yourself ample time to readjust when necessary.

Action 35 – College Major Backups

Set yourself up for success by considering possible backup options now. That way, if you begin to reconsider your college major choice, you'll already have other possibilities in mind.

Return to the list of majors you reviewed in the action step for Myth 33, available at the following link: bit.ly/careermythlinks.

Next, revisit the list of courses you found during the Myth 34 Action by noting which majors your selected courses fall into.

Based on your review of these lists, choose two backup college majors and list them here:

Backup 1: _____

Backup 2: _____

Myth 36

"Academic advisors aren't helpful for career planning."

Fact

Academic advisors and faculty members can serve as invaluable mentors for career planning. Although their role is focused primarily on academia, faculty can offer valuable insights related to career planning. For example, they may be able to offer unique resources to aid in the career planning process. In addition, many academic advisors have connections to both employers and recent graduates in their industry which can provide useful networking opportunities for jobs (Campbell & Burrows, 2020). Contrary to popular belief, academic advisors rarely try to sway students to pursue academia if they aren't interested, and most students choose to explore careers outside academia (NACADA, 2006).

Use your resources and seek out multiple mentors within your college's faculty to support you. Keep in mind that they were once in your same position trying to figure out what they were going to pursue. Be sure to regularly discuss your future planning, interests, and career development with your advisor. Share where you are in the process, ask questions, and solicit their support and advice. Use this information to frame academic decisions such as which classes and extracurricular activities to pursue. Academic advising offers a formal opportunity to have these conversations (Davidson et al., 2017).

Action 36 – Scheduling Advising

Recognize how helpful academic advisors can be in your career planning by making an appointment with an academic advisor or faculty member to discuss your career development.

Identify three academic advisors and/or faculty members that would be helpful to meet with. List their names below:

Advisor 1: _____

Advisor 2: _____

Advisor 3: _____

Schedule an appointment to meet with at least one of the people above. Share your current career interests and ask for advice about how to refine them. Reflect on this appointment afterward. What did you gain from your meeting?

_____

_____

_____

_____

_____

Myth 37

"Time off from college will help me make a career decision."

Fact

Time and effort help your career decision process, not necessarily time away from college. Merely permitting time to pass will *not* make your decisions any easier. When facing a complex career decision, it's important to give yourself the time you need to research and consider alternatives. College is an ideal setting for this, as it offers resources and accountability for the decision-making process. While time away can serve as a distraction, keep in mind it can also be useful to give yourself periodic breaks throughout the decision-making process to reduce stress and allow your mind to work. Stated differently, you can always take a break from career-related decisions during college, but leaving altogether may prove to be counterproductive (Vogt, 2007).

Take advantage of your university's resources and engage in the career decision-making process in small doses. Rather than leaving college, seek support within the college environment by discussing career-related stressors with a trusted mentor. Struggling to decide means you need help, not that you should avoid making one altogether. By the same token, working with a mentor to process these feelings can be especially helpful as it can strengthen your relationship and connection with the career planning process (Welsh & Campbell, 2016).

Action 37 – Mentorship

Expand your relationships by taking the time to talk with potential faculty and staff mentors. Rather than relying on one advisor, additional relationships can offer new perspectives, challenge your thinking, and be a source of encouragement. By seeking multiple mentorships, you will uncover their individual strengths, which in turn may shape your own goals and ambitions along the way (Welsh & Campbell, 2016).

You can even seek additional mentorships online. The website FindAMentor.com, also available at bit.ly/careermythlinks can pair you with a mentor by considering your interests and location.

Utilizing resources through your school and online, identify the names of three new people that you believe will be supportive mentors. List their names below:

Advisor 1: _____

Advisor 2: _____

Advisor 3: _____

Next, schedule an appointment to meet with one of them. Share your challenges related to career decision making and ask for their advice about how you can manage these challenges better. Reflect on this afterward. What did you gain from this meeting?

_____

_____

_____

_____

_____

Myth 38

"I can ignore career planning until after I graduate."

Fact

Ignoring career planning until after graduation is doing yourself a serious disservice. If you want to have the job of your dreams, it's best to start by planning early (Mills, 2017). Planning can begin with thinking about what you want to do, talking with others about possibilities, and gathering useful work experience. Developing a general idea of the workforce through broad exposure to various occupations will help you refine your interests while granting you a competitive edge.

In addition, college is a uniquely ideal time for career planning due to its abundance of resources available over four years (Wahlstrom & Williams, 2004). You'll never have more time later as additional responsibilities emerge following graduation. Whether it be family, increased financial responsibilities, or less access to immediate support systems, waiting until after you graduate will make finding the time needed for career development unnecessarily difficult.

So far, you've identified multiple mentors who can help you in your journey, but having a primary mentor can be uniquely helpful. Imagine planning to compete in your first ironman competition. While you might choose to train on your own, working closely with a personal coach to guide your preparation would be highly preferable. Career development can be viewed similarly; while it is possible to do it alone, having a designated career counselor to guide you through the process can be highly advantageous (Bolles, 2020).

Action 38 – Career Coaching and Counseling

Consider working with a career counselor or career coach during your time in college to guide you and help keep you accountable. A career counselor is typically a licensed counselor who specializes in helping with personal and professional concerns across the entire career development process. On the other hand, a career coach typically doesn't hold a professional license and is more focused on helping you meet your external goals, such as getting a job (NCDA, 2017). For more on career counseling, see Myth 19.

Most colleges and universities have career coaches available to help you. If your school doesn't provide career coaching, another available resource is the National Career Development Association directory (NCDA, 2020), available at bit.ly/careermythlinks.

Utilizing your school's resources and/or the NCDA website, identify three career coaches you might be interested in working with. Include their names and information below. Not everyone wants or needs career coaching, but it is useful to know where to find additional help available if it is ever desired.

1. Name: _____

   Contact Information: _____

   _____

   _____

   What might be helpful about working with them: _____

   _____

   _____

   _____

2. Name: _____

   Contact Information: _____

   _____

   _____

   What might be helpful about working with them: _____

   _____

   _____

   _____

3. Name: _____

Contact Information: _____

_____

_____

What might be helpful about working with them: _____

_____

_____

_____

Myth 39

"Career success is dependent on the coursework I complete."

Fact

Beyond your immediate coursework, there are many opportunities provided by your university that can positively impact your career success. Restricting your educational experience to solely focus on your mandatory coursework comes at the cost of missing out on several helpful resources. Keep in mind that colleges offer a lot more than just courses and lectures. In fact, students who didn't take advantage of these opportunities during college often pay extra for the same opportunities after college (Hettich & Landrum, 2014).

It may surprise you to know that coursework alone is not enough to stand out to an employer, but consider that other candidates likely completed similar requirements in order to obtain their degree. On the flip side, research suggests that activities outside of the classroom develop supplementary skills that employers *do* desire (Rubin et al., 2002). By complementing your education with skills acquired beyond the classroom walls, you can avoid being glossed over by potential employers. In fact, you might even become impossible to ignore.

You might also be surprised to learn just how beneficial these additional activities can be to your personal and professional development. Contrary to popular belief, related activities outside the classroom can aid in both your understanding of and satisfaction with course material (Strapp & Farr, 2010). Despite the less obvious relationship between extracurricular activities and future career success, these opportunities can help you become a versatile and competitive professional.

Unfortunately, most students are unaware of the benefits that these additional experiences offer (Hettich & Landrum, 2014). While this myth provides an overview, the next several will explore popular extracurricular activities for your consideration.

Action 39 – On-Campus Activities

Read the article about extracurricular activities, available at bit.ly/careermythlinks, and learn why they are broadly beneficial. Based on your newly acquired knowledge, answer the following questions:

What are the two most compelling reasons to get involved with extracurricular activities?

1. _____

_____

2. _____

_____

What two types of extracurricular activities you would like to try and why?

1. _____

_____

_____

2. _____

_____

_____

Myth 40

"University career centers are a waste of time."

Fact

Despite being chronically underutilized by students, university career centers can be a very helpful asset for those willing to take advantage of them. They can offer career assessments, interest exploration tools, career fairs, networking opportunities, resume development, and even interview coaching (Schaub, 2012). However, most students mistakenly underestimate these amenities and consequentially miss out on the benefits provided by career centers. Surprisingly, upwards of 40% of college students never use their university's career center (Joseph, 2018). Curiously, those who never step foot into their university's career center are the most likely to consider them "useless" (Phillips, 2021). This is likely influenced by the misguided stereotypes associated with the centers themselves, such as the falsehood that they only serve business majors. On the other hand, students who engage with these services regularly report them as beneficial and advantageous.

Recall from Chapter 2 our approach to developing a constructive mental framework. Instead of the self-sabotaging "This won't work for me," gently shift your mental narrative to the productive curiosity of "*How* can this work for me?" (Forleo, 2019). Expect to hear some cynical remarks from others, but don't let them discourage you. Instead remain humble and open minded, and calmly proceed with the plan. Keep in mind these inauspicious reviews are likely rooted in stereotype, not grounded in experience or empirical research.

Capitalize on your university career center's services by making an appointment with a consultant. Explain what you know so far about the career development process and where you currently see yourself. Ask for recommendations, available resources, and productive next-step actions. Chances are they will have a lot to offer; it is simply a matter of asking (Schaub, 2012).

Action 40 – Career Center

See what your university's career center has to offer. If your school doesn't have a career center, check out a local one instead. You can locate your nearest career center using the CareerOneStop website (BLS, 2022), available at: bit.ly/careermythlinks. Enter your location and search for your nearest location.

List ten services your career center offers below. Then, circle the top three services you are interested in trying.

1. _____

2. _____

3. _____

4. _____

5. _____

6. _____

7. _____

8. _____

9. _____

10. _____

Myth 41

"Student organizations are an interference to future success."

Fact

College student organizations, including honors societies, community service groups, sports teams, student government, Greek life, religious groups, and more, offer valuable and enriching experiences. Student organizations, especially sororities and fraternities, sometimes get a bad reputation from media spotlights that highlight negative behaviors such as drug use, alcohol abuse, hazing, and bullying (UNLV, 2020). Given this, it's understandable to be hesitant toward student groups and organizations. However, popular media perception does not portray the average experience.

Although these issues occasionally happen, the problems are often exaggerated for college student organizations (UNLV, 2020). In fact, student organizations are required to abide by federal, state, and university policies aimed at preventing these problems from occurring. While undesirable incidences still do occur, they are not confined to college campuses (Colbert, 2016).

In actuality, the benefits of student organizations far outweigh the potential drawbacks that a small percentage of students experience. For example, these organizations often provide opportunities for service, develop leadership skills, recognize achievements, and offer networking support (Colbert, 2016). A good example of this can be found in a survey conducted at the University of Arizona. The findings indicated that over half the students who completed the survey noted that joining a student organization helped them to strengthen their leadership skills, which is a highly desired trait among employers (Hegedus & Knight, 2016).

The key is finding the right student organizations to get involved with. You can do this by considering the potential positive and negative outcomes of joining. Keep in mind that you should find an organization that reflects your goals and values. To do this, consider the long-term consequences, both good and bad, of being affiliated with the group.

Action 41 – Student Organizations

Explore student organizations on your college campus. For student groups that may be particularly valuable for your future, check out national and international honor societies to join. For an official list of certified societies, review the Association of College Honor Societies, available at bit.ly/careermythlinks. Under the "For Students" tab, select "Certified Societies (Member Directory)" and search for societies in your field of interest.

Based on your search, what are two student organizations you are interested in joining? How might joining these organizations benefit you? List your responses below.

1. Organization Name: _____

Benefits of joining: _____

_____

_____

_____

2. Organization Name: _____

Benefits of joining: _____

_____

_____

_____

Myth 42

"Certain college majors are unemployable."

Fact

The dynamic skillset that college graduates develop throughout their education can be easily transferred to a wide variety of disciplines. In fact, these skills can be viewed as the fundamental base layer principles that enable widespread flourishing. Eugene Zechmeister, a Loyola University Director, said it best when he stated, "I know this will sound sacrilegious, but skills are actually more important than course content" (Clay, 1996, p. 1). While both skills and content are important, the essence of Zechmeister's takeaway rings true. The interpersonal, communication, leadership, and organizational skills gained throughout college are essential to potential employers. Keep in mind, many people thrive in jobs that may not seem inherently related to their field of study. However, this crossing of disciplines is not reason for concern. On the contrary, this diversification is not indicative of a poorly chosen major, but rather the flexibility of a good education (Rubin et al., 2002).

Coursework in a variety of majors offers a foundation of knowledge and skills to expand upon. Active participation in specialized opportunities beyond the classroom enhances career development and workplace readiness (Hettich & Landrum, 2014). One highly desirable opportunity is a research assistantship (RA), in which undergraduate students assist faculty members in studying their field. RAs offer unique experience and skill development opportunities, particularly for those who are interested in graduate study. Since research is the primary source of academic content, graduate schools often expect some level of research interest and involvement.

Serving as an RA can be beneficial in multiple ways. For example, it can help you better understand your discipline, gain valuable research skills, and learn how to read, conduct, and analyze studies. Furthermore, an RA can serve as a gateway to presenting at research conferences or writing for peer-reviewed publications. Likewise, you may enjoy the research itself and discover an unanticipated enthusiasm that could yield new career interests (Landrum & Davis, 2010). Equally as important, by working closely with a faculty member, you might spark a meaningful mentorship. This relationship can help steer your future interests in addition to providing meaningful references and compelling letters of recommendation.

Action 42 – Research Assistantships

Explore RA opportunities at your university and online. Begin by asking your instructors about their scholarly work and if there are any RA positions available. Also, search for opportunities online through the Council on Undergraduate Research (CUR), an international organization devoted to providing undergraduate research opportunities for faculty and students. Participation with CUR requires membership, which can be found at bit.ly/careermythlinks.

What available RA opportunities did you find on your college campus and online search?

_____

_____

_____

_____

_____

What about these opportunities sounds most interesting to you? Why?

_____

_____

_____

_____

_____

Myth 43

"I don't have time to do anything outside of taking classes."

Fact

It's no joke, taking classes is a large time commitment that can make it difficult to arrange additional activities. Often, people fail to look beyond the bare minimum coursework required to receive their diploma. Don't make this mistake. In order to take full advantage of the college opportunities you're paying for, you need to reach beyond the confines of mandatory coursework. Just because something isn't required for your diploma doesn't mean it's not essential to your future. Supplementing your education with additional activities helps further your career development and prepare you for your next steps.

That said, some college opportunities are more time-consuming than others. Serving as a teaching assistant (TA), for example, can benefit your future while simultaneously reducing your time demands compared to other activities. The role of a TA is to assist a faculty member in a specific course throughout an academic term. Common duties of a TA include answering student questions, leading study sessions, grading, monitoring class attendance, and sometimes providing a guest lecture (Indiana University Bloomington, 2020). At some universities, serving as a TA can earn course credit and take the place of another class.

Like a research assistantship, the benefits of serving as a TA are numerous, also developing transferable skills in both leadership and communication. Moreover, a TA position can provide the opportunity to better understand the field of teaching, how people learn, and see your college experience from a broader perspective (Indiana University Bloomington, 2020). For some, being a TA can be a review or aid with studying for qualifying exams, which can also boost time efficiency (Hettich & Landrum, 2014). For others, it is an excellent way to build a close mentoring relationship with a faculty member, which can lead to a meaningful ongoing connection as well as future references and letters of recommendation (Hettich & Landrum, 2014).

Unfortunately, not all schools allow undergraduates to serve as TAs. If this happens to be the case, consider kindly asking a faculty member if they might consider it. Keep in mind that the experience is more valuable than the ascribed label, so be creative in your pursuit by utilizing the available opportunities. Perhaps you might simply ask an instructor if they "want help" on a volunteer basis or they might be willing to offer you an independent study or internship credit for the experience instead (Hettich & Landrum, 2014).

Action 43 – Teaching Assistantships

Explore TA opportunities at your university by asking your instructors about available positions. If your school doesn't have an existing TA program, consider the merits of requesting the opportunity after educating yourself on what the role looks like. Visit the link provided to learn about TA programs at other schools, such as Carnegie Mellon (2002): bit.ly/careermythlinks.

After learning more about serving as a TA, what about this opportunity appeals to you?

_____

_____

_____

_____

_____

Which instructors and classes would you like to serve as a TA? Why?

_____

_____

_____

_____

_____

Depending on whether your school has an existing TA program, how might you pursue this opportunity at your school?

_____

_____

_____

_____

_____

Myth 44

"I should graduate as quickly as possible."

Fact

Although graduating early may offer tempting benefits like lower costs and an earlier entrance into the workforce (Hua, 2015), an early graduation also comes with potential consequences and risks. In fact, research shows that scurrying through college is a perfect way to miss out on unique opportunities while increasing the likelihood of not graduating at all (Alexander, 2016). Moreover, rushing through the college experience in favor of doing the bare minimum puts you at a disadvantage and represents a fundamental misunderstanding of what a four-year college degree is intended to provide (Scheele, 2005). Like speeding on a freeway, going through college as fast as possible feels efficient and effective, but in practice, it only turns out to add unnecessary risk.

The value of getting involved with additional experiences outside the classroom cannot be overstated. To quote career coach and strategist Adele Scheele (2005): "If I could, I would require every student in every major to take as many work and volunteer experiences as possible before graduating" (p. 89). Unlike high school, opportunities provided on the college landscape require your voluntary participation. No one will force you to participate in these supplementary activities. Your intrinsic motivation is key. Rushing through college to complete a degree at the expense of valuable experiences misses the essence of the unique opportunities college can provide.

Networking is a critical offering that is mistakenly disregarded far too often. This includes informally connecting with university alumni, attending job fairs, and going to formal networking events. Campus career centers often host these events to initiate the process of building a powerful network of connections. In fact, many schools have a core set of employers that they work closely with (Taylor & Hardy, 2004). Likewise, some colleges offer an elaborate database of contacts that are available on request. In short, networking events help you make connections with employers, find mentors beyond academia, prepare for interviews, and even provide a direct pipeline to jobs after graduation (Scheele, 2005). Missing these events in an effort to exit the college scene sooner is an avoidable misstep.

Action 44 – Networking Events

Check your university career center's networking resources and watch for job fairs on campus. If you don't have a career center, search for available job fairs in your city. For those with limited local resources, check out online networking resources, such as Doostang (2020), an online career networking community developed by Stanford University intended for students and graduates to connect with professionals and employers, available at bit.ly/careermythlinks.

Consulting resources from your university, your local community, and online, find professionals you'd be interested in connecting with to learn from their experience. Write down the contact information of at least three people you'd like to network with.

1. Name: _____

   Job Title: _____

   Organization: _____

   Phone: _____

   Email: _____

2. Name: _____

   Job Title: _____

   Organization: _____

   Phone: _____

   Email: _____

3. Name: _____

   Job Title: _____

   Organization: _____

   Phone: _____

   Email: _____

Myth 45

"Everything I need to be workplace-ready is available at my university."

Fact

As previous myths have introduced a vast array of on-campus opportunities, it is easy to disregard the value of venturing beyond the university walls during your college years. However, it is a mistake to limit yourself to on-campus opportunities when you can prepare yourself for the future with a wider variety of unique options by venturing across the street.

The next several myths will explore the value of engaging in off-campus activities, the most popular of which is a part-time job. In fact, according to the National Center for Education Statistics, upwards of 45% of college students have a part-time job (NCES, 2019). This is understandable; as the cost of higher education increases, the number of students who hold a part-time job also rises accordingly. However, the bulk of working students have a short-sighted perception regarding the value of their part-time jobs, with most viewing their work primarily as a source of income while discounting the other benefits they offer. For example, employers view part-time jobs as strong indicators of personal reliability, responsibility, and transferability of skills. This is why career counselor Peter Vogt (2007) encourages college students to recognize the desirable characteristics of part-time work. He says, "work is not a foreign concept to you… you are reliable… you are willing to sacrifice… and you are flexible and adaptable" (p. 160). To put it concisely, a part-time job allows you to kill multiple birds with one stone. You can make money, get off campus, engage in diverse activities, *and* usefully prepare for the future. Regardless of the job you undertake, you can focus on what pays well and what works with your schedule, but you can also consider how the job helps develop your individual, interpersonal, and technical skills, in addition to what it indicates regarding your further growth.

Action 45 – Paid Work

Consider whether a part-time job might be useful for you. First, consider the practicalities of your life and schedule, and whether a part-time job could fit your needs.

What are the benefits of holding a part-time job? For example, money might be an essential benefit for you. List at least three benefits.

1. _____

_____

2. _____

_____

3. _____

_____

What might be the drawbacks or challenges of holding a part-time job? For example, you might not have a car or access to transportation. List at least three drawbacks.

1. _____

_____

2. _____

_____

3. _____

_____

Next, consider the skills you might acquire from a part-time job. Below is a rank-ordered list of characteristics that employers expect recent graduates to demonstrate when they enter the workplace (Landrum et al., 2010). Identify where you are currently lacking and consider if a part-time job would strengthen this area. To do so, write down an experience you've had that demonstrates each skill. If you cannot list an experience for one, highlight it as a potential area to improve through part-time work.

1. Self-discipline, punctuality, and dependability

   Experience: _____

2. Work well with others

   Experience: _____

3. Meet others' needs, such as customers and clients

   Experience: _____

4. Set priorities and manage time efficiently to meet deadlines

   Experience: _____

5. Identify, prioritize, and solve problems

   Experience: _____

6. Effectively make decisions

   Experience: _____

7. Work independently without supervision

   Experience: _____

8. Effectively manage several tasks simultaneously

   Experience: _____

9. Adapt to changing circumstances

   Experience: _____

10. Function effectively during stress

    Experience: _____

Lastly, summarize what you've learned about yourself by listing the pros and cons of getting a part-time job off campus. What pros and cons are most compelling to you? What option works best for you? Why?

_____

_____

_____

_____

_____

_____

_____

_____

_____

_____

Myth 46

"Work experience only counts if I got paid."

Fact

Valuable work experience is not dependent on a paycheck. As discussed in previous myths, experience allows you to apply your academic knowledge to the real world. Furthermore, employers care more about your relevant skills and experiences than how much you were paid for a position (Bolles, 2020). In other words, all experience is valuable regardless of your hourly rate.

This also means that volunteering, although it doesn't provide monetary gains, is still beneficial. As stated by career counselor Peter Vogt (2007), "if you think volunteering does not pay at all, then you have to reexamine your definition of 'pay'" (p. 169). Volunteering still allows you to engage in direct experience and develop transferable skills and abilities. Regardless of pay, these experiences offer opportunities to clarify career interests, seek other opportunities, and develop professional connections (Lore, 2011).

Keep in mind that volunteer work can actually provide benefits that paid work cannot, such as the chance to observe positions that may otherwise be unavailable to you (Lore, 2011). For example, while a paid, entry-level employee would rarely work directly with a top CEO, a volunteer may receive the opportunity to connect with such a high-ranking individual. Furthermore, many companies show preferences for candidates who volunteer in their communities. A report by the National Association of Colleges and Employers (2012), *Job Outlook*, indicated that employers consider volunteer work a top attribute for ranking candidates in the hiring process.

Action 46 – Volunteering

Look for volunteer opportunities in your area that interest you. Your university might offer resources such as lists of or even partnerships with possible agencies. You can also use online search directories such as Volunteer Match, available at bit.ly/careermythlinks, or even a general search engine to search your city and the phrase "volunteer opportunities."

Research local volunteer opportunities. What are two possibilities that sound interesting to you and why?

1. Volunteer Position: _____

   Organization: _____

   What interests me about this position: _____

   _____

   _____

   _____

2. Volunteer Position: _____

   Organization: _____

   What interests me about this position: _____

   _____

   _____

   _____

Myth 47

"Most students get positions through on-campus recruiting."

Fact

While many companies recruit on campus, the majority do not. In fact, well-established on-campus recruitment programs are rare, so if your college campus has one, take advantage of it and consider yourself lucky (Taylor & Hardy, 2004). That said, even if there is on-campus recruitment at your school, it's important to avoid limiting your options to your own back-yard. As discussed in previous myths, it's valuable to extend your search off-campus and consider volunteer work. Doing so can yield another related and equally valuable strategy for experience: internships.

In college, you'll hear many people talk about internships; however, the term is imprecise and broad. Also referred to as "field experience," "externship," "practicum," and "college co-ops," these experiences can range from brief unpaid work at nonprofit agencies to long-term paid positions at large business corporations (Baird, 2014). The key feature of an internship is that it is a temporary experience. Within an internship, you generally perform entry-level work to learn about the business for educational purposes (Taylor & Hardy, 2004). Additionally, internships are often completed for college credit, although this isn't always the case. Internships may also be considered formal or informal. An informal internship refers to a self-created position subsequently deemed an "internship" (Hettich & Landrum, 2014). Consequentially, the line between volunteering, a job, and internships is fuzzy; and what ultimately counts as an internship is in the eye of the beholder.

Partaking in an internship is a worthy pursuit with numerous benefits. For instance, internships mirror the benefits of a job and volunteer position while granting the opportunity to learn more about a field and encourage career development. Likewise, internships also offer practical experience to develop transferable skills (Taylor & Hardy, 2004).

Internships can also provide unique perks in the way of prestige, specificity, and likelihood of getting hired. Given that a college internship is universally recognized, it may carry more prestige as a unique accomplishment than other experiences (Hettich & Landrum, 2014). Furthermore, internships also can denote specificity by emphasizing a specific career field (Vogt, 2007). For example, while volunteer experience at a creative arts agency might indicate general work experience, a "Creative Arts Internship" suggests a greater emphasis on the creative arts industry. With this, interns can often build field-specific skills along with more general transferable abilities. What's more, by working closely with others, interns increase their networking opportunities and obtain references from individuals who can speak directly to their job preparation (Vogt, 2007). Lastly, internships often lead to jobs. According to the National Association of Colleges and Employers (2011) *Internship and Co-Op Survey*, organizations reported that on average, 39% of their total hires came from internships and that organizations converted about 58% of their own internships into full-time employment.

Action 47 – Internships

Check out available internships in your area. Ask instructors and fellow students in your chosen discipline for internship recommendations. Many campuses have staff dedicated to coordinating field experiences. These staff often work in departments such as Career Services, or other departments such as "Cooperative Education" or "Community Learning" programs (Baird, 2014). You can use online internship search directories such as Chegg Internships or Intern Match, both available at bit.ly/careermythlinks. Keep in mind that you can approach agencies directly to build your own internship even if a formal position doesn't already exist (Bolles, 2020).

Research local internship opportunities. What are two that sound interesting to you and why?

1. Internship Position: _____

    Organization: _____

    What interests me about this position: _____

    _____

    _____

    _____

2. Internship Position: _____

    Organization: _____

    What interests me about this position: _____

    _____

    _____

    _____

Myth 48

"Studying abroad is a luxury I can't afford."

Fact

More than a luxury, studying abroad can be one of the most valuable experiences of a college education (Hettich & Landrum, 2014). Contrary to popular opinion, the benefits go far beyond typical tourist sightseeing and collecting fun memories with your peers. Although it usually involves additional costs, there are many reasons why the experience is worth it. Studying abroad is a gateway to interacting with diverse perspectives, understanding cultural differences, adapting to different situations, and gaining new knowledge that wouldn't be otherwise available. Accordingly, as you contemplate off-campus options for career development during college, you should strongly consider studying abroad.

Typically, studying abroad involves traveling to a different culture as part of a group or as an individual. As the term *studying* abroad implies, it generally occurs as part of an educational program consisting of classes that earn college credit while working in a different environment (Vogt, 2007). Unlike most other off campus experiences, studying abroad can appear deceivingly expensive. However, this short-sighted view fails to consider that the price might be negligible once the cost of a typical academic term on-campus is subtracted (Hettich & Landrum, 2014). Keeping this in mind, studying abroad can be a worthwhile investment if you can afford the additional costs.

The benefits of studying abroad on career development are surprisingly far reaching. In fact, according to over a decade of research, Gardner and colleagues (2008) identified four primary benefits that studying abroad can offer: interacting with people who hold different perspectives, understanding cultural differences in the workplace, adapting to situations of change, and gaining new knowledge from experiences. Furthermore, Gardner's research indicated that 45% of employers found value in these attributes. In terms of employability, students who study abroad may have a unique advantage over others. Currently, one in five jobs within the United States are linked to international trade, yet U.S. companies lose a staggering $2 billion a year due to insufficient skills in cross-cultural relations (Young & Remington, 2014). As international skills are often lacking in college students, studying abroad can be a particularly desirable experience among potential employers.

Action 48 – Study Abroad

Take a moment to review potential study abroad opportunities. Chances are that your college has specific staff dedicated to coordinate such programs. You can also explore opportunities online by using sites such as the International Student Exchange Program, available at bit.ly/careermythlinks. Click "Start a Search" and follow the provided prompts to narrow your search criteria based on preparation, needs, and interests. Keep in mind that you can also pursue a self-designed study abroad experience by building one yourself if a formal program doesn't already exist (Bolles, 2020).

After reviewing the available study abroad opportunities, what are two locations that sound especially interesting to you and why?

1. Location: _____

   What interests me: _____

   _____

   _____

   _____

2. Location: _____

   What interests me: _____

   _____

   _____

   _____

Myth 49

"I wasted my time in college."

Fact

Completing college is a major accomplishment and a valuable use of time. That said, the last several myths and activities presented several possibilities for additional experience during college, both on and off campus. While some high school and early college readers may find this information helpful to offer direction, upper-level students may find this information disheartening. If you happen to be reading this book after or near the end of your college career, you may have regret about what you did or didn't do during your time in college. If this is the case for you, don't let your mind spiral into unnecessary cynicism. Rather, simply recognize the negative thinking patterns and redirect your attention toward the positive. Realize that you may have stumbled onto a dreaded meta-myth. That is, a myth about career myths! As we continue to explore more myths, try to notice these meta-myths when they emerge.

Although the previous myths offered suggestions about ways to engage in career development throughout college, strict adherence to these suggestions isn't required for success. In fact, by working your way through college, you're necessarily engaging in many worthwhile activities. A college degree is a valuable investment in skill acquisition, personal development, earning power, and long-term career success (BLS, 2020). Nevertheless, learning about experiences that could have maximized the college experience can leave graduates feeling like they missed a golden opportunity. If you happen to be one of these disheartened readers, I challenge you to take a second look at your college career and recognize that you may have participated in far more valuable activities than you initially believed.

To quote the existentialist philosopher Søren Kierkegaard (1843), "Life can only be understood backwards; but it must be lived forwards" (p. 306). This is especially true when applied to career development. When we engage in experiences without the explicit purpose of career advancement, it can be difficult to recognize them as such. Without being aware of it, students frequently engage in formative career experiences that take place behind the scenes. Research suggests that while most students are aware that they're having important career preparing experiences in college, they're unable to identify and articulate those experiences (Vargas et al., 2015). In other words, it is only in looking backwards through the lens of career development that we can recognize our formative experiences.

Even if you never engaged in formal "volunteering," "internships," or "jobs," you may have gained similar knowledge and skills from informal activities during your time in college. In fact, when you look back on some of your experiences, you may be able to relabel them as such. For example, one of my clients once stated that he did not engage in any volunteer work during college. However, when we reviewed his past experiences, we discovered that he had a habit of collecting trash around his local neighborhood. We also noted that he served at a soup kitchen as a date activity with his girlfriend. By previously labeling these activities as a mere "habit" or part of "dating," he neglected to recognize these experiences could be easily reinterpreted as "volunteering."

It is important to note that marketable skills can come from your *entire* life and don't need to be sourced in formal experience. Rather, these skills can exist through informal experiences such as hobbies or avocations—meaningful pursuits that we pursue for enjoyment (Vogt,

2007). For example, you may enjoy buying and selling products online through sites such as eBay or Amazon. You could relabel this experience as a part-time job or instead refer to it as an occasional hobby. Either way, recognize the valuable transferable skills gained from this experience, including the technical skills of being able to navigate online platforms, pricing strategies, marketing and communication skills, and entrepreneurship. The key takeaway is that we develop and learn through all our experiences; the trick is being able to recognize and communicate our skills.

Action 49 – Experience Reflection

Brainstorm a list of all the experiences you've had outside the classroom during your time in college that could be viewed as an asset to organizations and employers. In general, employers are looking for applicants that possess transferable skills, which are talents and abilities that you can take from one job and use in multiple careers (Bolles, 2020).

Table 3.2 contains a list of five broad skill areas, which are divided into more specific job skills. This list is an adapted report from the National Association of Colleges and Employers (2011) on employers' rankings of the most important transferable skills. For each of these areas, write down experiences you can think of that demonstrate the skills. These experiences can come from anywhere, including school, hobbies, leisure activities, family, etc., but should be from your college years. As you think of them, relabel any that seem better described under formal titles we've discussed in previous myths about on-campus and off-campus experiences, including extracurricular activities (Myth 39), student organizations (Myth 41), research assistantships (Myth 42), teaching assistantships (Myth 43), part-time jobs (Myth 45), volunteering (Myth 46), internships (Myth 47), and study abroad (Myth 48). Remember that these experiences can be labeled with fitting titles after the fact, and experiences that don't fit these titles can still be valuable and worth noting.

Table 3.2 Transferable Skills

Transferable Skills	Experiences
Communication Skills: • Speaking effectively • Writing concisely • Listening attentively • Expressing ideas • Facilitating group discussion • Providing appropriate feedback • Negotiating • Perceiving nonverbal messages • Persuading • Reporting information • Describing feelings • Interviewing • Editing	

Transferable Skills	Experiences
Research and Planning Skills: • Forecasting, predicting • Creating ideas • Identifying problems • Imagining alternatives • Identifying resources • Gathering information • Solving problems • Setting goals • Extracting important information • Defining needs • Analyzing • Developing evaluation strategies	

Transferable Skills	Experiences
Interpersonal Skills: • Developing rapport • Being sensitive • Listening • Conveying feelings • Providing support for others • Motivating • Sharing credit • Counseling • Cooperating • Delegating with respect • Representing others • Perceiving feelings, situations • Being assertive	

Transferable Skills	Experiences
Organization, Management, and Leadership Skills: • Initiating new ideas • Handling details • Coordinating tasks • Managing groups • Delegating responsibility • Teaching • Coaching • Counseling • Promoting change • Selling ideas or products • Decision making with others • Managing conflict	

Transferable Skills	Experiences
Work Survival Skills: • Implementing decisions • Cooperating • Enforcing policies • Being punctual • Managing time • Attending to detail • Meeting goals • Enlisting help • Accepting responsibility • Setting and meeting deadlines • Organizing • Making decisions	

Myth 50

"My academic skills don't translate to the real world."

Fact

Your academic work matters long after college, but not necessarily in the ways you think. This is normal, as college students often find it difficult to identify exactly how academic skills translate to the real world (Vargas et al., 2015). It is important to know the value of your education so that you are confident in communicating your skills to potential employers.

Understanding begins with differentiating between the two types of curriculum you complete in college: the *overt curriculum* and the *covert curriculum* (Landrum & Davis, 2010). The overt curriculum addresses *what* we learn in school, and can vary depending on your program of study and course subjects. For example, the overt curriculum for a physics major addresses how the world works and how the universe is structured through learning about topics such as the laws of motion (Malnig & Malnig, 1984).

Conversely, the covert curriculum addresses *how* we learn in school and is largely consistent across courses and subjects. The covert curriculum comprises the "numerous, routine skill-related activities, behaviors, and attitudes that are transacted inside and outside of classrooms" (Hettich, 1998, p. 52). Put another way, the covert curriculum is the assortment of transferable skills gained from classroom activities. Returning to our earlier physics major example, the covert curriculum includes the ability to speak and write effectively, as demonstrated through writing term papers and delivering presentations. It also includes skills in punctuality, as demonstrated by consistently attending classes on time. These skills are considered part of the covert curriculum because they're hidden: while students focus on mastering the overt curriculum, they also gain the skills of the covert curriculum.

While focusing on the overt curriculum during your college years is essential to facilitate the covert curriculum, the skills acquired by the covert curriculum are ultimately what matter the most to employers and graduate schools (Hettich & Landrum, 2014). Students often fail to make the mental leap from overt to covert, thereby failing to grasp the true value of their education. Don't fall prey to that same mistake! Recognize how classroom activities and experiences provide valuable evidence of important transferable skills.

Action 50 – Course Experience Reflection

To help you recognize key academic experiences, let's return to the list you created in the previous myth's action. You first completed this list using the transferable skills you gained from experiences outside the classroom. You'll complete this list again, but this time you'll focus only on experiences you had in your college *courses*. As a reminder, we're doing this because employers and graduate schools desire applicants that possess transferable skills, meaning talents and abilities that you can take from job to job and use in multiple careers (Bolles, 2020).

Table 3.3 provides is a list of five broad skill areas, which are divided into more specific job skills. This list was adapted from a report by the National Association of Colleges and Employers (2011) on employers' rankings of the most important transferable skills. For each of these areas, write down experiences you had in the classroom that demonstrate the skills. These experiences may include class attendance and participation, note taking, papers, projects, activities, presentations, etc. Include as many experiences as you can think of, limiting yourself to tasks and experiences during your college years only. As you think of them, relabel any that seem better described under formal titles, such as "independent researcher," "technical writer," or "study group participant/organizer/leader." Remember that these experiences can be labeled with fitting titles after the fact, and experiences that don't fit these titles can still be valuable and worth noting.

Transferable Skills	Experiences
Communication Skills: • Speaking effectively • Writing concisely • Listening attentively • Expressing ideas • Facilitating group discussion • Providing appropriate feedback • Negotiating • Perceiving nonverbal messages • Persuading • Reporting information • Describing feelings • Interviewing • Editing	

Transferable Skills	Experiences
Research and Planning Skills: • Forecasting, predicting • Creating ideas • Identifying problems • Imagining alternatives • Identifying resources • Gathering information • Solving problems • Setting goals • Extracting important information • Defining needs • Analyzing • Developing evaluation strategies	

Transferable Skills	Experiences
Interpersonal Skills: • Developing rapport • Being sensitive • Listening • Conveying feelings • Providing support for others • Motivating • Sharing credit • Counseling • Cooperating • Delegating with respect • Representing others • Perceiving feelings, situations • Being assertive	

Transferable Skills	Experiences
Organization, Management, and Leadership Skills: • Initiating new ideas • Handling details • Coordinating tasks • Managing groups • Delegating responsibility • Teaching • Coaching • Counseling • Promoting change • Selling ideas or products • Decision making with others • Managing conflict	

Transferable Skills	Experiences
Work Survival Skills: • Implementing decisions • Cooperating • Enforcing policies • Being punctual • Managing time • Attending to detail • Meeting goals • Enlisting help • Accepting responsibility • Setting and meeting deadlines • Organizing • Making decisions	

Myth 51

"I have to go to graduate school."

Fact

You can succeed in life; no additional schooling required! Determining how much schooling is sufficient for your career development is a challenging question, with no one-size-fits-all answer. Deciding whether to conclude or continue your formal education requires thoughtful decision making that is individualized to your specific circumstances. Typically, nearing the completion of your bachelor's degree is a good time to decide whether you want to enter the workforce or pursue graduate school.

The reasons not to go to graduate school may surprise you, as they also represent many career myths. Some students consider graduate school because they don't know what else to do. In this way, graduate school is seen as a method to continue to gain skills and experience while affording a grace period to continue exploring interests. While undergraduate education works in this manner, graduate school is different. Bachelor's degree programs train students in general skills that transfer to a variety of settings while helping the student to explore a variety of career options. Graduate school, however, typically focuses on specialized training to prepare students for specific jobs (Green, 2013). In fact, holding a graduate degree can make you less marketable to certain industries. For instance, in the field of history, wide disparities exist between the high number of doctorate degrees awarded and available job postings using this degree. By comparison, this disparity disappears at the bachelor's level, since numerous job postings request a bachelor's degree in any major, including history (Ruediger, 2019). While the niche training of graduate school is required for certain careers, it is a poor choice for those uncertain of what they want to do.

Students can also falsely assume that a graduate degree will result in sweeping salary increases, making it a wise investment to pursue, even if career prospects remain uncertain. Once again, this line of thinking is accurate when pursuing a bachelor's degree but no longer applies for a master's or doctoral degree. While it remains true that salary rates rise and unemployment rates decrease as level of education increases, these increases diminish drastically with graduate school (BLS, 2020). For example, the median weekly earnings from a high school diploma to a bachelor's degree yields a whopping 67% increase, while the increase from a bachelor's degree to a master's degree is only 20%. Factoring in the added costs associated with earning a graduate degree, the financial gains associated with graduate school are negligible (Green, 2011). In other words, money alone is not a sufficient reason to pursue a graduate program.

So, what *is* a good reason to go to graduate school? Determine what you want to pursue for a career first. Revisit Chapter 2 of this book for guidance in how to do that. If a bachelor's degree doesn't allow you to do what you want to do, graduate school is an excellent option. For example, if you decide you want to become a licensed psychologist, graduate training is required. Ultimately, avoiding or delaying career decisions by prolonging school unnecessarily won't serve you in the long term. Instead, discern a career choice and move toward it by attending graduate school only if doing so enables you to do what you want (Landrum, 2010).

Action 51 – Graduate School

Consider if graduate school will help you achieve your career goals by researching available options. Begin by browsing graduate school options related to your major or that you might be interested in by visiting the link available at bit.ly/careermythlinks and browsing by major. Scroll down to explore a full list of available subjects. Click on subjects of interest to read about available options, particularly the "[Subject] Graduate Programs" sections, which lists possible degrees. You may need to engage in additional searching to better understand what these subject areas mean. Keep in mind that this site prominently displays sponsored listings for specific programs, which is not an ideal strategy because it limits search results to paid advertisements. Use this resource to explore possible graduate programs, but consult experts within your program area for appropriate search strategies to find specific schools.

Once your initial search is complete, answer the following questions:

Based on your understanding of your career goals and initial research of available options, do you believe graduate school is a good option for you? Why or why not?

_____

_____

_____

_____

_____

If you decide to pursue graduate school, what are two program types that sound especially interesting to you and why? Note that the question asks about program types rather than subject areas. For example, "Kinesiology" is a subject that includes program types like "Biomechanics" and "Sports Psychology." Be sure to research and identify program types for this question.

1. Program Type: _____

   What interests me: _____

   _____

   _____

   _____

2. Program Type: _____

   What interests me: _____

   _____

   _____

   _____

Myth 52

"Everyone else knows what they want to do after college."

Fact

If you've reached the end of your college education and you don't know what you want to do next, you're not alone; in fact, you're in the majority. The uncertainty that most college students face at this stage is a normal and expected part of the career development process.

Retrospective interviews on traditional college students conducted a decade after graduation found that only about one third of the students (35%) saw a direct career path consisting of related jobs or additional education that was linked to longer-term career choices. The rest (65%) said they spent the majority of their 20s participating in activities completely unrelated to later career paths (Selingo, 2016). Reasons for these activities included taking time away for personal or family reasons, traveling prior to "settling down," and choosing temporary jobs with a higher salary to pay off student loans. The most cited reason for engaging in these unrelated activities was for exploration and experimentation. In other words, the majority of people spent their early 20s trying to figure out what they wanted to do.

Further evidence of post-graduation uncertainty can be observed online. In fact, social networks have emerged that serve to unite graduates around this shared experience. For example, check out the subreddit aptly named "Quarter Life Crisis," which is an online discussion board created for college graduates in their 20s who are "having difficulty finding direction in their life" (Reddit, 2021): bit.ly/careermythlinks. As you'll see, many people still don't know what they're doing after college.

Even still, social comparison with others can be difficult, anxiety provoking, and counterproductive. Regardless of what others are doing, it is unsettling to graduate from college without concrete plans. Without plans, it can feel like leaping into the unknown without a safety net. That unknown is where fear lives. It means you might repeatedly try and fail. You could also end up in a job or activity that's unrelated to a later career path. Even if you feel certain about your plans after college, your plans may still need to change when unexpected circumstances emerge. Either way, failure and mistakes are inevitable, and attempting to fight them only magnifies the distress. Happiness researcher Arthur Brooks (2021) warns that, "fear of failure can have surprisingly harsh consequences for our well-being" (p. 3). He explains that this paralyzing fear can interfere with our ability to take risks, try new things, and can even lead to mental illness in the forms of anxiety and depression. But without these experiences, we may never find a career fit (Vogt, 2007). For these reasons, Brooks (2021) advocates that reinterpreting our failures as challenges and learning opportunities can lead to greater levels of happiness. For additional guidance on how to reframe failures, return to Myth 25.

Action 52 – Graduation Fears

Address your fears of post-graduation uncertainty and potential failures by increasing your feelings of courage. One way to boost your courage is to bolster your belief that you are able to bounce back and recover from missteps (Brooks, 2021). To do so, read about how others have found success after a blunder, and then reflect on how this can also apply to your own life.

Read the motivational article chronicling the initial failures and later accomplishment of 50 highly successful people, available at bit.ly/careermythlinks.

What are the most significant insights you gained from reading these stories? What do you want to remember as you face potential missteps in your future?

_____

_____

_____

_____

_____

_____

Myth 53

"I'll lose momentum after I graduate from college."

Fact

Momentum can be maintained after college though effective goal setting. Still, leaving school can be scary, and the concern is understandable. College provides an atmosphere in which growth is built into the curriculum, where you can move passively through developmental stages. After college, however, the responsibility rests squarely on your shoulders to guide your own development. While there's an exciting freedom innate in being the pilot of your own career path, students often worry they'll lose their drive and stagnate. This is particularly the case for students who envision long-term goals that require several intermediate steps, such as taking several gap years to earn money before returning to graduate school. Likewise, some students express concern that they'll end up stuck in a career they don't enjoy by default (Vogt, 2007).

Although it's true that learning in college is a more passive activity than working post-college, career development doesn't automatically occur during school. (If it did happen automatically, this chapter on career development and education wouldn't be necessary!) You've had to learn how to take the initiative yourself, and the personality you've forged won't change just because you graduated. The attributes and skills you've developed will carry forward with you through future phases of life (Brown & Hirschi, 2013).

It's also a falsehood to think that successful people race through preparatory steps while those who take longer lose momentum. In fact, it's becoming increasingly more common for students to take a break from formal education in order to work and gain experience prior to returning to school. These so-called "gap years" are being chosen more often by students and are more frequently advocated for because they help students refine their interests and better prepare for graduate study. In fact, the vast majority (90%) of undergraduate students in the United States are under age 25, while the majority of graduate students (60–80%) in the United States are above age 30, depending on the type of program (full-time or part-time) and type of institution (public or private; NCES, 2019). Interestingly, experts say that this structured time away from school increases students' chances of successful admission (Handelsman et al., 2014). As a matter of fact, most people who attend graduate school waited to do so and gained momentum in the process. The important part of maintaining momentum in your career development after college resides in having clearly defined goals and reminding yourself of them along the way (Mills, 2017).

Action 53 – Future Letter

Keep your goals present by writing them down to remind yourself of them in the future. You can do so by writing a letter to your future self (Mills, 2017). Imagine yourself in a year's time and express to your future self what you care about and what you want to keep in mind.

Letters to your future self provide a record of your life and personal development. This will serve as a time capsule for your current views, attitudes, philosophy, and outlook. For inspiration, you may want to consider the following questions:

- What goals do you have that you aspire to? What hopes do you hold for yourself in the future? What fears and obstacles do you wish to overcome?
- What is the ultimate and underlying reason why these goals matter to you?
- What internal resources do you inherently possess that will help you, now and always?
- How will you remember these things? What reminders, inspiration, etc. would you like to give yourself?

Include a copy of your letter below. Also consider uploading it to a website that will email the letters to you on a designated date, such as the link available at bit.ly/careermythlinks.

Dear _____

_____

_____

_____

_____

_____

_____

_____

_____

_____

_____

_____

_____

_____

_____

_____

_____

_____

_____

_____

_____

_____

_____

_____

_____

_____

_____

Love,

_____

References

Alexander, M. M. (2016). The early graduation gambit of Japanese high-school sojourners in the US: Organizing educational paths across borders. *Asia Pacific Journal of Education, 36*(3), 350–363. https://doi.org/10.1080/02188791.2014.959467

Association of American Medical Colleges (AAMC). (2021). *2021 facts: Applicants and matriculants data*. Medical Education Facts. www.aamc.org/data-reports/students-residents/interactive-data/2020-facts-applicants-and-matriculants-data

Association of College Honor Societies (ACHS). (2020). *Association of College Honor Societies*. www.achshonor.org

Auter, Z., & Marken, S. (2016, December 13). *One in six U.S. grads say career services was very helpful*. Gallup. https://news.gallup.com/poll/199307/one-six-grads-say-career-services-helpful.aspxn

Baird, B. N. (2014). *The internship, practicum, and field placement handbook* (7th ed.). Routledge.

Beggs, J., Bantham, J., & Taylor, S. (2008). Distinguishing the factors influencing college students' choice of major. *College Student Journal, 42*(2), 381–394.

Bolles, R. N. (2020). *What color is your parachute? A practical manual for job-hunters and career-changers* (2020 ed). Ten Speed Press.

Brooks, A. C. (2021, February 25). How to build a life: Go ahead and fail. *The Atlantic*. www.theatlantic.com/family/archive/2021/02/how-overcome-fear-failure/618130/

Brown, S. D., & Hirschi, A. (2013). Personality, career development, and occupational attainment. In S. Brown & R. W. Lent (Eds.), *Career development and counseling: Putting theory and research to work* (2nd ed., pp. 299–328). Wiley.

Bruni, F. (2018, August 17). How to get the most out of college. *The New York Times*. www.nytimes.com/2018/08/17/opinion/college-students.html

Bureau of Labor Statistics (BLS). (2020). *Unemployment rates and earnings by educational attainment*. U.S. Bureau of Labor Statistics. www.bls.gov/emp/tables/unemployment-earnings-education.htm#

Bureau of Labor Statistics (BLS). (2021). *Fastest growing occupations*. U.S. Bureau of Labor Statistics. www.bls.gov/ooh/fastest-growing.htm

Bureau of Labor Statistics (BLS). (2022). *CareerOneStop American Job Center Finder*. U.S. Bureau of Labor Statistics. www.careeronestop.org/LocalHelp/AmericanJobCenters/find-american-job-centers.aspx

Campbell, E. L. (2013). Anticipating work & family: Experience, conflict, & planning in the transition to adulthood. *Dissertation Abstracts International: Section B. Sciences & Engineering, 73*(8).

Campbell, E. L., & Burrows, M. A. (2020). LGBT college student career development: Goals and recommendations for faculty members. *International Journal of Innovative Teaching and Learning in Higher Education, 1*(2), 29–40. https://doi.org/10.4018/ijitlhe.2020040103

Carignan, N. (2021, January 29). *Community college vs. university: Pros and cons*. Mount Wachusett Community College. https://mwcc.edu/blog/community-college-vs-university/

Carnegie Mellon. (2002). *Obligations and expectations for undergraduate teaching assistants*. Eberly Center for Teaching Excellence. www.cmu.edu/teaching/resources/PublicationsArchives/UGTA_TAs-v2.pdf

Chamber of Commerce. (2020). *Student loan statistics*. www.chamberofcommerce.org/student-loan-statistics/

Clay, R. A. (1996, September). Is a psychology diploma worth the price of tuition? *APA Monitor, 27*, p. 54.

Colbert, D. (2016, March 3). *The importance of joining student organizations in college.* College Express. www.collegexpress.com/articles-and-advice/student-life/blog/importance-joining-student-organizations-college/

Cutrone, C., & Stanger, M. (2012, December 2012). 14 ways students can get more out of college. *Business Insider.* www.businessinsider.com/how-to-get-the-most-out-of-college-2012-12

Daugherty, G. (2020, November 6). *Is university prestige really that important?* Investopedia. www.investopedia.com/articles/personal-finance/051915/university-prestige-really-important.asp

Davidson, M., Davidson, S. M., & Campbell, E. L. (2017). Talking with students about faith-based career fears. *International Journal of Christianity and Education, 21*(3), 213–224. https://doi.org/10.1177/2056997117712529

Doostang. (2020). https://doostang.com

Eide, E. R., Hilmer, M. J., & Showalter, M. H. (2016). Is it where you go or what you study? The relative influence of college selectivity and college major on earnings. *Contemporary Economic Policy, 34*(1), 37–46. https://doi.org/10.1111/coep.12115

Forleo, M. (2019). *Everything is figureoutable.* Portfolio/Penguin.

Freedman, L. (2013). The developmental disconnect of choosing a major: Why institutions should prohibit major choice until the second year. *The Mentor: An Academic Advising Journal, 15.* https://doi.org/10.26209/MJ1561278

Gardner, P., Gross, L., & Steglitz, I. (2008). *Unpacking your study abroad experience: Critical reflection for workplace* competencies (CERI Research Brief 1-2008). Collegiate Employment Research Institute. https://ceri.msu.edu/_assets/pdfs/Unpacking-Your-Study-Abroad-Experience.pdf

Gelhaus, D. (2007). What can I do with my liberal arts degree? *Occupational Outlook Quarterly.* www.bls.gov/careeroutlook/2007/winter/art01.pdf

Green, A. (2011, December 21). *Grad school isn't an escape from a bad job market.* US News Careers. https://money.usnews.com/money/blogs/outside-voices-careers/2011/12/21/grad-school-isnt-an-escape-from-a-bad-job-market

Green, A. (2013, January 7). *6 career myths you shouldn't fall for.* US News Careers. http://money.usnews.com/money/blogs/outside-voices-careers/2013/01/07/6-career-myths-you-shouldnt-fall-for

Gross, A., & Marcus, J. (2018, April 25). High-paying trade jobs sit empty, while high school grads line up for university. *National Public Radio.* www.npr.org/sections/ed/2018/04/25/605092520/high-paying-trade-jobs-sit-empty-while-high-school-grads-line-up-for-university

Handelsman, M. M., VanderStoep, S. W., & Landrum, R. E. (2014). Questions (and answers) about graduate school. *Eye on Psi Chi, 18*(3). www.psichi.org/page/183EyeSprSum14jHande?&hhsearchterms=%22%22gap+year%22%22#.YEvmjC1h3JE

Harmon, L. W., Hansen, J. C., Borgen, F. H., & Hamer, A. L. (1994). *Strong interest inventory: Applications and technical guide.* Stanford University Press.

Hegedus, C. M., & Knight, J. (2016). *Student participation in collegiate organizations: Expanding the boundaries.* Leadership Educators. www.leadershipeducators.org/Resources/Documents/Conferences/Lexington/Hegedus.pdf

Hettich, P. (1998). *Learning skills for college and career* (2nd ed.). Brooks/Cole Publishing Company.

Hettich, P. I., & Landrum, R. E. (2014). *Your undergraduate degree in psychology: From college to career.* SAGE Publications, Inc.

Hua, K. (2015, June 24). Graduating from college early: Is the money saved worth missing senior year? *Forbes.* www.forbes.com/sites/karenhua/2015/06/24/graduating-college-early-is-the-money-saved-worth-missing-senior-year/?sh=6f3db48f45a0

Indiana University Bloomington. (2020). *Undergraduate teaching assistants (UTA) program.* Indiana Univeristy Bloomington College of Arts and Sciences Department of Biology. https://biology.indiana.edu/student-portal/undergraduate/undergrad-teaching-assistants.html

Indiviglio, D. (2010, May 17). Should more people skip college? *The Atlantic.* www.theatlantic.com/business/archive/2010/05/should-more-people-skip-college/56821/

Jones, J. (2022). *Auto loan statistics 2020.* Lending Tree. www.lendingtree.com/auto/debt-statistics/

Jordan, L. A., & Marinaccio, J. N. (Eds.). (2017). *Facilitating career development: Student manual* (4th ed.). National Career Development Association.

Joseph, S. V. (2018, August 11). What every college student should be doing for career success. *Forbes.* www.forbes.com/sites/shelcyvjoseph/2018/08/11/what-every-college-student-should-be-doing-for-career-success/#1eb2092c62c4

Kierkegaard, S. (1843). Søren Kierkegaards Skrifter. *Journalen, 167*(18), 306.

Landrum, R. E., & Davis, S. F. (2010). *The psychology major: Career options and strategies for success* (4th ed.). Pearson Education.

Landrum, R. E., Hettich, P. I., & Wilner, A. (2010). Alumni perceptions of workforce readiness. *Teaching of Psychology, 37*(2), 97–106. https://doi.org/10.1080/00986281003626912

Lobosco, K. (2017, May 5). No scholarship? Here's how to pay for college. *CNN Money.* https://money.cnn.com/2017/04/25/pf/college/pay-for-college/index.html

Lore, N. (2011). *The Pathfinder: How to choose or change your career for a lifetime of satisfaction and success.* Touchstone.

Malnig, L. R., & Malnig, A. (1984). *What can I do with a major in…? How to choose and use your college major.* Abbott Press.

Meier, K. S. (2018, August 9). *List of trade careers.* Chron. https://work.chron.com/list-trade-careers-7833.html

Mills, C. (2017). *Career coach: How to plan your career and land your perfect job* (2nd ed.). Crimson Publishing.

National Academic Advising Association (NACADA). (2006). *Concept of academic advising.* www.ship.edu/globalassets/advising/faculty/nacada-concept-of-advising.pdf

National Association of Colleges and Employers (NACE). (2011). *2011 internship and co-op survey.* www.workandlearnindiana.com/documents/research/internship_co_op_survey_research_brief_2011.pdf

National Association of Colleges and Employers (NACE). (2012, March). *Job outlook 2012: Spring update.* https://uncw.edu/career/documents/joboutlook2012spring update.pdf

National Association of Colleges and Employers (NACE). (2019). *Starting salaries by academic major.*

National Career Development Association (NCDA). (2017). *Introduction to credentialing.* https://ncda.org/aws/NCDA/pt/sp/credentialing_intro

National Career Development Association (NCDA). (2020). *National Career Development Association Directory.* https://ncda.org/

National Center for Education Statistics (NCES). (2017). *Beginning college students who change their majors within 3 years of enrollment.* https://nces.ed.gov/pubs2018/2018434.pdf

National Center for Education Statistics (NCES). (2019). *The condition of education 2019.* https://nces.ed.gov/pubs2019/2019144.pdf

Petrie, T. A., Petrie, H. G., Landry, L., & Edwards, K. B. (2002). *Strategic learning in college.* RonJon Publishing, Inc.

Phillips, P. (2021). *5 common myths about career exploration.* Next Step U. www.nextstepu.com/common-myths-career-exploration.art#.WVUmLcaZO3V

Primé, D. R., & Tracey, T. J. G. (2010). Psychometric properties of the career clusters interest survey. *Journal of Career Assessment, 18*(2), 177–188. https://doi.org/10.1177/1069072709354202

Ramsey, D. (2003). *Financial peace revisited.* Viking Press.

Reddit. (2021). *Quarter-life crisis.* Reddit. www.reddit.com/r/quarterlifecrisis/

Rubin, R. S., Bommer, W. H., & Baldwin, T. T. (2002). Using extracurricular activity as an indicator of interpersonal skill: Prudent evaluation or recruiting malpractice? *Human Resource Management, 41*(4), 441–454. https://doi.org/10.1002/hrm.10053

Ruediger, D. (2019, January 28). *The 2019 AHA jobs report.* American Historical Association. www.historians.org/publications-and-directories/perspectives-on-history/february-2019/the-2019-aha-jobs-report-a-closer-look-at-faculty-hiring

Schaub, M. (2012). The profession of college career services delivery: What college counselors should know about career centers. *Journal of College Student Psychotherapy, 26*(3), 201–215. https://doi.org/10.1080/87568225.2012.685854

Scheele, A. (2005). *Launch your career in college: Strategies for students, educators, and parents.* Praeger.

Selingo, J. J. (2016). *There is life after college: What parents and students should know about navigating school to prepare for the jobs of tomorrow.* William Morrow.

Strapp, C. M., & Farr, R. J. (2010). To get involved or not: The relation among extracurricular involvement, satisfaction, and academic achievement. *Teaching of Psychology, 37*(1), 50–54. https://doi.org/10.1080/00986280903425870

Taylor, J., & Hardy, D. (2004). *Monster careers: How to land the job of your life.* Penguin Group.

University of Nevada Las Vegas Student Involvement and Activities (UNLV). (2020). *Myth vs. fact.* University of Nevada Las Vegas. www.unlv.edu/sia/fraternity-sorority/myths

Vargas, K., Campbell, E. L., Sullivan, R., Johnson, Z., & Engelmann, C. (2015, April). *Mind the gaps: Proficiencies & pitfalls in college student career development* [Poster presentation]. Western Psychological Association annual meeting, Las Vegas, NV.

Vogt, P. (2007). *Career wisdom for college students: Insights you won't get in class, on the Internet, or from your parents.* Ferguson Publishing Company.

Wahlstrom, C., & Williams, B. K. (2004). *College to career: Your road to personal success.* South-Western.

Welsh, M., & Campbell, E. L. (2016). Relational mentoring: Fostering genuine connections with professors. *Eye on Psi Chi, 21*(2), 10–12. https://doi.org/10.24839/1092-0803.eye21.2.10

Young, S., & Remington, D. (2014, November 1). *Study abroad: Guiding students to demonstrate skills to employers.* National Career Development Association. www.ncda.org/aws/NCDA/pt/sd/news_article/98747/_self/layout_details/false

Chapter 4

Job Hunting

This chapter will break down myths surrounding the job search and application process, such as "networking is all about who you know" and "cover letters don't matter." Instead, we'll look at the facts and explore the actions to take to get the job you want. From picking up a quick side gig to landing your dream job, this chapter is for you, job hunters!

Myth 54

"No one will hire me."

Fact

Getting hired is possible! You've reached the point where it's time to start the job hunt, which can dredge up all sorts of fears and insecurities. Job hunters often worry that lack of experience, gaps in their work history, poor academic performance, and other issues may prevent them from getting a job. These challenges may require additional time and effort to land your dream job, but can all be overcome to find satisfying work. Most early job hunters begin with entry-level jobs and advance from there based on their education and growing experience. You don't need a perfect resume and educational background to get started. For most entry-level jobs, employers seek general abilities such as communication skills, reliability, and enthusiasm (Crosby, 2005).

Fears and uncertainties are understandable. The job hunt represents a step into the unknown; the future is unpredictable and uncontrollable. Success is possible but it's unclear what form it will take, or the length of time required until it occurs. Let's be realistic: this can be a hard process. Traditional job-hunting strategies yield a job offer less than half of the time, with estimates ranging from 47% to as low as 7% (Bolles, 2020). Thankfully, the strategies you'll learn in this book will vastly improve your chances, but still not to 100%. You're likely to face disappointments and rejections along the way and you'll need to put in continued effort until you land a job. It can be difficult to persevere in situations like this. When a long period of unemployment has passed or a long preparatory period has led into the job hunt, job hunters often have increasing apprehension and even hopelessness (Miller, 2010).

Belief in yourself is most important. How you handle adversity as you progress through this process is a good indicator of your ability to persevere toward your long-term goals. You

DOI: 10.4324/9780429261770-4

need to believe it's possible and you need to want someone to hire you. If you don't believe it, you won't be able to convince anyone else (Segal, 2017). Everyone has insecurities. Even the most successful people I've counseled question at times whether they have what it takes. Fears are a natural part of the human experience. What matters is whether you allow them to take you over and hold you back, or face them directly and persevere (Mills, 2017).

Action 54 – Developing a Hopeful Mindset

Job hunting is challenging; you *will* have doubts and fears at times. Plan ahead by developing strategies to bounce back and readjust to a hopeful mindset. There are numerous methods to inspire a positive and hopeful mood. For some people, it includes physical movement, spiritual practices, socializing and mentorship, and reading inspirational material. All these methods have been shown to boost mood and confidence during the job-hunting process (Miller, 2010).

Another effective method to try is listening to inspirational music. Music affects deep emotional centers in the brain, releasing dopamine, a powerful neurotransmitter associated with feelings of pleasure (Segal, 2017). Harness the power of music and plan ahead for times in the job hunt when your confidence may need a boost. Below, create an inspirational play-list of songs and commit to using this list when needed to refocus your job-hunting efforts. Focus your list on songs that help you to feel confident, powerful, capable, and inspired. Include at least ten songs below:

1. Song name: _____

   Artist: _____

2. Song name: _____

   Artist: _____

3. Song name: _____

   Artist: _____

4. Song name: _____

   Artist: _____

5. Song name: _____

   Artist: _____

6. Song name: _____

   Artist: _____

7. Song name: _____

   Artist: _____

8. Song name: _____

   Artist: _____

9. Song name: _____

   Artist: _____

10. Song name: _____

    Artist: _____

Myth 55

"The more applications I complete, the better my chances."

Fact

Haphazardly submitting loads of applications is a recipe for disaster—not to mention burnout. Finding a job is not a quick or easy process, and even in the best of circumstances, the rate of rejection is high (Asher, 2011). Don't make a hard task worse. Wasting time pursuing jobs that aren't a good fit not only interferes with your success, but it also actually increases your chance of failure by diverting your time and attention, depleting your energy and destroying your confidence (Morem, 2007). When it comes to job hunting, work smarter, not harder. Job searching should be an exercise in efficiency and in finding a fit. This is not a hunt for just any job—you're aiming for the best possible match for you by maximizing quality opportunities most likely to yield an offer. Don't apply for a job in Delaware if you're unwilling to live there, and don't waste your time on jobs that require a law degree if you don't have one. Reserve your time for the opportunities that match what you want with what they need. Accordingly, start with a large pool of possibilities and then weed out the ones you don't want or aren't qualified for. This leaves the opportunities most ripe for pursuing: job opportunities that you want and can attain.

Job-hunting methods are not created equal and while some have a great track record, others are pretty terrible (Bolles, 2020). Methods and success rates will be introduced here to help you set realistic expectations and identify a plan for your job hunt. These will also return to be expounded in later myths and activities in this chapter to help you maximize their effectiveness. The job market is competitive, and job seekers need to be flexible, creative, and assertive when seeking employment (Jordan & Marinaccio, 2017). Despite the varying effectiveness among job-hunting methods, a multimodal approach offers the best possibility of discovering a fit (Bolles, 2020).

I'll provide a brief rundown of the primary methods for identifying job opportunities. The strategies included here and their effectiveness may surprise you, since the most common strategies utilized by most job hunters are often the least effective in producing a job offer. Clearly, career myths are at play and help to explain the challenges and stressors so many job hunters encounter (Morem, 2007). Let's set the record straight and prepare for better outcomes by planning out your job search strategy ahead of time. While you don't want to discard the less effective strategies completely, balance your approach to favor the more effective ones. Note effectiveness rates and incorporate multiple techniques, but plan to devote more time and energy to more effective methods. To aid in this process, methods for identifying job opportunities are listed in order from least to most effective.

Look for employers' job postings on the Internet. This strategy includes searching a variety of places for job descriptions of existing job vacancies posted by employers. Companies' individual websites often include a jobs section, such as Walmart.com which has a "Careers" page to apply for current openings. Internet job postings can also be found on job boards for specific fields, such as HigherEdJobs.com for those wanting to work at a university. The most popular places to find job postings on the Internet are job search engine websites such as Indeed, Monster, CareerBuilder, Glassdoor, CareerArc, and LinkedIn. Although widely popular, applying to job postings on the Internet works on average just 4% of the time (Bolles, 2020). That means you'll likely need to apply on average for about 25 jobs to get one offer. Talk about discouraging odds! As you can see, you don't want to rely on job postings alone.

Self-employment. This strategy involves starting your own company and working for yourself. Hopefully, through this method, a job offer is guaranteed! However, self-employment isn't a universally good fit for everyone. Given that, the success of this option is a bit harder to quantify. According to the United States Small Business Administration (2018), about 80% of new businesses survive the first year, although only about 45% last five years, and less than 33% make it past ten years. Choosing to pursue self-employment is a big decision, so devote at least some time of your job-hunting energy to at least considering whether this might be an option for you.

Targeted campaigns of identifying and pursuing companies of interest. Rather than hunting for existing job openings, this method focuses on companies of interest. Targeted campaigns involve approaching companies and inquiring directly about employment. By doing so, you may stumble on "secret jobs" in the hidden job market. These are either openings that aren't posted or not yet posted (Jordan & Marinaccio, 2017). Sharing with them the additional value you can offer to the company, you may also have the opportunity to engage in job crafting, where a position is created for you. Shockingly, this method is highly effective and works 47% of the time (Bolles, 2020).

Networking to discover secret jobs in the hidden job market. Networking means connecting with people who are doing the kind of work you want to do (Jordan & Marinaccio, 2017). The best way to discover secret jobs in the hidden job market is through word-of-mouth, which can reveal jobs that aren't posted or publicly advertised. Secret jobs actually represent the vast majority of jobs. Statistics vary, but researchers suggest that as few as 15% of jobs are ever publicly posted, and at least half of newly employed workers didn't respond to a job post (Asher, 2011). Networking provides a powerful resource to not only discover current jobs but also encourage future job leads to be reported directly back to you. For this reason, networking yields about a 48% success rate and is considered the most successful job search strategy (Jordan & Marinaccio, 2017).

Action 55 – Job Search Strategy

Develop your overall job search strategy. How much time and energy do you plan to devote to your job search? (e.g., "I plan to spend the next three months finding a job. I'll devote 10 hours per week engaging in job search activities during this time…")

_____

_____

_____

_____

_____

Given what you've learned about each of the strategies presented, how do you plan to divide your time between these strategies? Consider dividing your time based on your willingness to engage in each method, keeping strategy effectiveness in mind. Indicate your answer below by drawing out the ratio of how you'll spend your time with each of the following methods: 1) collecting and applying for employers' job postings on the Internet, 2) considering and pursuing self-employment, 3) identifying and pursuing companies of interest, and 4) discovering secret jobs in the hidden job market through networking. Figure 4.1 depicts an example pie chart.

Figure 4.1 Example Pie Chart

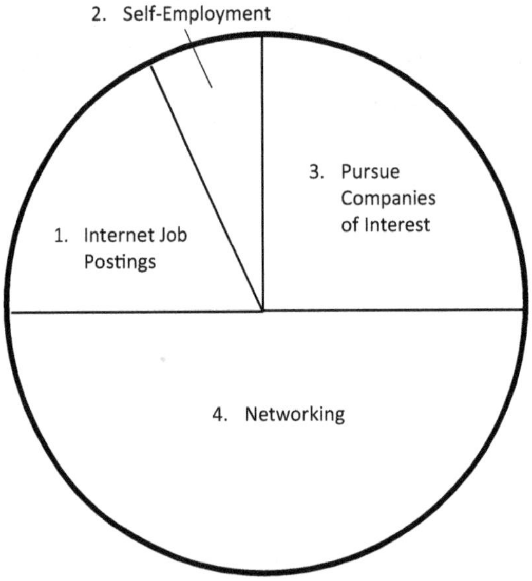

In Figure 4.2, create a pie chart as a visual representation of what percentage of your time you'll devote to each of these four areas:

Figure 4.2 Pie Chart

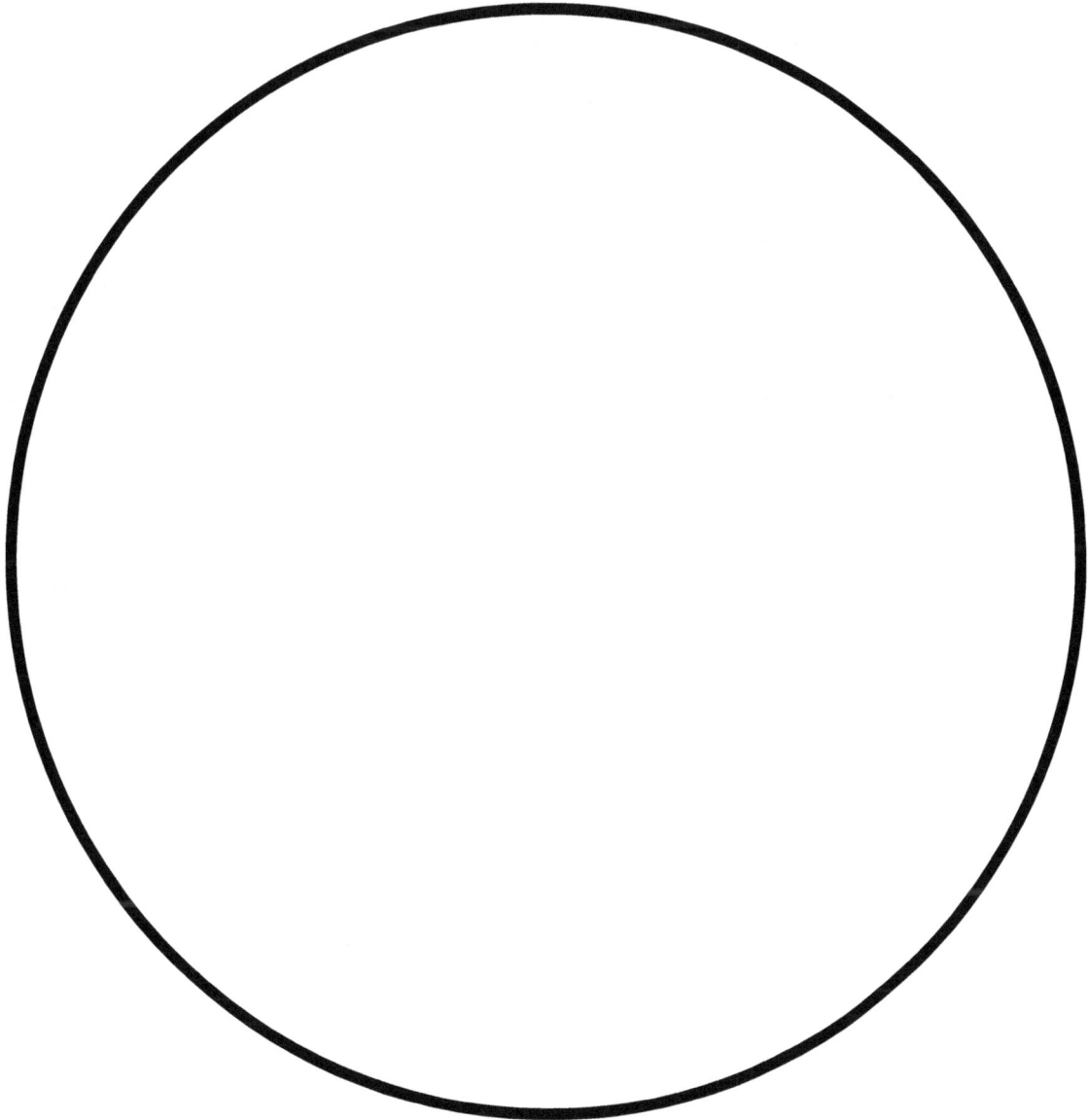

Translate your drawing into a written plan. How much time and energy do you plan to devote to each method?

1. Internet job postings: _____

   _____

   _____

2. Self-employment: _____

   _____

   _____

3. Pursue companies of interest: _____

   _____

   _____

4. Networking: _____

   _____

   _____

Myth 56

"Networking is an annoying attempt to cheat the system."

Fact

Connecting with others is an enjoyable and mutually beneficial process. The problem is that networking has developed a bum rap. It conjures up images of awkward rooms of strangers forced to mingle and exchange unwanted sales pitches. We can thank too many required "networking events" for this one. The truth is that networking means connecting with people who are doing the kind of work you want to do (Jordan & Marinaccio, 2017). Using networking as a job search method means relying on relationships with other people and social connections to identify job leads (Huang & Western, 2011). These word-of-mouth leads are the best way to discover secret jobs that aren't otherwise publicly advertised, which actually represent the vast majority of jobs. Statistics vary but research indicates that up to 85% of jobs are obtained through networking (Asher, 2011). For this reason, networking is considered the most successful job search strategy (Jordan & Marinaccio, 2017).

Relationships are everything. A strong personal network is essential for successful job hunting and building one can be an enjoyable and rewarding process (Bolles, 2020). Networking doesn't have to be awkward, or uncomfortable, or involve spontaneously imposing yourself on unsuspecting strangers. Instead, networking can and should be about forming connections and having enjoyable conversations with other like-minded people. The most effective form of networking involves starting with the people you know and then branching out through their networks to meet others (Taylor & Hardy, 2004).

The reason this is valuable is due to the relative power of weak versus strong ties (Jome & Phillips, 2013). Strong and weak ties refer to the intensity of relationships in your network. Strong ties are those you're in regular direct contact with, such as family members and friends. Weak ties are those with whom you have infrequent or indirect contact, such as acquaintances and friends-of-friends. When it comes to networking for job leads, research suggests that using weak ties, rather than strong ties, is a more effective strategy to finding a job (e.g., Granovetter, 1995; Hodges et al., 2010).

Thus, part of finding your next job will be building relationships—personal and professional—with people who will help connect you to them. Just as you don't yet know what your future job will be, you also might not yet know the key relationship that will connect you to it. Thus, it's important that your job search includes both a search for job leads as well as valuable connections, since both will likely be needed for success (Taylor & Hardy, 2004).

Action 56 – Networking

Now that we've reviewed the importance of networking, we need to begin identifying people in our social network. While we'll begin engaging in networking in later myth activities, for now just begin by thinking of the supportive people you have directly available to you. These people represent your strong ties. Although weak ties are the connections that will be most helpful in your job search, we access them first through strong ties. So, start with strong ties and we'll build from there.

To brainstorm strong ties in your social network, begin by thinking of people you know who you admire, and who you think may have helpful wisdom to offer regarding your future. They may come to mind because they have a great job that you're interested in, or they tend to offer great tips and supportive comments, or you suspect they may have job leads or know someone who might, or they've just generally been a good person to go to when you're working on a problem. Regardless, brainstorm who in your world might fit this description and include them on the brainstorming grid below.

Complete the brainstorming grid in Table 4.1. Several roles are offered to get you thinking, but don't limit yourself to the categories provided. Feel free to generate other roles, include multiple people in certain categories, or skip ones that don't apply. We're just trying to start thinking about people that make up our social network who may lead you to your next job.

Table 4.1 Brainstorming Grid

Role	Name	Email	Phone Number
Family members			
Friends			
Neighbors			
Church members			
Online acquaintances			
Classmates			

Role	Name	Email	Phone Number
Teachers and school mentors			
College acquaintances			
Professors and college mentors			
Coworkers			
Volunteer acquaintances			
Other			
Other			
Other			

Myth 57

"My social media is only for personal use."

Fact

Your social media presence offers a useful networking tool. Popular social networking sites such as Instagram, Facebook, Twitter, Pinterest, and YouTube may be appealing for entertainment purposes and maintaining private social connections, but they offer additional networking capabilities in the professional realm, too. Learning how to use social media effectively is essential in today's job market.

Failing to take advantage of such opportunities means missing out. Virtually all job recruiters look at social media, and 44% of the time, employers hire based on positive exposure online (Bolles, 2020). Carefully controlling your social media presence also serves to protect against negative exposure. Whether you use your online presence for job hunting or not, recruiters and employees will likely search online to discover information about you. Even information intended to be personal can be discovered and used to make hiring decisions. In fact, 57% of employers reported rejecting a job applicant for negative online exposure (Bolles, 2020). But if you believe that avoiding social media altogether can remedy this issue, think again; according to a Harris Poll survey, 47% of employers declined job interviews to applicants who didn't have a searchable social media presence (CareerBuilder, 2018). Since it can either work for you or against you, it's best to take control of your online presence now and use its power for good.

The best ways to engage proactively online is to be thoughtful about using your social media presence as both a personal and professional public representation of yourself. Before you post anything, think about the broad audience of personal and professional contacts who might see it, both now and in the future, and ask yourself whether the post represents you in positive ways (Bolles, 2020). Use social media to not only connect with friends and family but potential networking contacts as well. Lastly, join networking groups and subcommunities of interest online (Hettich & Landrum, 2014). For example, I run a Facebook group for students and alumni of our university's undergraduate psychology department. Together, the group offers fruitful opportunities for networking and provides individuals with needed advice, mentoring, and job offers. Simply based on the shared experience of attending the same school and holding similar interests, people in the group are willing to go to great lengths to support each other. Online communities such as these offer direct access to weak ties, which can ultimately be your most powerful networking connections.

Action 57 – Social Media

Use social media to your advantage through the following steps:

1. If you aren't yet on social media, consider joining. Top recommended social media sites include LinkedIn, Facebook, Instagram, and Twitter. We'll learn specifically about LinkedIn with the next myth.
2. If you already have a social media presence, search for networking contacts. Review your networking grid from the previous myth and connect with anyone missing from your online networks. In doing so, your social media accounts may suggest other networking contacts you hadn't previously recalled or considered. Add these contacts to your grid; also request to add these connections to your social media accounts. Bonus points if you send them a quick note to say hello!
3. Search for networking groups. If you have specific interests, especially in jobs or industries, search for groups based on these interests and ask to join. Other possibilities for online communities include groups you're affiliated with in person, such as churches, schools, clubs, and honors societies. General networking groups can be useful as well.
4. Lastly, learn specific strategies for how to harness the positive power of social media. Visit the following link to a YouTube video for tips and then answer the following questions: bit.ly/careermythlinks.

What did you learn from this video?

_____

_____

_____

_____

_____

How will you implement what you learned?

_____

_____

_____

_____

_____

Myth 58

"Networking is all about who you know."

Fact

If you're following this train of thought, you're really missing out. As discussed in previous myths, the power of networking occurs through your weak ties—those with whom you share mutual connections but don't yet have direct contact (Jome & Phillips, 2013). Networking isn't about who you know but rather about who you don't yet know.

Understanding this key feature of networking unlocks the ability to use it effectively. The value is in expanding your social network and connecting with new people in your areas of interest. One way to accomplish this is through reaching out first to your strong ties, which are the people you already know. Understand that your strong ties are meant to serve as a starting point to access others (Hodges et al., 2010). We've already started this strategy in previous myths by identifying our strong ties and we'll continue building on this strategy in later myths.

For now, it's valuable to understand that in addition to our other networking strategies, we can also use the power of social media to expand our social networks. The benefit of this approach is that it puts the power of networking in your hands without relying solely on others. Such a mindset not only permits more control over our approach, but also helps combat the idea that you cannot network due to lack of direct connections or present social standing. Social networking provides a new space to self-promote and to discover and cultivate valuable relationships (Gitomer, 2011).

Broadening your social network online is possible through a variety of social networking sites such as Facebook and Twitter; however, LinkedIn is recommended as your primary social networking platform for professional development (Jordan & Marinaccio, 2017). Unlike other platforms that were originally created to connect a person with family and friends, LinkedIn was designed to be a professional networking site. It is the largest online professional network, used by over 133 million people in the United States and 500 million people world-wide (LinkedIn, 2020). Deemed the "Swiss army knife of job sites" (Bolles, 2020, p. 142), LinkedIn provides a variety of functions that are helpful for professional networking and job hunting, such as expanding your professional social network with a few clicks of a button. After creating a profile, you can begin by adding your strong ties to your network, such as family, friends, classmates, and coworkers. You can also follow and request additional connections with people, companies, and topics of interest. From there, LinkedIn offers recommendations for additional connections and new sources to follow. The more connections you make, the more the LinkedIn algorithm adapts to your networking foci and provides increasingly useful suggestions for new networking connections (LinkedIn, 2020).

Action 58 – LinkedIn Profile

Heed the advice of career development expert, Richard Bolles (2020): "LinkedIn... be sure to get on it, if you're not already." For more in-depth instruction on how to create a LinkedIn account and how to optimize your profile, use the resources available at bit.ly/careermythlinks. Watch the video and follow the instructions provided. Consult the tutorials for additional tips and instruction.

Use the following checklist to guide the creation and optimization of your LinkedIn profile, which was adapted from a LinkedIn assignment created for Gustavus Adolphus College (2020):

_____ Profile: Create a LinkedIn profile

_____ Photo: Include a professional headshot

_____ Write a headline: Create a unique headline

_____ Professional summary: Include a concise summary paragraph

_____ Experience: Include at least two paid or unpaid jobs/activities

_____ Education: Use your University/School name to connect with Education LinkedIn Alumni Network; as applicable, include your degree, specialization, and years

_____ Skills and expertise keywords: Add at least five skills to your profile

_____ Recommendations: Include at least one recommendation

_____ Location and industry: Add location and industry to profile

_____ Create a unique URL: Change to a unique and professional URL

_____ Get connected: Join at least two groups

Myth 59

"Self-employment isn't a realistic career option."

Fact

Before you spend too much time looking for a job, maybe consider creating one. As we consider all these possibilities, keep self-employment in mind. It's not a good fit for everyone, but it's important to first consider any option before ruling it out.

Self-employment may feel out of reach simply because it's unfamiliar, but it's actually quite common. As many as 80% of workers toy with the idea of working for themselves at some point in their careers (Bolles, 2020), and many ultimately decide to do so. Self-employment continues to be a significant source of jobs in the United States. Of all U.S. workers, roughly one in ten are self-employed (Hipple & Hammond, 2016). You would be remiss not to join the majority and at least seriously consider the possibility, especially if you might be the 10% of job seekers who are best suited to working for themselves.

Typical candidates for self-employment often struggle to find a fit in the traditional job market and don't find satisfaction in working for someone else (Miller, 2010). Through trial and error, their paths eventually lead to self-employment. Thus, self-employment is more common among older populations. When categorized by age, those aged 65 years and older are the highest group of self-employed workers, making up over 25% of all self-employed workers (Hipple & Hammond, 2016). Although self-employment can wait until later in your vocational journey, it doesn't have to. Plenty of people of all ages and industries work for themselves. Don't let intimidation stop you; taking the time now to assess whether self-employment is right for you could save you the frustration and discouragement of a career path that doesn't really fit you.

Action 59 – Self-Employment

Consider the possibility of self-employment by assessing whether it is a good fit for your personal characteristics. One way to do so is to do your research: read about what is involved in self-employment and how to take steps in owning your own business, and then evaluate whether that seems like a desired and appropriate fit for you. The Internet is full of great resources for self-employment, such as the Small Business Administration (SBA, 2020), available at bit.ly/careermythlinks. The SBA is a federal program dedicated to help start, manage, and grow small businesses. They have lots of helpful articles, advice, and even contacts for local networking and support to get you started.

Assessments to measure whether your personal characteristics are well-suited for self-employment can be another useful place to start. Review activities from Chapter 2 of this workbook for a comprehensive selection of assessments to learn more about your personal characteristics. A helpful starting point to check on your fit with self-employment is the Small Business Readiness Assessment by the SBA, available at bit.ly/careermythlinks.

Take the assessment and answer the following questions to determine if self-employment may be suitable career option for you.

What were your Small Business Readiness Assessment results?

_____

_____

_____

_____

_____

Remember that tests such as these can offer feedback but you are the ultimate authority on you. Critically evaluate your results based on your understanding of yourself. Are your results on the self-employment assessment accurate or not? In what ways do they seem accurate or inaccurate?

_____

_____

_____

_____

_____

Based on this information, what role might self-employment play in your job options moving forward?

_____

_____

_____

_____

_____

Myth 60

"If it's meant to be, I'll get the job."

Fact

Providence is not in the business of delivering nice things to your doorstep; that would be Amazon. While fate has certainly played a role in many famous success stories, opportunities don't typically appear with a chorus of angels or a shower of fairy dust. Instead, opportunity must be pursued. Job searching takes time and effort – likely a lot more than you had hoped or planned for. As career coach Darnell Clarke (2018) notes succinctly: "your job is to find a job."

In previous myths, we learned about various strategies for job hunting, including online job boards, targeted campaigns, and networking. The following myths will introduce you to each of these search strategies in more detail, starting with online job boards. Using job boards is the most common and well-known strategy, but it's not especially effective. This strategy includes searching for job descriptions of existing job vacancies posted by employers. While people do get jobs from online postings, the competition is fierce and only a small percentage of individuals have success. It's a numbers game, so if you use this strategy, be prepared to apply for a lot of jobs. For example, many career coaches subscribe to the "5-25-100 rule" (Clarke, 2018), which targets submission of at least five applications per day for 25 applications per week and totaling 100 applications per month. As you can see, finding employment requires full participation and commitment.

Reviewing online job postings are most often used to find existing job vacancies posted by employers; however, they have additional value to other more effective search methods, such as targeted campaigns of companies of interest and networking. Job postings provide the opportunity to browse available jobs to get a sense of possible job duties, salaries, market demand, and organizations available. Understanding the job market better prepares job seekers to engage in networking and launch a targeted campaign of companies of interest (Jordan & Marinaccio, 2017).

All this is to say, use online job boards wisely. Although there are several sites to choose from, my favorites are Indeed, Monster, Career Builder, and Simply Hired; overall, I most recommend Indeed due to its size, number of industries, and unmatched update frequency (Polner, 2021). Use these sites to search for specific positions as well as to gain a sense of the overall job market and opportunities. When you find specific postings of interest, don't apply for any of the jobs through the search website; apply directly with the company's website instead. Online job boards often include outdated postings, so check the company's website first to ensure the job is still open (Clarke, 2018). Applying directly to the company also shows an elevated level of interest and may set you apart from the large number of online job seekers (Taylor & Hardy, 2004).

Action 60 – Job Boards

Learn how to use job boards by following the steps and reporting your findings below:

1. Visit Indeed.com, also available at bit.ly/careermythlinks, and create an account. For more in-depth instruction for how to create an Indeed account and how to optimize your profile, Indeed has helpful video tutorials on their YouTube channel available at bit.ly/careermythlinks. Consult this resource for additional tips and instruction.
2. Conduct a job search on Indeed by completing the "where" and "what" search boxes. For "where," include your preferred city and state. Under "what," search for what you're interested in doing if you have a specific occupation in mind. If not, search by your qualifications instead. Begin with your highest level of completed education (e.g., "Bachelor's degree"). Depending on the location, hundreds of jobs may result from your search.
3. On the results screen, refine your search criteria using the options at the top of the page. Choose your preferred "job type," either "full-time" or "part-time." Select the most fitting category for "experience level," which in many cases is "entry level" for those entering the job market or changing industries. For "date posted," limit your search to "last 14 days" to see the most recent postings. After this first search, plan to return for new postings at least once a week; subsequent searches can limit to "last 7 days."
4. Scroll through the available options and click on postings of interest. Read through the job posting and note the duties and qualifications. If you're still interested and generally meet the qualifications, click the "save job" button. Note the 5-25-100 rule and compile a list of at least five jobs of interest. List them below, including pertinent information and additional notes, including questions or concerns you have about the position:

Job Posting #1

Job Title: _____

Organization: _____

Location: _____

Website: _____

Why I'm interested: _____

_____

_____

_____

Additional Notes: _____

_____

_____

_____

Job Posting #2

Job Title: _____

Organization: _____

Location: _____

Website: _____

Why I'm interested: _____

_____

_____

_____

Additional Notes _____

_____

_____

_____

Job Posting #3

Job Title: _____

Organization: _____

Location: _____

Website: _____

Why I'm interested: _____

_____

_____

_____

Additional Notes: _____

_____

_____

_____

Job Posting #4

Job Title: _____

Organization: _____

Location: _____

Website: _____

Why I'm interested: _____

_____

_____

_____

Additional Notes: _____

_____

_____

_____

Job Posting #5

Job Title: _____

Organization: _____

Location: _____

Website: _____

Why I'm interested: _____

_____

_____

_____

Additional Notes _____

_____

_____

_____

Myth 61

"There aren't any good jobs available right now."

Fact

The job market is tough but there are more opportunities than you think. In the past few myths, you've moved forward in your job-hunting process by considering self-employment and checking job boards. From those strategies, you may already have an abundance of career prospects to pursue. If that's so, congratulations! You're well on your way to finding a job, although your experience is atypical. Chances are that most of you ruled out self-employment and checked the job boards to find only a handful of viable options. That's a recipe for discouragement.

Given that most people search job boards as their only job search strategy, it's unsurprising that discouragement is high among job seekers (Kanfer et al., 2001), which interferes with their ability to continue searching (Slebarska et al., 2009). Many on the hunt for jobs conclude that none are available and fall prey to the negative belief, "I can't get a job." This is the point where they stop looking. Vocational psychologists refer to the "I can't do it" attitude as low self-efficacy. Self-efficacy is the belief that you have the capability and control to get yourself a job (Kanfer et al., 2001). Self-efficacy is essential for job attainment; when self-efficacy is high, it predicts active job searching behaviors and successful employment outcomes. This means that when you believe in yourself and your ability to get a job, you're more likely to keep hunting until you do so.

We need to keep trying beyond the typical methods and incorporate the job search strategies we know work best. Although less well known, one of the most effective job search methods is targeted campaigns (Bolles, 2020). Targeted campaigns involve identifying and pursuing companies directly, regardless of whether they advertise current vacancies. By doing so, you may stumble on secret jobs in the hidden job market (Jordan & Marinaccio, 2017). Sharing with them the additional value you can offer to the company, you could engage in job crafting, where a position is created for you. Essentially, targeted campaigns flip the job search process: ordinarily, the process starts with a company generating a posting on a job board and you responding with an application. In this approach, you're in a passive position with little control over your options, completely at the mercy of what's presented to you. The process is also cumbersome for employers, given the time and expenses involved with generating a job posting and conducting a search. With targeted campaigns, on the other hand, the control lies with you as the active agent. You start and guide the process by approaching companies of interest and asking for a job, putting them in the passive position of responding to your request. We can see the mutual benefit of this approach: it raises job seeker self-efficacy and offers employers the benefit of acquiring motivated employees without the time and expense of a job search. As a result, this method is highly effective and works 47% of the time (Bolles, 2020). Despite its effectiveness, targeted campaigns are often avoided due to job seekers' discomfort and uncertainty about how to do so (Miller, 2010), so we'll begin with how to conduct a targeted campaign in our action below and build on it throughout this chapter. As you'll discover, targeted campaigns work best when used in conjunction with networking, which we'll learn about next.

Action 61 – Identify Organizations

Let's start planning for a targeted campaign, beginning with identifying organizations of interest. Begin by finding out the types of organizations with positions that interest you. Research often yields a broader variety of organizations than you might initially expect. For example, if you are interested in teaching, you might initially limit your search of employers to schools; however, plenty of other organizations such as private research firms, educational consultants, military bases, and training academies also hire teachers. So, begin your targeted campaign by considering multiple kinds of organizations in your search and exploring places in each area that may be of interest you.

Take the following steps in your targeted campaign:

1. Choose your identified career area that you would like to pursue further. Return to Chapter 2 for guidance on how to choose a career area.
2. Research the kinds of places that employ this career by visiting the Occupational Outlook Handbook (OOH), available at bit.ly/careermythlinks. Search your identified career in the upper right-hand corner and click on the appropriate occupation link. Click the "work environment" tab and read about typical types of organizations that employ this career. Consider which kinds of organizations sound most interesting to you to help narrow your search.
3. Using a general search engine, such as Google, search your local area for the types of organizations you discovered. Include your city and state, and the type of organization in the search bar to yield specific names of organizations, such as "Spokane Washington" (your city and state) and "hospital" (the type of organization).
4. A second method for discovering specific organizations is to return to Indeed. As you'll discover, job boards offer more than just current openings. On Indeed's homepage, complete the search bar with the name of your chosen career interest in the "what" text box and your city and state in the "where" text box. Click the "company" tab at the top of the page, revealing a drop-down menu of company names that employ your career of interest.
5. A third method for finding specific organizations is to return to LinkedIn. Click "advanced search," input your career interest in "keywords," and your city and state in "location." Scroll down the left column to "current company" to reveal local places where your career is employed.
6. Finding companies to target can be tricky, so continue hunting using all the steps above until you have ten possible agencies. This will give you a large pool to draw from. Visit the websites for each organization and read their "About" sections, including vision and mission statements, if available. Consider how eager you are to work for them and what specifically interests you about each agency. Check each website for a "careers" or "employment" section to see if they're currently hiring for posted positions. If so, add those positions to the application list you developed from job boards in the previous myth.
7. You now have a top ten list of local companies that employ people to do the kinds of work you want to do. Rank your list by level of interest from top to bottom. List them below, including the company name, website, and why you're interested/what you like about the company. A targeted campaign involves contacting these companies and

asking if they're hiring, or would consider hiring you. Feel free to contact them now—
we know that's an effective approach. If you're hesitant to contact, just start with the
list and we'll use it in combination with networking for a more guided approach.

Company #1

Name: _____

Website: _____

Why I'm interested: _____

_____

_____

_____

Company #2

Name: _____

Website: _____

Why I'm interested: _____

_____

_____

_____

Company #3

Name: _____

Website: _____

Why I'm interested: _____

_____

_____

_____

Company #4

Name: _____

Website: _____

Why I'm interested: _____

_____

_____

_____

Company #5

Name: _____

Website: _____

Why I'm interested: _____

_____

_____

_____

Company #6

Name: _____

Website: _____

Why I'm interested: _____

_____

_____

_____

Company #7

Name: _____

Website: _____

Why I'm interested: _____

_____

_____

_____

Company #8

Name: _____

Website: _____

Why I'm interested: _____

_____

_____

_____

Company #9

Name: _____

Website: _____

Why I'm interested: _____

_____

_____

_____

Company #10

Name: _____

Website: _____

Why I'm interested: _____

_____

_____

_____

Myth 62

"The most qualified applicant gets the job."

Fact

Having the necessary skills and education is vital for impressing an employer, but it is not always the most influential factor in hiring decisions. There is no doubt that being able to excellently perform the tasks a job requires is something that an interviewer seeks in a future employee, but knowledge and abilities are not enough. Studies consistently demonstrate that the largest hiring factor is networking, with at least half of applicants reporting that social networks played a key role in securing a position (Granovetter, 1995; Hodges et al., 2010). Social connections are far more influential than many job seekers realize.

Confusion also surrounds what specific steps you should take to network. Networking is not about turning yourself into a social butterfly at networking events, nor is it saying, "Please give me a job" to the woman you met on the bus. Instead, networking involves meeting, socializing, and talking with as many people as you can about careers and companies that interest you until you speak with someone who can help you land a job (Jordan & Marinaccio, 2017). Building a network can be as easy as chatting with your best friend, calling a former classmate, or having coffee with a mutual acquaintance.

Networking is more effective when you start with a plan (Jordan & Marinaccio, 2017). Approach individuals with the goal of conducting an informational interview, or a career-focused conversation intended to help you make informed career decisions by gathering information and building your social network (Taylor & Hardy, 2004). Ask your interviewee for 20 minutes of their time, preferably in person. Think of yourself as a journalist uncovering facts, so write down questions to ask ahead of time and plan to take notes. Be sure to thank your informational interviewee for their time and follow up the next day with a thank you note to express your gratitude again (Lore, 2011).

Informational interviewing questions should focus on three areas: 1) career and company information, 2) feedback and advice, and 3) building your network (Jordan & Marinaccio, 2017). Career and company information includes questions about your chosen career, such as, "What do you find most satisfying and most frustrating about your job?" (Lore, 2011, p. 141) and "Can you tell me about the types of finance positions with XYZ Company?" (Jordan & Marinaccio, 2017, pp. 8–13). Feedback and advice refer to sharing your career interests, plan, and preparation, and then asking follow-up questions. For example, "Would you mind taking a look at my resume?" (Jordan & Marinaccio, 2017, pp. 8–13) and "If you were in my position, how would you go about getting into this field?" (Lore, 2011, p. 141). Building your network involves making plans for continued contact with your interviewee and requesting new contacts to interview, such as, "May I contact you if other questions arise?" and "Can you refer me to other people… who could answer further questions?" (Lore, 2011, p. 141). This final question can lead to subsequent informational interviews, thus building your network.

Action 62 – Informational Interviews

Conduct informational interviews with three people in your existing network by following these steps:

1. Select five people to interview from the networking grid you created in Myth 56. Consider choosing people you feel most comfortable with or who you believe may be most helpful to your job search.
2. Prepare and memorize questions to ask them. For ideas of questions to ask, simply do an online search for "informational interview questions" and you'll get ample lists of possible questions. A few key questions are included below. Adjust the questions and wording to best fit your relationship and the person's expertise.
   a. Career and information
      i. How did you get into the work you do now?
      ii. What do you find most satisfying and most frustrating about your job?
   b. Feedback and advice
      i. Explain your career interests and preparation for the field (e.g., "I'm interested in becoming a mediator. I earned a bachelor's degree in political science and am currently working in retail…"). Also share a copy of your targeted campaign list of top ten companies you're most interested in working for (developed in the previous myth action), for your interviewee to examine.
      ii. If you were in my position, how would you go about getting into this field?
      iii. What suggestions and feedback do you have about my preparation and plans?
      iv. What words of wisdom do you have for me at this point in my search?
   c. Network building
      i. Can you refer me to other people who could answer further questions?
      ii. Who else could I talk to about my interests who might know other careers and companies like what I want to do?
      iii. If you don't know of anyone, who do you think might know?
3. Send a thank you note following the interview.
4. Continue informational interviews with suggested contacts that emerge from this initial discussion. Keep a networking log of all your contacts using the format below. Complete the log here for one of your five informational interviews.

Name: _____

Company: _____

Phone Number: _____

Email: _____

Relationship/Referred By: _____

Discussion Notes: _____

_____

_____

_____

_____

_____

Referrals: _____

_____

_____

Myth 63

"Everything you need is online."

Fact

Online job-hunting resources are booming but remember that the Internet is only one of your critical tools. While much career development can be done online, certain aspects of the process benefit from moving beyond online platforms into the real world, and job hunting is one of them.

Networking is the best method for job hunting, and it requires that you expand your search through direct contact, preferably face-to-face meetings. Executive coach Ginny Rehberg explained, "if we're going to help someone, we have to know them first. Nobody will help you until they get close enough to smell you" (Taylor & Hardy, 2004, p. 283). Research agrees—trust, connection, and altruism increase with face-to-face contact as opposed to remote methods (Newman et al., 2002). Whenever possible, try to meet in person.

As we network and engage in a targeted campaign, also recall from earlier in this chapter that we're ultimately attempting to discover secret jobs in the hidden job market through networking. Through connecting with people who are doing the kind of work you want to do, you're using the best method to discover secret jobs in the hidden job market by uncovering jobs that aren't posted or publicly advertised. These secret jobs represent the vast majority of jobs, and we need to get people talking with you—and about you—to discover them (Jordan & Marinaccio, 2017).

This process occurs through expanding your network from your strong ties to your weak ties (Jome & Phillips, 2013). Recall that strong and weak ties refer to the intensity of relationships in your network. Strong ties are those you're in regular direct contact with, such as your friends and family members. Weak ties are those with whom you have infrequent or indirect contact, such as acquaintances and friends-of-friends, and these are the key to obtaining job leads (e.g., Granovetter, 1995; Hodges et al., 2010). The people who connect your strong ties to your weak ties are called "bridge people" (Bolles, 2020). When conducting informational interviews with your strong ties, your bridge people will refer you to a weak tie contact who will lead you closer to a job prospect. In this way, your strong tie serves as a bridge to a weak tie with a secret job lead.

Action 63 – Secret Jobs

Continue to build your network and access secret jobs by building on the informational interviews that you started in the previous myth action. Remember, you interviewed five of your strong ties and asked them for a referral to someone else who could help you (i.e., a weak tie). Hopefully your initial interviews revealed that some of your strong ties are also your bridge people.

Based on the referrals provided in your first round of informational interviews, conduct a second round of informational interviews with your referral contacts. When requesting a meeting, mention your shared connection and referral source by saying, "[shared contact] suggested I contact you" or "I was referred to you by [shared contact]." Conduct the interview by engaging in the same process as the first round, including taking notes using the networking log format provided. After that, keep going! Continue to ask for referrals and conduct informational interviews in subsequent rounds.

In Figure 4.3, complete the diagram for your first, second, and third round of contacts to watch your network grow. Include the name of each of your contacts in the boxes.

Figure 4.3 Networking Diagram

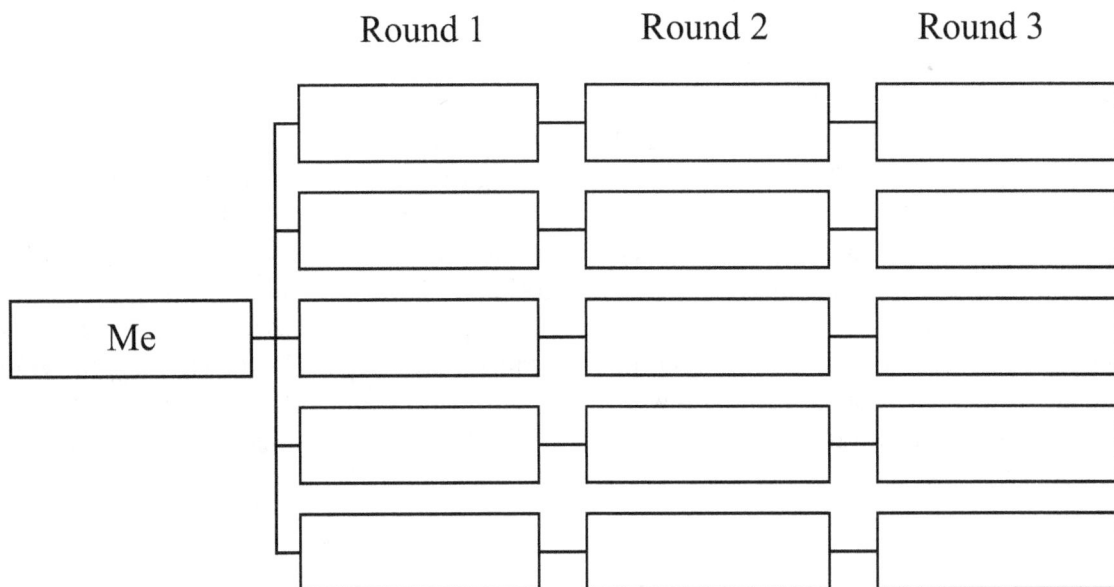

Myth 64

"A job portfolio should be all about me."

Fact

Your job portfolio needs to be tailored for each position and emphasize fit. You can start a general job portfolio by making it all about you to collect an anthology of every awesome thing you've ever done but this shouldn't be your final product. Given that you've likely done a multitude of noteworthy activities in your life, submitting all of them in a job portfolio would present as arrogant rambling to an employer (e.g., "My car is ridiculously clean. I'm great at balancing things on my nose. Did I also mention that I always replace the empty paper towel roll?"). A good writer brainstorms their next novel by brain dumping every engaging plotline they can think of, but they don't just stitch all their ideas together and call it a story. Instead, they sort through their ideas and edit down to a singular cohesive plotline. They may discard extra good ideas or save them to use for future novels. Similarly, your job portfolio needs to follow a similar process of generating ideas and then editing them down to tell a focused and cohesive story about your fit with a particular job. A job search is ultimately about finding the right connection between you and a job, which means your portfolio shouldn't focus on you but rather on your fit with a specific job (Vogt, 2007). This can't be accomplished by creating one-size-fits-all job portfolio and instead requires a carefully curated portfolio for each position. Keep a copy of that complete portfolio as a reference from which to draw information for future tailored versions.

Now that you have several job search strategies in motion, it's time to get started developing your job search portfolio. The next several myths will address job portfolio components and subsequent activities will guide you through developing each of these important documents. A job search portfolio is a collection of documents that showcase your fit with a particular position (Junge, 2012). Although your job portfolio needs to be tailored for each position and emphasize fit, learning how to create each one and developing an initial draft are critical first steps. Thus, the exact components will differ from position to position, but generally a job portfolio includes the following: 1) elevator pitch, 2) cover letter, 3) qualifications summary and work samples, 4) resume, 5) references, 6) applications, 7) interview responses, and 8) thank you notes (Taylor & Hardy, 2004).

The elevator pitch is the shortest and most straightforward part of your job portfolio. By engaging in networking, I find that many of my job-seeking clients at this point often have developed their pitch without realizing it. An elevator pitch is a brief introduction of yourself that summarizes key career-related information. The reason it's called an elevator pitch is that it should be short enough to present during a brief elevator ride; aim for about 30 seconds. The elevator pitch is useful in a variety of career-related contexts, such as in-person networking and interviewing, as well as written correspondence, including cover letters and social media profiles. It's the answer to the question, "Tell me about yourself" (Segal, 2017, p. 140). Although the answer will vary depending on who you're talking to, having a general starting point will help you be ready to offer a powerful synopsis of yourself.

Action 64 – Elevator Pitch

Create an elevator pitch using the Who-What-Where approach. Ask yourself the following three questions: 1) Who are you? 2) What are your skills? 3) Where do you want to work?

Who are you? Start with your name and follow it with a description of either your job title or a description of your work or work aspirations. Examples include, "My name is Elizabeth and I'm a psychologist who specializes in career counseling" or "My name is Elizabeth and I'm dedicated to helping people find the career of their dreams." Write your answer by completing the blanks below:

My name is _____

and I'm _____

What are your skills? Describe your primary qualifications and strengths in a single sentence. For example, "My strengths include dual-practice licenses and over a decade of experience, with special expertise in conveying empathy and building strong relationships with my clients." Someone new to a field might say instead, "My strengths include a bachelor's degree and two years of work experience, with a passion for helping those in crisis using my specialized skills of empathy and nonjudgement." Write your answer by completing the blanks below:

My strengths include _____

_____

_____

Where do you want to work? Include a sentence about where you want to go next in your career development journey. For example, "I'm looking for a job that will put my counseling skills to work." If appropriate to the situation, you can also include a request with your explanation, such as, "If you know of anyone who's looking for a caring helper, I would be so grateful if you let me know" or "If your company is in need, I'd be thrilled to work here." Note the two components of these sentences, starting with "If," followed by a given circumstance (e.g., "If you know of anyone hiring" or "If your company is hiring") and then your request of them in that circumstance (e.g., "please tell me" or "please consider hiring me"). When writing your own, begin with the circumstance of, "If you know of anyone who's looking…" since that language works best for general networking situations, which you'll encounter most often. Keep in mind the other options but for now, write your answer from a networking perspective by completing the blanks below:

I'm looking for _____

If _____

then please _____

You now have all the components for a solid elevator pitch! Simply take your answers to the three questions above and re-write them out here. Memorize this pitch so you can share it quickly and easily in all your future career encounters.

_____

_____

_____

_____

_____

_____

_____

_____

Myth 65

"I have nothing of value to include in a job portfolio."

Fact

When starting to compile your qualifications for a job portfolio it can be daunting to determine what to include and how to include it. Most people begin by spontaneously recalling their most notable activities in general; however, the most vital information and relevant value is often left unclear to specific employers (Bolles, 2020). For example, you may list previous jobs of lawn mowing and babysitting in your job portfolio when applying for a job in customer service. You as the applicant may clearly see a connection between your previous work and the desired job; however, without directly connecting the dots, the value may be unclear to a potential employer.

Instead, it can be helpful to start with "backward brainstorming" by beginning with the final goal in mind and working backward. Think about what employers want first and then brainstorm what you have done that demonstrates and communicates those skills in a clear and concise format. Backward brainstorming starts with a brain dump of every experience you can think of that demonstrates your skills. For example, beginning with the earlier example of a desired customer service job, an applicant may highlight the customer service aspects of previous babysitting and lawn mowing jobs, as well as volunteer work, extracurricular activities, and group projects in school that all demonstrated superior people skills needed for a customer service job. In this example, the connection between past experience and future goals is clear. Notice how backward brainstorming yields a greater number of qualifications and more focused connections to the desired job.

Job portfolios should include all information that communicates how you would be an asset to organizations and employers (Junge, 2012). You don't have to have been paid for an experience to count. Experience can include anything—paid or unpaid work, volunteering, internships, extracurricular activities, school projects, hobbies, home tasks—anything is fair game to highlight your qualifications and get you to the interview. In general, employers are looking for applicants that possess transferable skills. Transferable skills are talents and abilities that you can take from job to job and use in multiple careers (Bolles, 2020).

Action 65 – Experience List

Before we begin compiling your job portfolio, we need to identify and compile your many qualifications to include. Table 4.2 offers a list of five broad skill areas, which are divided into more specific job skills. This list is an adapted report from the National Association of Colleges and Employers (2011) on employers' rankings of the most important transferable skills. These lists were also used in Chapter 3 for compiling qualifications gained in school, so include information learned about yourself from Myths 49 and 50 here as well. For each of these areas, write down experiences you've had that demonstrate the skills. These experiences can come from anywhere, including school, hobbies, leisure activities, family, etc. Limit to experiences you've had in the past ten years and include as many experiences as you can think of. Include everything that comes to mind for now. When you transfer it to a resume format, you can decide what to exclude.

Table 4.2 Transferable Skills

Transferable Skills	Experiences
Communication Skills: • Speaking effectively • Writing concisely • Listening attentively • Expressing ideas • Facilitating group discussion • Providing appropriate feedback • Negotiating • Perceiving nonverbal messages • Persuading • Reporting information • Describing feelings • Interviewing • Editing	

Transferable Skills	Experiences
Research and Planning Skills: • Forecasting, predicting • Creating ideas • Identifying problems • Imagining alternatives • Identifying resources • Gathering information • Solving problems • Setting goals • Extracting important information • Defining needs • Analyzing • Developing evaluation strategies	

Transferable Skills	Experiences
Interpersonal Skills: • Developing rapport • Being sensitive • Listening • Conveying feelings • Providing support for others • Motivating • Sharing credit • Counseling • Cooperating • Delegating with respect • Representing others • Perceiving feelings, situations • Being assertive	

Transferable Skills	Experiences
Organization, Management and Leadership Skills: • Initiating new ideas • Handling details • Coordinating tasks • Managing groups • Delegating responsibility • Teaching • Coaching • Counseling • Promoting change • Selling ideas or products • Decision making with others • Managing conflict	

Transferable Skills	Experiences
Work Survival Skills: • Implementing decisions • Cooperating • Enforcing policies • Being punctual • Managing time • Attending to detail • Meeting goals • Enlisting help • Accepting responsibility • Setting and meeting deadlines • Organizing • Making decisions	

Myth 66

"A good resume will land me a job."

Fact

A single resume won't work for every job. The primary purpose of a resume is to help an employer decide to interview you (Jordan & Marinaccio, 2017). The resume is crucial to earning you face-to-face time to connect with employers and acts as brief personal marketing material to persuade your reader to invest time getting to know you in an interview. Constructing a compelling and persuasive resume takes time and effort (Vogt, 2007). Think like an advertising executive who works tirelessly with their team to develop a winning marketing campaign. So too will you devote the same energy to effectively market yourself to your audience of employers. Consequently, we'll spend the next several myths learning about resumes and how to construct a winning document that can be tailored for each position.

The importance of your resume cannot be overstated. For many positions, the resume represents the first interaction with a potential employer and the primary opportunity to launch the persuasion process toward choosing you for hiring (Jome & Philips, 2013). Like all the documents in your job portfolio, your resume should be revised and tailored for each and every job position you apply for, no matter how fantastic your original document. You may have a general version of a resume that lists every single one of your strengths, experiences, and skills, but it is more important to discerningly choose aspects of yourself and your experiences that match best with what an employer is looking for to present in a specific resume. Though your application materials may be impressive, lean into the challenge of marketing yourself in such a way that employers will quickly understand your features and assets regarding a distinct position. Crafting application materials in such a way is an opportunity to effectively display your best self for each position.

Action 66 – Resumes

Before we begin constructing your resume, it's helpful to have a full understanding of the process. There is no specific formula for developing a good resume, but the following resource offers helpful guidelines. Focus now on learning about resumes prior to jumping in to creating one yourself. The resume guide is from the Rockport Institute, a career coaching resource for career changers; however, the information is valuable for anyone constructing a resume at any stage of the career development process. Read the guide, "How to write a masterpiece of a resume" (Rockport Institute, 2017), available at bit.ly/careermythlinks. List the top three tips you learned from this resource:

1. _____

_____

_____

2. _____

_____

_____

3. _____

_____

_____

Myth 67

"I should use templates to make the best resume."

Fact

Avoid the allure of perfectly polished templates, as they are a hidden path to major problems down the road. Resume templates are pre-prepared documents with formatting already in place, such as fonts and line spacing. Templates do the legwork of designing the resume and authors simply fill in the blanks with their individual content. Although templates are readily available, user-friendly, and offer superb design quality, they limit control and customizability. A resume template may serve your immediate purposes but is likely to stifle your needs moving forward. For example, a resume template usually includes pre-set spacing between entries, which saves you from having to fiddle with your document to achieve a pleasing and consistent design. However, you might need to reduce the spacing or even completely redesign the structure to include multiple columns for the extra experience you gain in the future. The trade-off of using a template is to avoid the initial stress of designing a resume from scratch at the beginning, but you cause yourself endless frustrations when you outgrow it. Your resume serves as a living document that requires extreme flexibility to shift with your evolving needs with each new application; taking the time at the beginning to build a document from scratch will ultimately pay off (Sundberg, 2021). Do your future self a favor and don't take the lazy route—take the time now to build your own beautifully designed document free from template restrictions.

Nevertheless, there's no need to reinvent the wheel (or the resume, as it were). You can still use templates and resume examples to gather ideas; just implement them into your own blank document to keep them adaptable. We'll start with some general guidelines that most resumes follow, although the most important guideline to follow is what highlights you best. Surveys suggest that the average hiring manager spends less than ten seconds reviewing a resume (Bolles, 2020); thus, your focus should be on making a document "pop" with professional, impactful, and appealing elements. Balancing professional and impactful elements is challenging within a succinct structure. Resumes are typically one to two pages in length, and most are written in size 10- to 12-point type and use standard fonts such as Helvetica and Times New Roman (Morem, 2007). Job-hunting resources offer endless dos and don'ts for resume writing (e.g., GradLeaders, 2016; Rockport Institute, 2017; Sundberg, 2021), but consistently agreed-upon "rules" to writing resumes don't exist.

Hence, there is no specific formula for developing a good resume. As career development experts Jordan and Marinaccio (2017) explain, "a resume is as unique as the individual creating it" (pp. 8–32). Employers are just people like you and me and have their own preferences that don't follow universal guidelines. We can't predict what resume design every employer will prefer, but we can make our best guess based on what we know about ourselves and our preferred industry. For example, a highly creative applicant might appeal to eccentric graphic design employers with an unconventionally bright orange resume with varied font styles and icons. Alternatively, a highly meticulous applicant might appeal to traditional business employers with a conventional white paper resume highlighting impeccable consistency to customary design elements on one page in Times New Roman.

As these disparate examples reveal, a successful resume is one that captures your unique qualifications that piques an employer's interest for addressing their needs. Given that you know your own qualifications and are familiar with the needs you're interested in filling, your opinion on what best advertises your ability to fill that gap is far more crucial than consulting unspecific suggestions for resume design.

Action 67 – Resume Design

Develop your vision for what your resume might look like, based on your assessment of what best highlights your unique qualifications to meet the needs of employers in your interest area. One method for beginning this process is looking at several examples to get a sense of what design elements most appeal to you. Scroll down the pages to see resumes listed by industry.

Spend about 30 minutes looking at as many resumes as you can, both within and outside of your industry and education level. As you browse examples, consider your qualifications while adopting the perspective of a hiring manager in your chosen industry. View the documents through the lens of needing to sort through resumes quickly to pick who you want to spend time interviewing for a job. Focus first on resume design, meaning the overall layout, general scheme, and eye-catching features that comprise an overall experience of the document. Begin by scanning several quickly—for ten seconds or less—and pick out your favorite resume designs. Review resumes and narrow down to your three favorite designs. We'll return to these resumes in future myth activities, so note where to find these resumes for later.

Answer the following question in the space provided below. What design elements do you like about these resumes that you want to duplicate in your own resume?

_____

_____

_____

_____

_____

Myth 68

"I have to follow the conventional rules of resume formatting."

Fact

Continue to break convention and forge your own path with your resume. As with resume design, the format of your resume should be determined by what highlights you best to your chosen industry. Resume format refers to the organizational elements of the document, including categories, headings and subheadings, and content structure. When resume resources present different "kinds" of resumes, they're usually referring to format (e.g., Grad Leaders, 2016; Rockport Institute, 2017).

Determine your preferred format prior to writing your resume so it can provide you an outline for construction. Much like a carpenter building a house, resume formats serve as a blueprint to build your resume in an organized and planful fashion. There are many different formats to choose from, and the one you choose should be based on what best highlights your qualifications and minimizes your weaknesses (Morem, 2007). Formatting also includes what sections and headings you'll include in your resume. Sections will vary somewhat based on your overall format, but some common elements remain. Resume authors often base the decision of which and how many categories to include based on space limitations. Although you certainly will want to adapt and edit based on space limitations, decide ahead of time which categories require inclusion on your resume, and which are optional, based on importance of content (Grad Leaders, 2016).

Action 68 – Resume Format

Learn about the different types of resumes and decide which one suits you best. Visit bit.ly/careermythlinks to learn about types of resume formats. Each format is presented briefly with links to additional information and examples of each one, including who might benefit most from using each type of resume format.

After learning about the different types of resume formats, which do you like best and why do you believe it will work best for you?

_____

_____

_____

_____

_____

Next, determine what sections and headings you most want to include in your resume. Decide which ones are required and which can be optional, based on pertinence and space allowances. For guidance, read the resume guide from the Campus Career Coach, a career coaching resource for college students, although the information is applicable to anyone writing a resume. Visit bit.ly/careermythlinks and read the Campus Career Coach resume guide (Grad Leaders, 2016), particularly the segment titled, "What sections should I include on my resume?" (p. 2). The guide dictates which categories are required and optional for a resume but, as we've discovered, the ultimate choice is yours. Decide on which sections are required and optional for your resume and list them here:

Required Sections:

_____

_____

_____

_____

_____

Optional Sections:

_____

_____

_____

_____

_____

Myth 69

"It is completely acceptable to exaggerate your skills on a resume."

Fact

Remain truthful about everything on your resume. Resist the temptation to lie or overstate your experience to appear more qualified. Employers often verify at least some of the information on your resume and if dishonesty is discovered, you risk blowing the interview or even being hired only to later lose the job (Morem, 2007). The risk of exaggeration isn't worth it.

The trick is to truthfully translate your skills and experience into language that best fits the needs of each position. Tell your story by focusing on facts and what you did in ways that are relevant to the job you seek. Doing so requires that your resume is altered for each application (Bolles, 2020). While alterations to the overall design and format may be required, the primary changes for each position will mostly be on what qualifications you choose to include and how you describe them (Mills, 2017). For example, you might include previous experience in a retail job on your resume for a retail manager position, whereas you might include previous experience writing papers in school on your resume for an editorial assistant position. Furthermore, you might include both experiences on both resumes, but might describe them differently on each resume. For a retail manager, you might highlight aspects of teamwork and communication skills through working with people in retail and collaborating with teachers and classmates on papers in school. For an editorial assistant, you might instead highlight aspects of detail orientation and writing mechanics through careful record keeping in retail and superior written communication abilities in school. Notice how the facts of what you did in each position remain truthful but the aspects that you choose to highlight vary to tell a story about your fit for the position.

When deciding what specific information to include on a resume, consult resources you used in previous myths based on the resume design and format you chose. From there, review the qualifications you listed in Myth 65 and choose the ones that seem to best tell how you fit in the position you seek. Remember that resumes can include all kinds of experience, not just paid experience.

Once you have the qualifications you plan to include on your resume, you need to develop descriptions of them. Include the name of your position, the company, location, and date. Then list descriptors of what you did in that position. For examples, return to the types of resume formats used in Myth 68, available at bit.ly/careermythlinks. Find the resume format you chose (e.g., "Combination Resume") and click the link to see examples.

The next aspect of resume writing is translation, where you need to convert the language you use to describe your experiences to fit the language of the new position. Aim to include in your descriptions two to four bullet points or sentences for each entry and start each one with a positive action verb, such as "created" and "produced" (Mills, 2017). For an exhaustive list of resume writing verbs, consult the link available at bit.ly/careermythlinks.

Action 69 – Resume Descriptions

Learn how to translate one experience to another by following the steps below. Repeat this process for all aspects of every resume you create.

Begin with a target job position in mind and obtain a list of desired job qualifications. If this is a posted position on a company website or job search board, the job description will often include desired qualifications. Given that most jobs are not obtained through a posted position and we're utilizing a variety of other search strategies, chances are such a list isn't already provided. If this is the case, develop the list yourself.

One resource for developing your own list is the Occupational Information Network (O*NET, 2021), available at bit.ly/careermythlinks. O*NET is a database of occupations that includes detailed information on job tasks, tools or technology, knowledge, skills, ability, education, interests, work styles, wages, and employment information. You may recognize this site from previous myths in Chapter 2, but given its tremendous value for learning, we're using it again. O*NET also helps with developing job search materials such as resumes and is especially useful for translating job descriptions.

Enter the name of your chosen job into the search bar labeled "Occupation Quick Search." From the available list, choose the best option for your interests. For example, you might search "office support" and choose "office clerks" or "office and administrative support workers" from a list of related options. Don't hesitate to explore several related titles if you're uncertain which one to select. A summary report for your chosen occupation is then presented. Consider the "Tasks" section at the top of the page your list of desired job qualifications, or the story you want your resume to tell. This section is also a representation of the kind of language you want to use to tell your story, and the terminology you want to highlight and include from your qualifications.

Next, return to the O*NET homepage and start a new search for a position you've already held and want to include on your resume. Enter the job name into the "Occupation Quick Search" and choose the best fit from the results. Review the "Tasks" section and consider this a good starting point description for the job you held, tailoring it to the specifics of the work you did.

Now compare the tasks sections for the job you had and the job you want, looking for similarities and overlaps. Use your resourcefulness and creativity to view your previous work from the perspective of what your desired job requires. How might your previous work prepare you to do that? What in your previous position demonstrates you have those abilities?

For example, I worked with a client who had previous experience as a restaurant server, and we decided it would benefit him to include that experience on a resume for a job as a mental health counselor. Although different on the surface, translating his experience afforded the opportunity to tell a story about fitting qualifications.

Below is how the original resume entry for the restaurant server read. Note how the focus was primarily on the needs of working with food and food handling, appropriate for food service work:

- Delivered exceptional and quick food and beverage service.
- Answered questions about menu selections and made recommendations when requested.
- Cleaned and maintained a safe working and eating environment.

Based on the needs of a mental health counselor, below is how the entry was changed through translation. Note how the information still accurately described the work performed, but the focus shifted to working with people, keeping accurate records, and respecting human concerns, all of which are important for counseling.

- Utilized effective communication skills to resolve complaints and ensure satisfaction.
- Effectively collected and processed sensitive information including dietary restrictions, customer bills, and monetary payments.
- Enforced organizational regulations with exceptional, helpful, and assertive service skills.

Choose one of your previous experiences and practice translating the description into the language of your desired position. Follow the steps described above to search O*NET for the position you had and the position you want and look for commonalities. Describe your previous work in translated language targeted to your desired position below:

Position Title: _____

Company: _____ Location (City, State): _____

Dates Worked (Month and Year): _____ to _____

Job Description: _____

_____

_____

_____

_____

_____

Myth 70

"Self-promotion is the same as lying."

Fact

This myth of self-promotion seems opposite to the preceding myth of "It is completely acceptable to exaggerate your skills on a resume." Some job seekers do need a reminder not to exaggerate, but I've found most people already know they shouldn't lie on a resume. In fact, it's my experience that far more struggle with self-promotion than exaggeration. But self-promotion is the opposite of lying and is essential to job seeking. Self-promotion involves recognizing your legitimate strengths and qualifications and highlighting them in the best light possible. To avoid lying, many of my career development students and clients seem to overcompensate by downplaying their qualifications and minimizing their achievements. Likewise, my research on college students revealed that most don't feel comfortable communicating their qualifications (Vargas et al., 2015). By trying to avoid lying, a new problem of failing to self-promote occurs instead.

Self-promotion, especially in your job portfolio materials including your resume, is essential to success. Business expert Tom Peters (1997) wrote a magazine article entitled, "The Brand Called You" where he first coined the term "personal branding" to explain this necessity. Referring to self-promotion and how people market themselves, the term highlights the importance of building a professional presence and reputation by directly advertising your many assets. Give the article a read: available at bit.ly/careermythlinks; it'll shift your perspective on the appropriate approach to your job search language. Although mainstream culture ordinarily scorns boastful self-promotion and rewards modest self-talk instead, the language you use about yourself in job seeking needs to be more positive and assertive (Bolles, 2020). If this differs from your typical manner of speaking, it'll likely feel like bragging. That's okay—allow yourself to be boastful. The job seekers I work with typically end up striking the right balance when they allow themselves to fully express their gifts in a way that feels prideful. This allows them to communicate their personal brand through the appropriate, humble, and accurate self-promotion that makes for a winning job portfolio. Even if you go way overboard in the other direction and end up sounding like a conceited blockhead, that's an easier fix than failing to self-promote, and future myth actions will guide you in obtaining feedback that will catch those mistakes before an employer ever sees them.

Action 70 – Writing Your Resume

Embracing your most self-promotional language, it's time to write your resume! Do so by combining the foundational work you've done in previous myth activities. Review Myth 65 for your qualifications, Myths 66 and 67 for your resume design, Myth 68 for formatting, and Myth 69 for resume descriptions. Focusing on the target of your desired job, put what you've learned together and create your resume in a Word document.

Use a checklist to make sure your resume has everything you need. A helpful resource is the Resume Review Checklist by Enelow and Kursmark (2019), authors of the book, *Modernize Your Resume: Get Noticed…Get Hired*, available at bit.ly/careermythlinks. Review the site for explanations of each checklist item. Feel free to adapt some of the items, especially if the resume format you chose differs from the sections listed here. The heading for each of the resume review checklist items are included below for you to check off when each one is complete:

_____ Name and contact information

_____ Headline and summary

_____ Professional experience

_____ Job descriptions

_____ Achievements

_____ Education section

_____ Keywords

_____ Readability

_____ Visual presentation

_____ Resume

Myth 71

"Don't sweat the small stuff—a few resume errors are expected."

Fact

Make every effort to avoid any resume errors. This is a time to sweat the small stuff—even a few mistakes can render you disqualified from an applicant pool. Mistakes on a resume suggest one of two things: either you don't really care about getting the job—in which case employers won't really care about hiring you—or that you do care about getting the job, and this sample of your best work is still below par. Neither is a good look. Research consistently suggests that employers are dissuaded by resumes that aren't aesthetically pleasing and that contain errors (Jome & Phillips, 2013). Robert Half, founder of an employment service called Accountemps, coined the term "resumania" to describe the many blunders that occur on resumes (Half, 2017). Avoid resumania by aiming for a flawless document that is well-constructed, accurate, and grammatically correct to present your best self.

After completing your resume, review the document carefully several times looking for mistakes. Career expert Susan Morem (2007) suggests to "proofread, proofread, then proofread again" (p. 52). Continue until you're confident that your resume is error-free. Even then, your resume is still likely to contain errors (Vogt, 2007). I'm continually stunned by my ability to miss needed edits in my own writing. You might relate to the experience of reading a sentence over and over, never realizing a vital was missing. See what I did there? This occurs whenever you work on any kind of document for a long period of time. The time, energy, and personal importance invested makes it difficult to be impartial, and the familiarity with its contents makes it impossible to remain objective (Morem, 2007).

Include others in your editing process by sharing your resume with trusted friends and colleagues. It can be especially helpful to ask those who are employers and have experience reviewing resumes, as well as people with an eye for detail and are skilled at proofreading, grammar, and spelling (Taylor & Hardy, 2004).

Action 71 – Editing Your Resume

After editing your resume until you deem it error-free, ask three people to look at your resume and offer feedback. Provide your editors with guidance on what feedback would be most helpful. The Resume Evaluation Checklist available from Monster.com resume expert Kim Isaacs (2020) is available at bit.ly/careermythlinks. Provide your resume editors with a copy of this checklist and ask them to complete it, as well as note any specific errors they see on the resume document. Discuss the checklist with them afterward to ensure your understanding of their feedback. Make needed changes to develop a polished resume.

What feedback did you obtain from your editors? List the areas they suggested improvement in (e.g., appearance, writing style):

Editor #1

Name: _____

Resume Areas for Improvement: _____

_____

_____

_____

_____

_____

Editor #2

Name: _____

Resume Areas for Improvement: _____

_____

_____

_____

_____

_____

Editor #3

Name: _____

Resume Areas for Improvement: _____

_____

_____

_____

_____

_____

Myth 72

"Cover letters don't matter."

Fact

Never submit a resume without a cover letter. *Psychology Today*, a popular behavioral science media outlet, presents several reasons people give for omitting cover letters: ' "These days, the application forms don't even allow cover letters.' Or 'The applications are read by computers.' Or 'Cover letters all sound the same, yet they're hard to write. Not worth the effort' " (Nemko, 2017, p. 5). These are all myths and represent faulty understanding. Instead, successful job hunters give reports such as the following: "Make it personal and specific to THAT job. I was directly told in two interviews that my unique cover letter got me in the door." (Bolles, 2020, p. 155). Employers read cover letters and including a personalized one communicates that you really want the job (Washington, 2000).

A cover letter is a short business letter that accompanies a resume and is another essential document in your job portfolio (Jordan & Marinaccio, 2017). Cover letters function to increase your chances of getting noticed and generate interest in your resume. It can sometimes be seen as optional since applications often won't ask for it specifically, but this added touch can set you apart from other applicants (Washington, 2000). You can briefly introduce yourself and express your interest in and expertise for the position. As explained by career experts Taylor and Hardy (2004), "If the resume is the movie, the cover message is the preview" (p. 210). Fast-moving, short, and persuasive, the cover letter offers a brief narrative snapshot of the more detailed particulars included in your resume. By highlighting specific details of your attributes, skills, and experience, you can begin with a clear statement of your personal brand to capture your employer's attention, producing added interest in your resume (Taylor & Hardy, 2004).

Not an easy feat to accomplish, so take time and multiple revisions to craft your cover letters as purposefully as your resumes. Like resumes, cover letters should be completely customized for each position. Target cover letters directly to your reader and keep them under one page. Focus entirely on fit with the position and sell yourself through concise and action-oriented language. Use the opportunity to highlight accomplishments from your resume, provide a useful overview, or perhaps offer an explanation that is otherwise unclear from your resume. For instance, a cover letter could explain why someone with 20 years of experience as a high school math teacher is applying for a job as a chef by conveying an authentic desire for the career change along with transferable assets developed through previous experience. Such an explanation contextualizes the information on the resume and persuades the reader to investigate further (Yate, 1992).

Action 72 – Cover Letters

In this section, you'll learn how to write your own winning cover letters. To begin, the Internet offers numerous resources and examples to use as a guide.

Learn more about how to write cover letters by reading the guide available at bit.ly/careermythlinks. Take notes below on the step-by-step process presented in the guide. While the guide offers solid instruction, I offer one caveat: continue to avoid templates and create your own cover letters instead. As with our resume writing process, the guide also provides a checklist to use when reviewing and editing your cover letter, ensuring a flawless document.

Next, browse cover letter examples available at bit.ly/careermythlinks. This site offers cover letters listed by industry. Spend about 20 minutes looking at as many cover letters as you can, both within and outside of your industry. As you browse examples, employ a similar strategy to the one used for reviewing resume examples. Consider your qualifications while adopting the perspective of a hiring manager in your chosen industry, i.e., needing to sort through heaps of applications quickly to pick who you want to spend time interviewing for a job. Begin by scanning several quickly—for ten seconds or less—and pick out your favorites. Review cover letters again and narrow them down to your three favorites. You'll want to use these cover letters as your primary cover letter examples, so be sure to save them for future reference.

Answer the following prompts in the space provided below. Describe the structure of a cover letter below, as presented in the cover letter guide. What should be included in each of these sections?

Contact Details: _____

_____

_____

_____

Hiring Manager/Department Information: _____

_____

_____

_____

Greeting: _____

_____

_____

_____

Opening Paragraph: _____

_____

_____

_____

Body _____

_____

_____

_____

Closing Paragraph: _____

_____

_____

_____

Formal Sign-Off: _____

_____

_____

_____

What design elements do you want to duplicate in your own cover letter?

_____

_____

_____

_____

_____

Myth 73

"I have to perfectly match a job description to apply."

Fact

A lack in some listed characteristics doesn't mean you're automatically disqualified. Given the steep competition and low success rates for successfully applying to job openings, it seems reasonable to avoid wasting your time on an application unless you're certain you'll be considered. While applying for jobs well above your qualifications *is* a waste of your and an employer's time (Vogt, 2007), placing rigid standards of demanding certainty or overqualification before applying for a job is also wasteful.

Your perspective on your match with a job description is imprecise. Nevertheless, you can broadly discern whether you're qualified for a job and follow your intuition. For example, most of my students know that completing a one-semester internship at a nonprofit organization is unlikely to prepare them to direct such an organization. Instead, a full-time staff position might be an appropriate place to start. Notice the word "might" in the previous sentence; they *might* be qualified for a full-time staff position. An example of this would be an applicant who meets all the qualifications except for one full year of previous experience, given that the internship was only one semester. However, perhaps the experience at the agency itself might compensate for the missing months of experience, or possibly other tangentially related experiences might also be counted to sum one full year – or perhaps not. Ultimately, we can't be sure. These kinds of jobs are a close call in which you might be qualified. Career counselor Peter Vogt (2007) calls these situations "borderline jobs" (p. 212) to emphasize the uncertainty regarding your fit. For these jobs, assume your perspective might be inaccurate. If you're strongly interested and after full consideration believe you might have an outside shot at the job, then certainly apply.

The reasons to do this stem from your limited perspective on the employer's needs. Job postings represent the ideal candidate, although employers often need to adjust based on the best applicants available. Although not often stated in the job description, employers may be flexible on certain requirements. Sometimes this is indicated through "required" and "preferred" qualifications, such as, "bachelor's degree required, master's degree preferred." If you meet the required qualifications, apply. Furthermore, it's often unclear from the job description the employer's prioritization and strictness of each qualification. This is particularly the case for niche skills (Vogt, 2007). For instance, an employer may be most interested in a candidate who is fluent in both Spanish and English and although other characteristics are listed on the job description, they're willing to accept most anyone who possesses the primary prerequisite language skills. Finally, knowing whether you meet the criteria or not requires deep consideration and creative thinking (Mills, 2017). I can't tell you how many times I've worked with someone who's said to me, "I don't have experience doing that," when I know they possess years of experience outside traditional work settings. For example, clients will often skip applying to jobs that require "childcare experience," without considering the years of babysitting they provided for family and friends. Similarly, my college students frequently pass over jobs requiring "leadership experience," with no acknowledgment for their informal leadership in student clubs and group projects. In these instances, applicants need to search all their previous experiences—not just the obvious paid job titles they held—and give full consideration of whether they could possibly meet requirements. Creativity and flexible thinking are necessary, and if you struggle with doing so, soliciting outside perspectives can help generate possibilities. A career coach can be especially helpful in this process (Jome & Phillips, 2013).

As Vogt (2007) advises, "If you cannot decide whether to pursue a particular job opening or not, adopt this seven-word motto: better to apply than not to try" (p. 212). With a solid resume and cover letter developed using the action strategies presented in the previous myths, you're now ready to apply for jobs, including those you are qualified for as well as borderline jobs.

Action 73 – Application Checklist

It's time to apply for more jobs, including the borderline ones. Return to Myth 60 and follow the action strategy for using job boards; this time focus your search on finding borderline jobs. These might be positions you'd initially passed up but now recognize as possible.

Choose one to apply for. Practice using your creative thinking to highlight your qualifications and possible ways you meet the job description, even in areas where it might be a stretch. Prepare your application and, before you send it, use the following checklist to ensure your application is ready. Make sure you do this for every job application. This checklist is adapted from the original based on Taylor and Hardy's (2004) Final Checklist:

_____ Customize your resume

_____ Attach your resume in the appropriate format (pdf preferred to maintain formatting)

_____ Customize your cover letter

_____ Attach your cover letter in the appropriate format

_____ Complete the online application

_____ Complete and attach any other requested documents

_____ Proofread everything

_____ Create an electronic file for this job with the job description; your completed application, cover letter, and resume; and any other submitted documents

_____ Mark a follow-up date on your calendar two weeks from the time you send your application

Myth 74

"Expect quality job interviews conducted by skilled interviewers."

Fact

Most employers have little experience or training in how to conduct an interview appropriately and effectively. Although most applicants assume their interviewers will be experienced and well-prepared professionals who will guide them smoothly from one question to the next with warmth and engagement, this is rarely the case (Jordan & Marinaccio, 2017). More often, the people in charge of interviewing have no training, little experience, and haven't had time to prepare for the interview. They may be as nervous as the person they interview and unclear on what they're looking for or how to objectively assess it (Jome & Phillips, 2013). Well-meaning but unknowing hiring managers may ask highly personal questions—and illegal ones, due to their discriminatory nature—such as, "Are you married?" throwing applicants further off-guard (Taylor & Hardy, 2004, p. 324). Unsurprisingly, research by Derous (2007) concluded that expectations of job applicants differed dramatically from the realities reported by recruiters.

As such, adjust your expectations about the job interview. It might not be the welcoming and organized experience you imagine; it could be a chaotic mess, or anywhere in between. Anticipate and ready yourself to encounter a variety of possible interview scenarios. That said, don't let the possibility of a chaotic interview diminish the importance of the event. Landing an interview is a big deal. It communicates that an employer is interested enough to take time out of their busy schedule to seriously consider you for the job you want. Your hard work paid off and your job portfolio documents were successful in getting you noticed (Landrum, 2009). Time to celebrate that accomplishment!

With an interview offer, you've reached one of the most important steps in the hiring process (Jome & Phillips, 2013). Previous steps such as resume writing are all directed at landing here. The function of the interview is to determine the match between you and the organization (Jordan & Marinaccio, 2017). Interviews may involve one conversation or comprise multiple stages of the hiring process, with interviews with different levels of management at each stage. Given the importance and uncertainty of the process, interviews can be a significant source of anxiety for many job seekers (Jome & Phillips, 2013). Even now, hearing about all these unknowns might raise your anxiety even further.

Fortunately, you can reduce that anxiety by taking ownership of the parts under your control, educating yourself about the process, and preparing for a variety of unknowns. Discard the fantasy of an ideally structured interview and envision instead what you want to communicate in the interview, regardless of what questions are asked. The key to cultivating a successful interview is to make it a conversation. This gives you the opportunity to provide the information you need without relying on interviewer prompts, which also takes pressure off the interviewer. You're more likely to be hired if you and your interviewer talk for an equal amount of time (Bolles, 2020). If either of you dominate the conversation, your hiring prospects decline. Besides, interviewing is truly a two-way street: the employer is interviewing you and you are also interviewing the employer. As Taylor and Hardy (2004) explain, "A job interview should be a conversation in which you and the employer build a common vision. Both ask questions; both give answers; both decide if the job and the candidate are a good fit" (p. 303).

Crucial to pulling this off is to prepare, prepare, prepare. The person who gets hired isn't the one who can do the job best; it's the one who knows the most about how to get hired from a job interview (Bolles, 2020). Accordingly, learn about and develop effective interviewing skills. Know exactly what information you want to share regardless of what prompts you're asked, as well as what questions *you* want to ask. Doing so helps you to plan for all contingencies. You'll be ready to share needed information if you're asked the exact question you'd planned, such as, "Why are you a good fit for this job?" Otherwise, you'll be prepared to contribute information you're not asked by saying, "I wanted to be sure to explain why I think I'm a good fit for this job." Know what you want to say in advance so you can focus on finding spaces in the conversation to say it, as well as prioritizing good conversation and connection during the interview.

No matter how many interview questions an interviewer asks you or how many interviews you do in the future, interviews are essentially looking for answers to three primary questions (Bolles, 2020). These are the answers you should prioritize in your preparations, as well as practicing how to share this information regardless of how questions are phrased:

1. Tell me about yourself. (i.e., What would you be like to work with and what difference could you make to the organization?)
2. Why do you want to work for us?
3. Tell us about your strengths and weaknesses. (i.e., Why should we be interested in you?)
4. What questions do you have for us?

You will return to these questions again and again throughout your interviewing future, although your answers will shift with time, experience, and focus. Since networking opportunities are often a form of informal interviewing and you never know when your next interview will be, it is helpful to have answers to these questions prepared for your current interests (Bolles, 2020).

Action 74 – Interviews

Get prepared by learning about effective interviewing. The Robert Walters Group, a professional recruitment firm, offers *The Complete Interview Guide* (Walters, 2020). Start by reading the guide available at bit.ly/careermythlinks.

Consider your immediate job prospects. What interview audience would be most helpful to you focus on to answer questions? Answer the following interview questions with your identified audience in mind. Include answers that take 20 seconds to a minute to say comfortably out loud. Write your answers in the spaces provided below.

1. Tell me about yourself. (i.e., What would you be like to work with and what difference could you make to the organization?)

   _____

   _____

   _____

   _____

   _____

2. Why do you want to work for us?

   _____

   _____

   _____

   _____

   _____

3. Tell us about your strengths and weaknesses. (i.e., Why should we be interested in you?)

   _____

   _____

   _____

   _____

   _____

4. What questions do you have for us?

_____

_____

_____

_____

_____

Since half the interview should be spent listening, write four questions for your prospective employer:

Question #1 _____

_____

_____

Question #2 _____

_____

_____

Question #3 _____

_____

_____

Question #4 _____

_____

_____

Myth 75

"People don't actually notice thank you notes."

Fact

Thank you notes impact employers' hiring decisions (Junge, 2012), so always send one after a job interview. Writing just a simple note expressing gratitude for an interview opportunity or another professional interaction communicates multiple valuable messages: it shows that you believe that the employer's time and energy is incredibly valuable, that you are aware of how to be courteous, and you are someone who will go the extra mile. Any of these traits may be what sets you apart from other candidates competing for the same job. In our fast-paced culture, it's typical for interactions to be surface-level and singular. A thank you note demonstrates your commitment to a relationship with the company as well as the individuals you interacted with during the interview process.

Sending a thank you note has become somewhat of a standard practice, so it is important to think about how to make your note stand out compared to others. One way to do this is to highlight the most significant aspects focused on during your interview, followed by the inclusion of some details that came up during your interaction with the employers (Jordan & Marinaccio, 2017). You may have discovered that you have a similar interest to an interviewer or have additional skills that may be of use to the company that weren't mentioned—acknowledge these details where it seems appropriate. For example, you might include, "I thought you might also like to know that I have professional social media experience." (Jordan & Marinaccio, 2017, p. 8–50). When deciding on the format to use for the thank you note, be mindful of the culture of the company. A smaller, more personal organization may appreciate a handwritten card, while a technologically focused company might prefer a thoughtful email.

Action 75 – Thank You Notes

Review how to write an interview thank you note and review examples. A helpful thank you note guide is available at bit.ly/careermythlinks. Read the guide and leave notes below on what to include in each section of your thank you letters:

First paragraph: _____

_____

_____

_____

Second paragraph: _____

_____

_____

_____

Third (optional) paragraph: _____

_____

_____

_____

Closing paragraph: _____

_____

_____

_____

Myth 76

"Salary negotiation is frowned upon."

Fact

Interestingly, most employers are impressed by salary negotiation, if performed in a business-like manner (Junge, 2012). Salary negotiation can be tricky and uncomfortable, so many simply avoid it and passively take whatever they're offered. Doing so can communicate a lack of appreciation for your value or an unwillingness to protect your worth. Conversely, the pursuit of salary negotiation demonstrates a level of proficiency and confidence that employers appreciate. If you're willing to advocate for yourself, chances are you'll champion for the company, too.

Initiate salary negotiation once an employer officially offers you a job and outlines the salary and benefits package accompanying the offer. If they offer the position only without explaining the salary and benefits, ask for them. Although presented as absolute, hiring managers typically leave some wiggle room when making an initial offer to account for negotiation (Bolles, 2020). You might want to start with buying yourself time by asking, "Do you mind if I take a couple of days to consider your offer?" (Moore, 2019, p. 5). Research comparable jobs in your area to determine typical pay and weigh the offer against your findings. You can then follow up by email, by phone, or in person. Expect salary negotiation to involve back-and-forth discussion before mutually agreeing on a final number. Engage in a forthright conversation about your desire for the job, expectations, and compensation needs. Aim for a win-win result, where you feel valued for your contributions and your employer feels satisfied in providing suitable compensation.

Finding the exact words to use can be an added challenge. Glassdoor.com, a website devoted to insights about jobs and companies, offers a wealth of information about salaries and salary negotiation. For instance, Glassdoor contributor Emily Moore (2019) offers some valuable phrases to use in salary negotiations. Communicate your eagerness through comments such as, "I am excited by the opportunity to work together" (p. 1) and expressions of gratitude for their offer and willingness to discuss terms. Initiate salary negotiation with questions such as, "Is that number flexible at all?" (p. 3). Follow up with counteroffers using phrases such as, "Based on my research…" (p. 2) and "similarly situated employees" (p. 3) to share your expectations. Once you arrive at a consensus, convey sincere thanks for their offer and willingness to engage in the process with you.

Action 76 – Salary Negotiation

Read tips for negotiating salary. In addition to Glassdoor, another helpful online resource for salary negotiation is CareerOneStop, a job and career search website for the U.S. Department of Labor (BLS, 2022). Read the CareerOneStop guide to salary negotiation, available at bit.ly/careermythlinks. Follow the steps, including finding out the typical pay for your desired position. Given this information, fill in below what you believe would be reasonable pay for the job you want. Consider providing a salary range you would be willing to accept. Explain why you believe this number is reasonable:

Salary Range: _____ to _____

Why? _____

_____

_____

_____

_____

_____

Myth 77

"I'm not what employers want."

Fact

Job rejection hurts. After reading all the myths in this chapter and engaging in every job-hunting action presented, you may still be without a viable job offer. Job hunting is taxing, and no techniques work all the time. At this point, disheartened job seekers often resort to the negative self-statement, "I'm not what employers want." The underlying belief is that a "good" candidate engaging in effective job-hunting strategies should receive a job offer within a reasonable amount of time. When this doesn't occur, the applicant concludes that the problem must be that they aren't a "good" candidate. The blame-game of "I'm too…" usually follows, followed by any challenges or deficiencies to blame, such as "I'm too old," "I'm too inexperienced," or "I'm too shy" (Bolles, 2020, p. 212). Negative beliefs are even stronger when we know certain characteristics carry a bias among some employers. Unfortunately, too many job seekers encounter biases, even in our diverse workforce. Race, ethnicity, age, gender identity, and sexual orientation can all work for or against job candidates, as can veteran status, physical and mental disabilities, and current or prior legal troubles (Jordan & Marinaccio, 2017).

Despite these hardships, the truth is that if you've paid attention to all the job-hunting strategies in this workbook, you're likely a good candidate. Sometimes finding a fit takes longer and requires more attempts than we'd prefer, so you just need to keep at it (Taylor & Hardy, 2004). If you're invited for several interviews and are continually rejected, you can ask interviewers for feedback. Bolles (2020) suggests using the following script: "I'd appreciate some advice. I've been on several interviews at several different places now. From what you've seen, is there something about me in an interview that you think might be causing me not to get hired at those places? If so, I'd really appreciate your giving me some pointers so I can do better in my future hiring interviews" (p. 192). This also is a clever way to turn a former job interview into an informational interview and networking meeting!

If you suspect employer bias based on your identity characteristics and circumstances, reach out for assistance and support. Employers by law are not permitted to discriminate in their hiring process due to a variety of multicultural identity characteristics such as race, age, gender, religion, and disability status (EEOC, 2021). For more information, visit the U.S. Equal Employment Opportunity Commission website. Additional support for applicants with disabilities can be found at the American Association of People with Disabilities website. For those who are justice involved, meaning those who have been through the corrections system and have a record of an offense, job search support is available through CareerOneStop. Visit bit.ly/careermythlinks to access these resources.

Keep in mind that although you may have encountered rejection, you can't generalize about what all employers will and won't want (Bolles, 2020). You have skills and abilities that many employers want; you just haven't found the fit with them yet. Critical to finding them is keeping optimism high. Research findings emphasize the importance of maintaining a positive outlook and self-concept through the job search process, since both are linked to more positive employment outcomes (Kanfer et al., 2001). Unemployability has more to do with state of mind than state of being. Keep hope alive and keep at it.

Action 77 – Job Rejection

Confidence in the face of rejection is incredibly challenging. Strive to maintain optimism and positive self-concept in the face of rejection by emphasizing your strengths; focus on what you have rather than what you might lack. Return to your motivational song list created in Myth 54 to get pumped. Then review your skills by visiting the career search website, the Occupational Information Network (O*NET, 2021). O*NET provides skill lists, available at bit.ly/careermythlinks. Skills are listed by categories (e.g., Social Skills); clicking the link for each category reveals a list of associated skills. Each of the skills are hyperlinked to a list of careers that require that skill.

Review each of the skill names and descriptions in each category and make a list of all the skills you possess. Click the links to see the many jobs that need your skills. Use this list as a reminder of the many gifts you possess to keep your hopes and self-esteem high during the continued job search process.

I possess the following gifts that employers want and need, and will help me to be successful in finding a job:

_____

_____

_____

_____

_____

Myth 78

"Accepting any job offer is the best strategy."

Fact

If you play the job-hunting game long enough, you'll eventually come out a winner and get an offer. Congratulations! It feels great to get the "yes" you've worked toward, but don't let the fever of excitement turn to desperation by immediately accepting whatever gets offered to you. Accepting any job offer isn't the best strategy; carefully evaluating whether the offer is right for you is a far better approach (Junge, 2012).

Give yourself time to consider options and discuss it with trusted others. Jobseekers often erroneously believe that hiring managers are ready to abdicate offers at any moment to another candidate, feeling pressured to give an answer immediately to secure their spot. The reality is the employer chose you as their top choice and is willing to wait a reasonable amount of time for you to make your final decision. If you ask for more time, be reasonable, respectful, and direct. Explain your reason for wanting time and be specific about how much time you need. Here's an example of what you might say: "I have another offer pending, but I am very excited about this offer. I will call them and ask for a decision by Wednesday. May I call you then?" (Taylor & Hardy, 2004, p. 351). If the reason is instead that you need to sleep on it or talk with your family, be honest about that as well. Provide a date and method by which you'll give them an answer.

Once you decide, communicate either decision to the hiring manager. Whether or not you choose to accept the job offer, take care to preserve the connection you made with the employer. By the time an offer gets extended, you and the employer have invested a good deal of time and energy into each other. They quite literally invested in your success and showed confidence in you, which is *such* an honor. Express respect and appreciation for their effort and interest with a sincere "thank you." If you accept the job, explicitly communicate your acceptance in writing through an acceptance letter (Taylor & Hardy, 2004).

If you choose to decline, carefully craft a gracious response. As career coach Michael Junge (2012) states, "There's an art to saying yes, and perhaps an even greater art to saying no" (p. 139). Thank them for the offer and let them know how much you value and respect them. Consider that although you may not want the job offer, you and the employer have a fair amount in common in terms of your career interests and would likely benefit from including each other in your future network. For example, in the small world of academia, professors from local universities in similar disciplines often work closely together. When applying for and accepting a university professor position, I declined other positions with professors at nearby schools. By carefully and respectfully declining offers, I maintained connections with professors who remain crucial members of my professional network a decade later. Likewise, let your hiring manager know that you value them—as professionals and human beings—and ask to stay in touch.

Action 78 – Accept and Decline Offers

Learn the protocol for how to accept and how to decline job offers. The Balance Careers (2021), a practical career advice website, offers helpful guides. Read their guides for accepting or declining a job offer, available at bit.ly/careermythlinks. Leave notes below on what to include when accepting and declining job offers.

Accepting Job Offers

_____

_____

_____

_____

_____

Declining Job Offers

_____

_____

_____

_____

_____

References

Asher, D. (2011). *Cracking the hidden job market: How to find opportunity in any economy*. Ten Speed Press.

Bolles, R. N. (2020). *What color is your parachute? A practical manual for job-hunters and career-changers* (2020 ed). Ten Speed Press.

Bureau of Labor Statistics (BLS). (2022). *CareerOneStop*. U.S. Bureau of Labor Statistics. www.careeronestop.org

CareerBuilder. (2018, August 9). *More than half of employers have found content on social media that caused them NOT to hire a candidate, according to recent CareerBuilder survey* [Press release]. http://press.careerbuilder.com/2018-08-09-More-Than-Half-of-Employers-Have-Found-Content-on-Social-Media-That-Caused-Them-NOT-to-Hire-a-Candidate-According-to-Recent-CareerBuilder-Survey

Clarke, D. (2018, August 27). *How to search for employment using job boards in 2019* [Video]. YouTube. www.youtube.com/watch?v=CLZeG4oFcNw

Crosby, O. (2005). Career myths and how to debunk them. *Career Outlook Quarterly*. www.bls.gov/careeroutlook/2005/fall/art01.pdf

Derous, E. (2007). Investigating personnel selection from a counseling perspective: Do applicants' and recruiters' perceptions correspond? *Journal of Employment Counseling*, 44(2), 60–72. https://doi.org/10.1002/j.2161-1920.2007.tb00025.x

Enelow, W., & Kursmark, L. (2019). *Modernize your resume: Get noticed ... get hired* (2nd ed.). Emerald Career Publishing.

Gitomer, J. (2011). *Social boom*. Pearson Education.

Grad Leaders. (2016). *Resumes*. The Campus Career Coach. https://thecampuscareercoach.com/wp-content/themes/campus-career-coach/guides/resumes.pdf

Granovetter, M. S. (1995). *Getting a job: A study of contacts and careers* (2nd ed.). University of Chicago Press.

Gustavus Adolphus College. (2020). *LinkedIn assignment for college students*. https://gustavus.edu/career/documents/LinkedIn-Grading-Rubric-1.pdf

Half, R. (2017, January 25). *The seven deadly (resume) sins: Top resume mistakes to avoid*. Robert Half. www.roberthalf.com/blog/writing-a-resume/the-seven-deadly-resume-sins-top-resume-mistakes-to-avoid

Hettich, P. I., & Landrum, R. E. (2014). *Your undergraduate degree in psychology: From college to career*. SAGE Publications, Inc.

Hipple, S. F., & Hammond, L. A. (2016). *Self-employment in the United States*. U.S. Bureau of Labor Statistics Spotlight on Statistics. www.bls.gov/spotlight/2016/self-employment-in-the-united-states/home.htm

Hodges, N., Karpova, E., & Lentz, H. (2010). An investigation of women's early career experiences in the textile and apparel industries. *Journal of Family and Consumer Sciences*, 39(1), 75–89. https://doi:10.1111/j.552-39334.2010.02046.x

Huang, X., & Western, M. (2011). Social networks and occupational attainment in Australia. *Sociology*, 45(2), 269–286. https://doi.org/10.1177/0038038510394029

Isaacs, K. (2020). *Resume evaluation checklist*. Monster. https://resumepower.com/docs/ResumeChecklist.pdf

Jome, L. M., & Phillips, S. D. (2013). Interventions to aid job finding and choice implementation. In S. D. Brown & R. W. Lent (Eds.), *Career development and counseling: Putting theory and research to work* (2nd ed., pp. 299–328). Wiley.

Jordan, L. A., & Marinaccio, J. N. (Eds.). (2017). *Facilitating career development: Student manual* (4th ed.). National Career Development Association.

Junge, M. B. (2012). *Purple squirrel: Stand out, land, interviews, and master the modern job market.* CreateSpace.

Kanfer, R., Wanberg, C. R., & Kantrowitz, T. M. (2001). Job search and employment: A personality-motivational analysis and meta-analytic review. *Journal of Applied Psychology, 86*(5), 837–855. https://doi.org/10.1037/0021-9010.86.5.837

Landrum, R. E. (2009). *Finding jobs with a psychology bachelor's degree: Expert advice for launching your career.* American Psychological Association.

LinkedIn. (2020). *What is LinkedIn and how can I use it?* www.linkedin.com/help/linkedin/answer/111663/what-is-linkedin-and-how-can-i-use-it-?lang=en

Lore, N. (2011). *The Pathfinder: How to choose or change your career for a lifetime of satisfaction and success.* Touchstone.

Miller, D. (2010). *48 days to the work you love* (2nd ed.). B&H Publishing.

Mills, C. (2017). *Career coach: How to plan your career and land your perfect job* (2nd ed.). Crimson Publishing.

Moore, E. (2019, September 22). *11 words and phrases to use in salary negotiations.* Glassdoor. www.glassdoor.com/blog/words-phrases-to-use-salary-negotiations/

Morem, S. (2007). *How to get a job and keep it: An essential guide to landing your ideal job and making the most of it* (2nd ed.). Ferguson Publishing.

National Association of Colleges and Employers (NACE). (2011). *2011 internship and co-op survey.* www.workandlearnindiana.com/documents/research/internship_co_op_survey_research_brief_2011.pdf

Nemko, M. (2017, August 1). 14 career myths: Common sense often trumps conventional wisdom. *Psychology Today.* www.psychologytoday.com/us/blog/how-do-life/201708/14-career-myths

Newman, J. C., Des Jarlais, D. C., Turner, C. F., Gribble, J., Cooley, P., & Paone, D. (2002). The differential effects of face-to-face and computer interview modes. *American Journal of Public Health, 92*(2), 294–297. https://doi.org/10.2105/AJPH.92.2.294

O*NET (2021). *O*NET OnLine.* www.onetonline.org

Peters, T. (1997, August 31). *The brand called you.* Fast Company. www.fastcompany.com/28905/brand-called-you

Polner, E. (2021, November 1). *Best job search websites.* The Balance Careers. www.thebalancecareers.com/top-best-job-websites-2064080

Rockport Institute. (2017). *How to write a masterpiece of a resume.* https://rockportinstitute.com/resources/how-to-write-a-masterpiece-of-a-resume/

Segal, A. M. (2017). *Know yourself grow your career: The personal value proposition workbook.*

Slebarska, K., Moser, K., & Gunnesch-Luca, G. (2009). Unemployment, social support, individual resources, and job search behavior. *Journal of Employment Counseling, 46,* 159–170.

Sundberg, J. (2021). *Don't use a resume template if you want to land a new job.* Undercover Recruiter. https://theundercoverrecruiter.com/dont-use-resume-template-if-want-land-new-job/

Taylor, J., & Hardy, D. (2004). *Monster careers: How to land the job of your life.* Penguin Group.

The Balance Careers. (2021). *The Balance Careers.* www.thebalancecareers.com

U.S. Equal Employment Opportunity Commission (EEOC). (2021). *US Equal Employment Opportunity Commission.* www.eeoc.gov

U.S. Small Business Administration. (2018, August). *Frequently asked questions about small business*. US Small Business Administration Office of Advocacy. www.sba.gov/sites/default/files/advocacy/Frequently-Asked-Questions-Small-Business-2018.pdf

U.S. Small Business Administration (SBA). (2020). *U.S. Small Business Administration*. www.sba.gov

Vargas, K., Campbell, E. L., Sullivan, R., Johnson, Z., & Engelmann, C. (2015, April). *Mind the gaps: Proficiencies & pitfalls in college student career development* [Poster presentation]. Western Psychological Association annual meeting, Las Vegas, NV.

Vogt, P. (2007). *Career wisdom for college students: Insights you won't get in class, on the Internet, or from your parents*. Ferguson Publishing Company.

Walters, R. (2020). *The complete interview guide: Helping you land the perfect role*. Robert Walters Group. www.robertwaltersgroup.com/content/dam/robert-walters/global/files/complete-interview-guide/Interview-guide-web.pdf

Washington, T. (2000). *Resume power: Selling yourself on paper*. Mount Vernon Press.

Yate, M. J. (1992). *Cover letters that knock 'em dead*. Bob Adams.

Working

This chapter will debunk myths about working, including "my first job will determine the rest of my career" and "making more money will make me happier." Instead, we'll look at the facts and explore the actions to find success and satisfaction with work. If you're already working a job and questioning your next steps, Chapter 5 will help you assess your present circumstances, maximize your success, and consider possible changes if needed.

Myth 79

"My first job will determine the rest of my career."

Fact

No single action will determine the rest of your career. Career development is a dynamic, lifelong process that remains unfixed through its entirety. Every choice you make throughout that process has an impact and involves some risk, but there is always flexibility. You can always change your mind and explore new directions— in fact, most people do. The average American worker switches jobs every three years and at least twelve times throughout their lives (BLS, 2019). First jobs are particularly terrible predictors of future occupations, and your career path is likely to change in all sorts of ways—job titles, companies, even the entire industry you work in, are all likely to change. Talk to any mid-career worker and you will likely be shocked by how different their first job was from their current one.

Consider a first job for right now rather than forever. Remember that you are always free to make other choices and explore new directions as you learn more about yourself and the world of work. Use your first job as an opportunity to learn about your interests and skills in a job setting, how organizations work, and what makes workers successful. Accomplish these goals by talking with supervisors and coworkers about their experiences and request feedback about your performance. Important information about your career development can only be gained with direct experience (Campbell, 2013), so now is the time to accumulate that valuable understanding. As you learn more about yourself and the work world, you can make more informed decisions about subsequent job choices.

DOI: 10.4324/9780429261770-5

Action 79 – Life Events Timeline

Reinforce the notion that your first job is just one step of many in your overall career development journey. To do so, create a timeline of significant life events that have occurred in your life and impacted your career development to date. This exercise was adapted from the "My Life Events" exercise developed by career coach, Corinne Mills (2017). The exercise can be helpful whenever a current event feels overpowering, allowing you to see it in a broader context.

Refer to the example in Figure 5.1 to help you. In the blank diagram in Figure 5.2, plot key moments, events, and experiences in your life. Start from birth on the left-hand side until the current date. In the spaces provided on the "age" line, starting with "0" for birth, indicate the age you are now on the last line on the right, then indicate equal age increments in the lines in between. For example, if you're now 20, the age increments would be 0, 4, 8, 12, 16, and 20. Next, include your first job on the timeline by marking with a dot when in your life it takes place and write "first job" either above or below the line, depending on whether you view it as a positive experience or a negative experience. The height of the dot represents the extent to which the experience was positive or negative on a one to five scale, with one being "a little" and five being "completely." Continue adding dots and descriptors for additional entries, for a total of at least ten, and then connect the dots by plotting a line, as shown in the example. Additional example entries could include:

- early life experiences
- educational interests, experiences, and achievements
- paid and unpaid work
- favorable events, such as meaningful relationships or personal achievements
- challenging or traumatic events, such as relationship conflicts or health issues
- other significant events and experiences, such as travel, hobbies, and modeling by others

Figure 5.1 Example Timeline

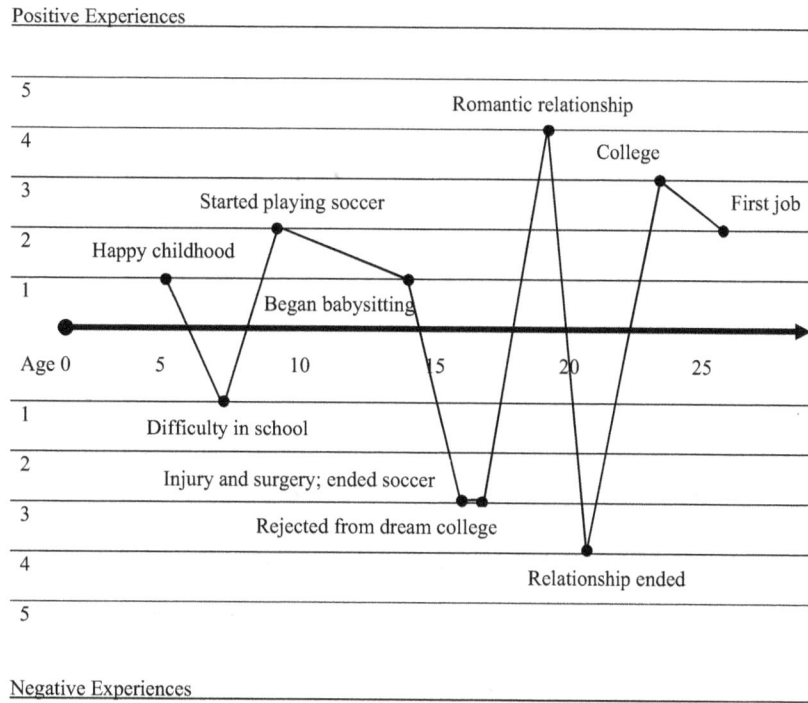

Positive Experiences

5				Romantic relationship	
4				College	
3		Started playing soccer			First job
2	Happy childhood				
1		Began babysitting			

Age 0   5   10   15   20   25

1	Difficulty in school	
2	Injury and surgery; ended soccer	
3	Rejected from dream college	
4	Relationship ended	
5		

Negative Experiences

Figure 5.2 Timeline

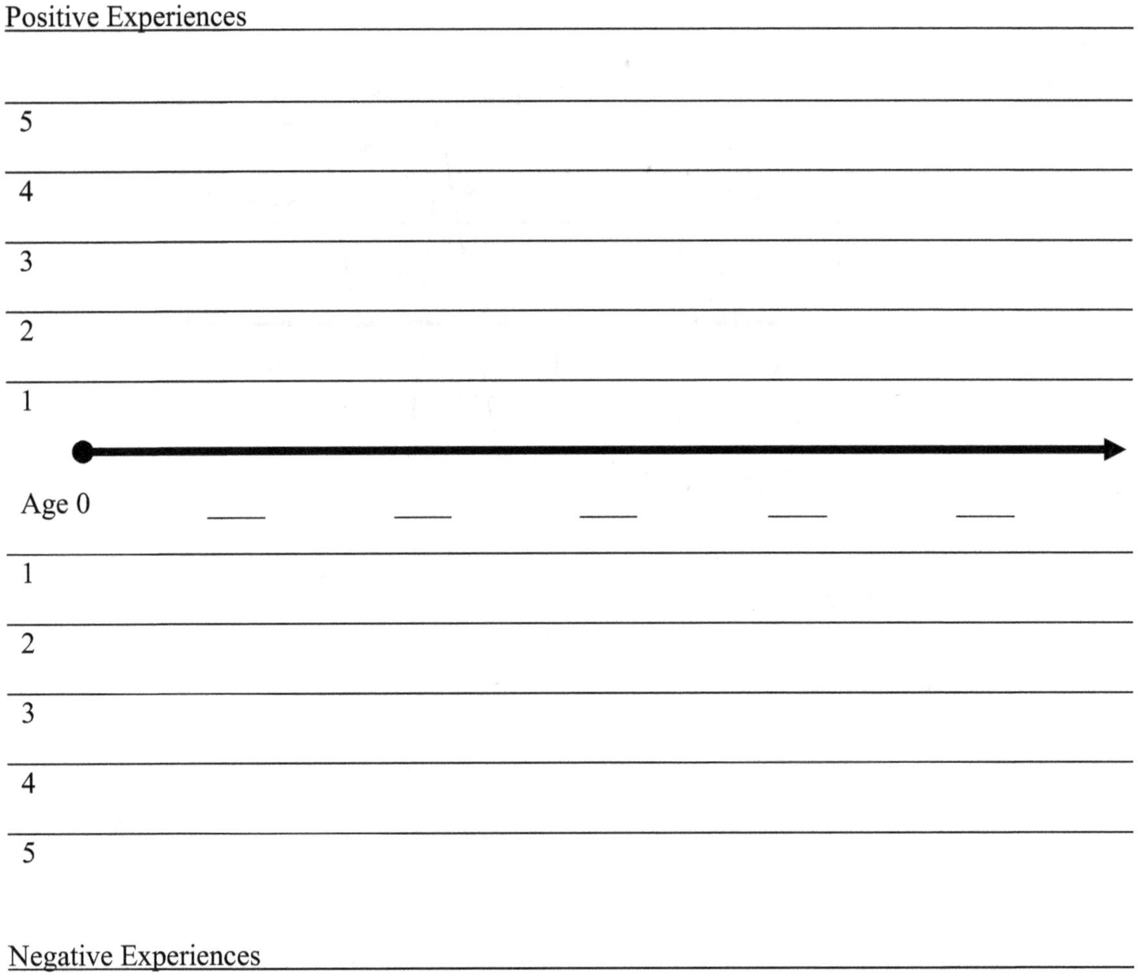

Positive Experiences _____

_____

5 _____

4 _____

3 _____

2 _____

1 _____

Age 0   ____   ____   ____   ____   ____

1 _____

2 _____

3 _____

4 _____

5 _____

Negative Experiences _____

Review the timeline of your career development to date and see what you notice about the overall course, happiest and most difficult times, and present day in context. Write down at least three key points that emerge for you from this exercise:

1. _____

_____

2. _____

_____

3. _____

_____

Myth 80

"I will get ahead by simply doing my job well."

Fact

While hard work and quality job performance are crucial aspects of career success, they usually will not prove to be enough on their own to make significant progress. You must not assume progress is based on your work results alone. Advancing your career takes displaying special skills that match the required skills needed for your desired position (Lore, 2011). Showcasing these skills within your current position and taking on responsibilities that show your aptitude for promotion can greatly improve your chances. It is also important that you display the right skills to the right people. Different employers may desire different skills, so pay close attention to the people around you. Whether they are looking for a team player or a go-getter, be sure to fulfill that specific role and show them why you are a great fit for your job.

Begin to develop a strong professional relationship with your coworkers and supervisors. In large corporations, you may not have the opportunity to interact with your boss directly, but these individuals can give you a great leg up in cultivating a successful career. They will often be the ones who look for and recommend the employees that they see fit for advancement. If you have a positive relationship with your superiors and show them your ability to fit into job positions, you are much more likely to be referred to the people in charge of promotions (Blair, 2009). You may even get a special choice or advanced notice of upcoming promotions, even further helping your chances.

Action 80 – Work Success

Start your job off on the right foot by focusing on job success from day one. Learn strategies for how to succeed at a new job and make plans to implement them (Raynier, 2019). Watch a video with new job success tips, available at bit.ly/careermythlinks. Then answer the following questions:

What is your learning style and how do you plan to use it at your job?

_____

_____

_____

_____

_____

What is your goal or "mini target" for this week at work?

_____

_____

_____

_____

_____

What else do you want to keep in mind for achieving job success?

_____

_____

_____

_____

_____

Myth 81

"I won't be accepted for being different."

Fact

You can't possibly have an issue that will keep all people from accepting you at work. Unfortunately, however, there is hardly a group you can name that does not face bias from some direction. You'll find people with prejudices everywhere, including at work (Campbell & Burrows, 2020). Bolles (2020) explains that workers are "human beings, glorious in their individuality and lamentable in their humanness, including their prejudices" (p. 223). These may interfere with gaining acceptance for aspects about you, but only from some people. No matter what issue you have, or think you have, you're never barred from acceptance from all others.

People vary greatly in their multicultural characteristics, including their values, beliefs, religion, socioeconomic status, sexual orientation, language, lifestyle, age differences, and countless other factors. Some of these factors are protected by law, and employers are not permitted to discriminate in their hiring process due to race, gender, ethnicity, age, national origin, and disability (Jordan & Marinaccio, 2017). Regrettably, discrimination still occurs and can sometimes be difficult to detect since it can be subtle, unconscious, or hidden.

You're not alone in fears about being accepted by others at your job. Many people worry about facing barriers at work, especially racial minorities and women (Jome & Phillips, 2013). Work can already be challenging, and rejection fears can make it dreadful. Anticipated discrimination restricts job activity since individuals tend to avoid situations where they expect to encounter judgment. Experiences of discrimination can also have a lasting impact on career decisions, limit career success, and harm mental and physical well-being (Fouad & Kantamneni, 2013). No one should have to face such difficulties and yet the occupational segregation in the United States' labor force is a clear indication that these challenges exist.

Nevertheless, all people—including you—have inherent worth and value as human beings, and your differences make you invaluable to the work world. People with diverse backgrounds and attributes bring different ideas, experiences, and perspectives to an organization. A diverse labor force working together provides a rich set of skills and creativity that make us all better and more capable. As our population grows increasingly diverse and globalized, we need to utilize every segment of the talent pool to achieve the best possible outcomes. By doing so, we can all learn from innovative ideas and novel approaches, provide more opportunities, and open broader networking channels and lucrative interactions across the globe (Sue & Sue, 2008). Consequently, efforts to recruit and retain a diverse and inclusive workplace are not only the kind and loving approach, but also advantageous for everyone's success and well-being.

Action 81 – Appreciating Differences

Reflect on the importance of diversity and inclusion for yourself and others at your job. Consider your concerns and those of others, as well as your role in promoting an atmosphere of acceptance for all. Answer the following questions:

What makes me different from others? What are my concerns about how others will treat me?

_____

_____

_____

_____

_____

What are possible differences in others that I'll encounter at work that I'm unfamiliar or might be uncomfortable with?

_____

_____

_____

_____

_____

What can I do to support myself regarding my concerns about being accepted by others at work?

_____

_____

_____

_____

_____

What can I do to support others with their concerns about being accepted by others at work?

_____

_____

_____

_____

_____

Myth 82

"It's not supposed to be fun—that's why it's called work!"

Fact

Every job offers unique ways to find fun and fulfillment. It's not an employer's duty to make a position entertaining and pleasant; even individuals who genuinely love their occupation can identify aspects of the job that are less than ideal. Nevertheless, remember that you're compensated in numerous ways for your work in the form of job experience, salary, and employee benefits. Your work is an area where you can extend beyond your own needs and serve those around you, which is often rewarding and enjoyable in itself (Dik & Duffy, 2012). You can still experience deep satisfaction at work, particularly if you have a job that is stimulating, challenging, and engaging.

Typically, however, we tend to focus much more on what's wrong than on what's right in our lives. For example, you're more likely to remember points of criticism rather than praise during an employee review. This is due to something called the negativity bias, or our tendency to focus on negative experiences over positive ones of equal intensity (Colman, 2015). Evolutionarily speaking, the negativity bias aids our survival, as focusing on potential problems and dangers help keep us alive. It's a good thing our ancestors developed the negativity bias—they learned to ignore the pretty butterfly floating in their direction to attend more closely to the rockslide also crossing their path! Unfortunately, this same survival mechanism now leads us to emphasize threats to our sense of selves in the same way. Rather than keeping us alive, it often leaves us pessimistic and dissatisfied with what appear to be overwhelmingly negative circumstances, when in reality our positive and negative experiences are more balanced.

Increase your job satisfaction by resisting the negativity bias through gratitude. Gratitude is an easy way to embrace the good in our work through consciously recognizing and acknowledging the positive things about our jobs. When we focus on the good things we have and express appreciation for them, we can radically reframe our experience toward enjoyment and fulfillment (Neff & Germer, 2018). A job won't be enjoyable all the time but engaging in regular appreciation for even little positive aspects can make it far more pleasant.

Action 82 – Gratitude List

Remind yourself of the positive aspects of your job by keeping a gratitude list. I love using a gratitude app on my smartphone because it sends me reminder prompts so I can easily record my responses. A link to a list of gratitude apps is available at bit.ly/careermythlinks. You can also keep it simple by jotting them down with pen and paper. For maximum benefit, develop a habit of regularly writing down your responses. Boost effectiveness by periodically reviewing your old responses to recall the many aspects of your life that inspire gratitude.

List something about your job that you're grateful for here to get you started:

_____

_____

_____

_____

_____

Myth 83

"My job will always be a source of happiness."

Fact

We learned in the previous myth that your work can be a source of fulfillment, but that doesn't mean it will be a constant source of happiness. Job satisfaction is not a given, and there will probably be times in your life when your work is rather a source of frustration or boredom. Starting with the aspiration for your workplace to be a constant source of joy and fulfillment leads to disappointment in job positions (Lent & Brown, 2013). There are things outside of your control that may happen in the workplace, such as being passed up for promotion or struggling to collaborate with a specific coworker. Knowing that unhappiness will be at least a part of your professional experience, it's important to adjust your expectations to reflect that reality. Be on the lookout for facets of your job that do bring you joy, and when you encounter a season of unhappiness, recognize it as a normal and common part of life (Burnett & Evans, 2016).

When you experience unhappiness in your job, it's essential that you identify other healthy sources of joy to tap into. Working in a position that causes you to be unhappy can be incredibly draining and necessitates engagement in activities that fulfill you in meaningful ways outside of work (Miller, 2010). How you go about obtaining this renewal will vary depending on your personal interests and personality. For example, if you are more extraverted, you might find happiness in setting aside a couple nights a week to spend time with a large group of friends. Those who are introverted might plan a weekly date with a close friend. In addition to activities with other people, you may also find refreshment through personal hobbies, indulging in your favorite pastimes when you aren't at work—plan a trip to go rock climbing, start a blog, or find the coffee shop with the best latte in town. For general inspiration on how to recognize and increase your levels of happiness in all areas of life, check out some of my favorite podcasts on the subject: *The Art of Happiness* by social scientist Arthur Brooks (2018), and *Ten Percent Happier* by former news anchor Dan Harris (2016).

Action 83 – Sources of Happiness

Explore sources of happiness in your life to strengthen positive feelings and increase engagement in the activities that promote them. Try out an activity termed the "good time journal," adapted from Burnett and Evans' (2016) book, *Designing Your Life.* The purpose of this activity is to keep a log of daily activities when you were engaged, meaning that you were excited, focused, and/or having a good time. Over the next three days, make a list of activities that produce these positive feelings. Include a brief note of what you did (e.g., "ran three miles" or "fixed the kitchen sink"), and then rate your level of engagement according to the scale in Table 5.1.

Table 5.1 Engagement Scale

1	2	3	4	5
Low Engagement		Moderate Engagement		High Engagement

Activity   Rating

_____

_____

_____

_____

_____

_____

_____

_____

_____

_____

_____

_____

_____

_____

_____

_____

_____

_____

After the three days, return to your list and reflect on your happy times. Summarize what you learned about sources of happiness from this exercise:

_____

_____

_____

_____

_____

_____

_____

_____

Myth 84

"I don't have time for self-care."

Fact

Self-care doesn't require a big time commitment, and it's crucial for career and life satisfaction. Hopefully, the last few myths have reminded you that your work is one of many important ingredients in creating a fulfilling life. In addition to what we learned in the previous myth about recognizing and cultivating happiness in all areas of life, we also need to engage in self-care to keep thriving. Life gets busy when you're working, and it can be hard to fit in extra healthy activities, but taking a few minutes every day for self-care is vital. When we don't prioritize our self-care, everything suffers, including our work enjoyment (Lent & Brown, 2013).

Self-care is the simple act of taking care of yourself (Beck, 2011). Far more than one-time celebratory treats or rewards, self-care is a continual undertaking of listening to your body and mind's unique needs and addressing them in the moment. Self-care doesn't require a lot of time, energy, money, or resources—simply awareness and a few minutes to engage in something healthy and effective. By regularly engaging in self-care, you can reduce your stress level and increase feelings of satisfaction and well-being (Neff & Germer, 2018).

Maslow's Hierarchy of Needs, as seen in Figure 5.3, can be helpful when considering self-care activities. Psychologist Abraham Maslow (1968) suggested that people are motivated to fulfill basic needs before moving on to more advanced ones, which he ordered in a specific hierarchy. People start at the bottom of the pyramid and move up as needs are satisfied. Whenever a lower-level need arises, people move down the pyramid until that need is satisfied once again. Movement is continual and requires frequent checks to determine current needs. According to Maslow, the ultimate goal of all people is self-actualization, a state of fulfillment where people can develop to the full extent of their capabilities. Using this hierarchy, we can ask ourselves what we might need at any given moment to guide what self-care activity we choose.

Figure 5.3 Hierarchy of Needs

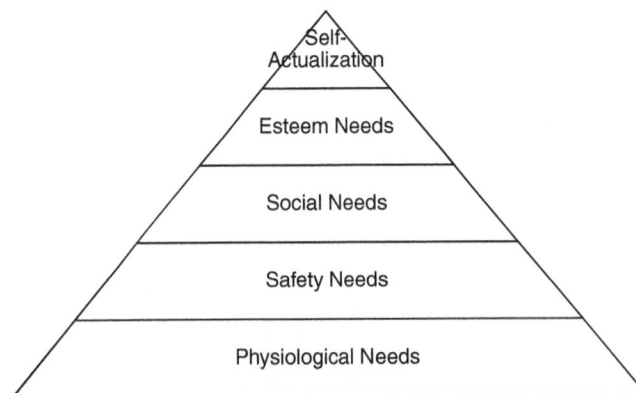

Maslow's Hierarchy begins with basic physiological needs, which include necessities for survival such as food, water, breathing, and sleep. When needs arise at this level, self-care might include pausing to take a drink of water, having a snack, or a brief nap. You might notice that your breathing is fast and shallow when stressed, necessitating some slow, deep breaths.

As we move up to the second level of the hierarchy, we find safety needs; these involve feeling secure and protected from harm. Self-care at this level would involve providing yourself with appropriate reassurance and security. Examples include offering reassuring self-statements such as, "you're okay" and "you're safe." A relaxing environment free from disruption can also be rejuvenating—shut off your phone, escape to a hot shower or bath, or step outside for a while. You might close your eyes or retire to a dark room to ground yourself when overwhelmed by outside racket.

Next, social needs represent the necessity of feeling loved and belonging with others. Self-care at this level could mean reaching out. For instance, you might call a family member, talk to the person in front of you in the grocery checkout, play with your pet, ask someone for help, or offer yourself compliments by being your own best friend.

Esteem needs include feeling appreciated and respected, and recognizing our own self-worth. Self-care at this level involves boosting self-assurance and reminders of strengths and achievements. Starting a compliments file of nice things people say about you can be helpful. Engaging in rewarding activities such as hobbies can also offer a confidence boost. My favorite (albeit slightly embarrassing) self-care activity is celebrating a success by doing an "I'm awesome" dance, much akin to the celebratory dances football players do in the end zone after scoring a touchdown. Even reminders of doing this gives me a chuckle!

Action 84 – Self-Care Activities

Brainstorm your own self-care activities. For added inspiration, start by watching a video about self-care (How to Adult, 2017), available at bit.ly/careermythlinks. Also consider Maslow's Hierarchy of Needs, including physiological, safety, social, and esteem needs. Note that your self-care activities should be unique to your needs. What's restorative for one person may not be for someone else, so it's essential that you have a list of activities that work for you. Make a list of at least 15 self-care activities below.

What self-care activities are effective for taking care of you?

1. _____
2. _____
3. _____
4. _____
5. _____
6. _____
7. _____
8. _____
9. _____
10. _____
11. _____
12. _____
13. _____
14. _____
15. _____

Myth 85

"Job burnout means you're weak and can't handle stress."

Fact

Burnout is an occupational hazard and can strike anyone, especially those who sustain high levels of stress. As previous myths elucidated, a key feature of thriving in your work is maintaining overall wellness by intentionally increasing happiness and self-care. Included in that is awareness of job burnout and efforts to prevent it from happening to you.

Job burnout is a condition of chronic stress and discouragement characterized by feelings of misery and dread. It has a profoundly negative impact on physical and mental health and can interfere with all areas of life, including your sense of accomplishment and identity (Toppinen-Tanner et al., 2005). According to researchers Maslach et al. (1996), the symptoms of burnout are threefold: 1) emotional exhaustion and feeling overextended by job demands; 2) depersonalization, characterized by callousness and disconnection from oneself and sense of purpose; and 3) reduced personal accomplishment through feeling incompetent and powerless to meet job demands. Burnout appears to have a variety of causes related to the worker, the job environment, and the fit between the two, but the most important factor appears to be awareness and responsiveness to burnout triggers (Lent & Brown, 2013). As such, prevention and early detection of job stressors are key.

Remain on the lookout for signs of lingering stress in your job and take steps to manage it. Burnout may ultimately require a career switch, but isn't an automatic sign that you need to change jobs—it's a sign that something needs to change to prevent the burnout from continuing. Consider the different factors involved in burnout to effectively identify strategies for all of them: 1) yourself, 2) the job environment, and 3) the fit between the two. Changes can occur in all these areas. For example, you might change yourself by focusing on stress reduction strategies, self-care, time management, and boundary setting. Consider modifying your current job environment by altering your physical workspace, such as switching to a standing desk or taking walk breaks. You might instead talk with your supervisor about adjusting job duties or expectations. After all other options are tried, you then might reconsider the fit between yourself and your job and pursue a career change.

Action 85 – Preventing Job Burnout

Plan to handle job burnout by learning more about the warning signs and ways to address it by reading the job burnout article by the Mayo Clinic (2021), available at bit.ly/careermythlinks. Then answer the following questions:

What signs of burnout will you look for in yourself?

_____

_____

_____

_____

_____

What strategies will you use to prevent burnout? Consider strategies for yourself, your job environment, and the fit between you and your job in your answer. Include at least ten burnout prevention strategies overall.

1. _____

2. _____

3. _____

4. _____

5. _____

6. _____

7. _____

8. _____

9. _____

10. _____

Myth 86

"I can't have a career and a family—I must choose one or the other."

Fact

You certainly can have a career and a family, and there are plenty of strong examples of working parents who live out this truth. But while it's feasible to have both, it is by no means easy. If you place a high level of importance on both work and family, it will require significant effort including planning, communication, flexibility, and being a part of a solid community to make it happen. Saying, "yes" to every demand placed on you at work and every parental responsibility is an impossibility, but even though we're limited by time and energy, it's possible to prioritize responsibilities in a way that honors your role as a family member and as an employee.

The false dichotomy between having a family and a career is engrained in most western cultures, particularly for women. This black-and-white way of thinking suggests that there is only one way to have a career and one way to have a family, when, in reality, individual's experiences of work and family are incredibly diverse (Campbell et al., 2015). Many parents take time off work to devote themselves to raising their children and many ultimately return to school and earn a degree. Couples sometimes can coordinate their work schedules to allow for optimum family time while both pursue their career goals. You might consider examining your own thoughts around this topic, identifying any rigid ways of thinking, and then challenging those thoughts with plausible alternatives. Additionally, when researching companies in a job search, be sure to find a professional community that is willing to respect and support your priorities (Groysberg & Abrahams, 2014).

Action 86 – Work–Life Balance

Learn more about multiple life roles and how to balance them. Mind Tools (2021), an online resource for personal and professional development, offers a useful Life Career Rainbow worksheet to help you do so, available at bit.ly/careermythlinks. Read the article and complete the pie chart exercises and reflection questions as instructed. Include your answers below.

Current Roles Pie Chart: In Figure 5.4, indicate the proportion of time you currently spend on each of the following eight life roles: child, student, leisurite, citizen, worker, parent, spouse, homemaker.

Figure 5.4 Current Roles Pie Chart

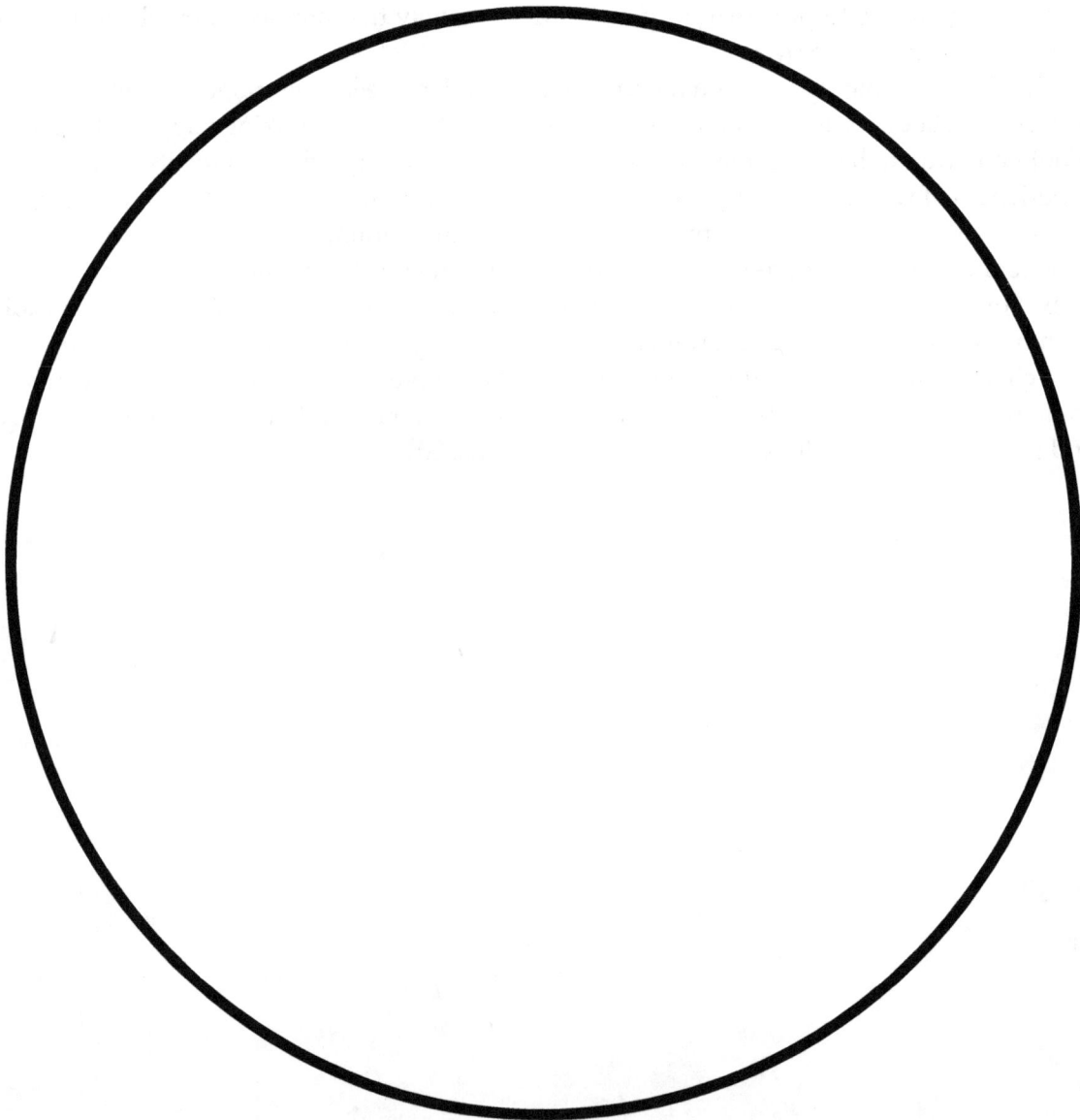

Current Ideal Roles Pie Chart: In Figure 5.5, depict an ideal scenario, indicating the proportion of time you currently would like to spend on each of the eight life roles.

Figure 5.5 Current Ideal Roles Pie Chart

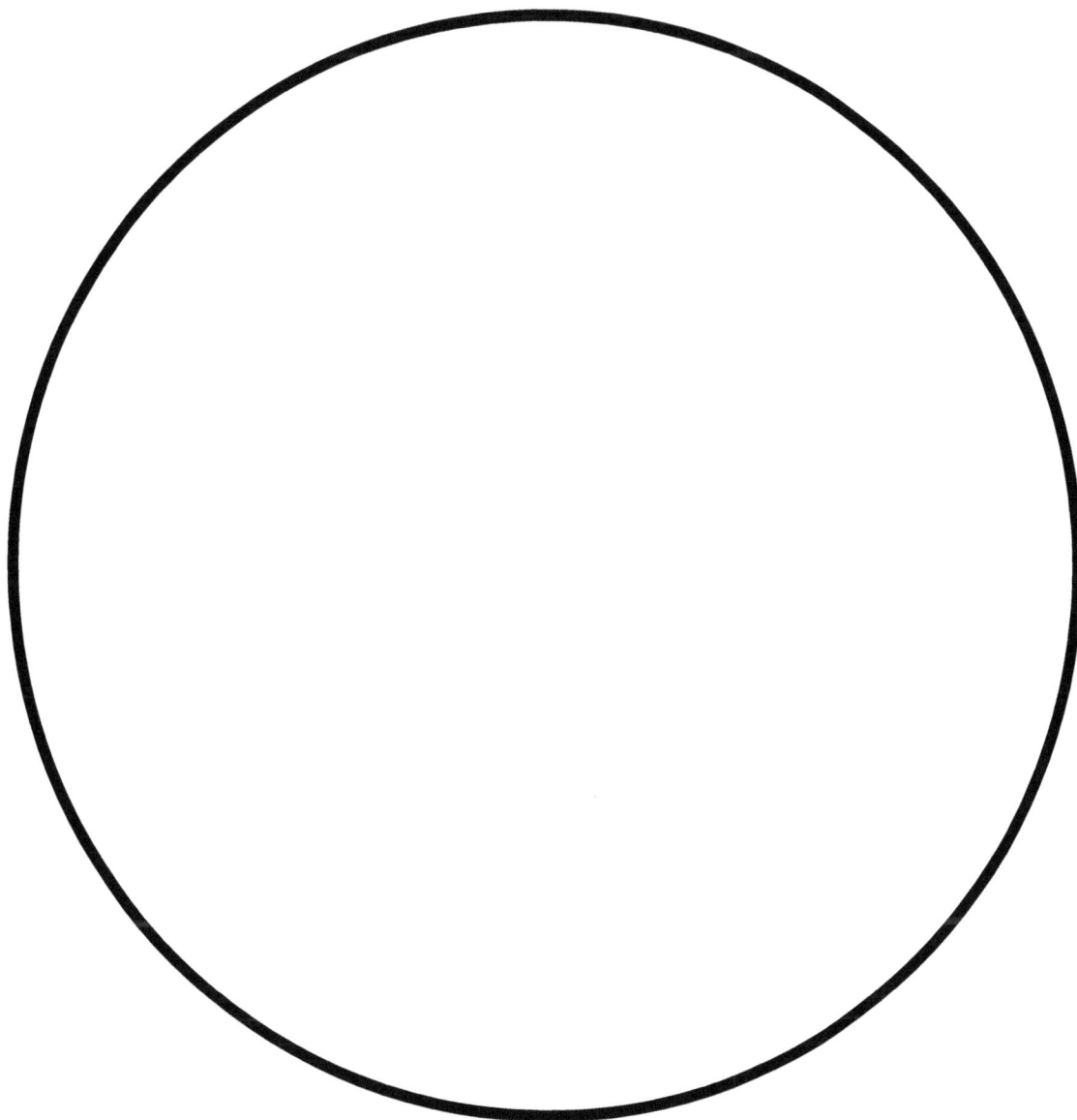

Five-Year Ideal Roles Pie Chart: In Figure 5.6, indicate an ideal scenario five years from now, showing the proportion of time you would like to spend on each of the eight life roles.

Figure 5.6 Five-Year Ideal Roles Pie Chart

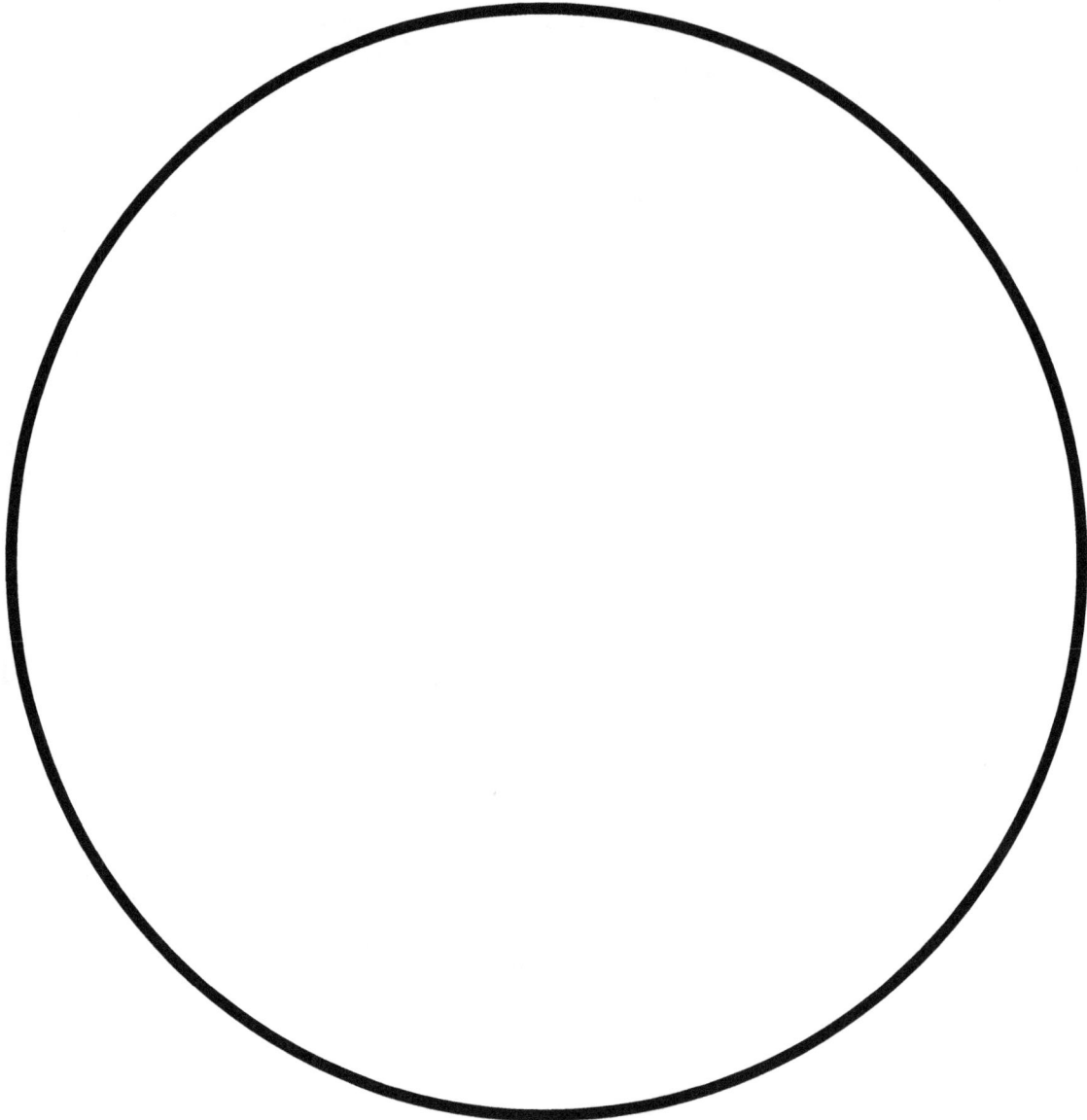

Compare your current pie chart from Step 1 to your ideal pie charts in Steps 2 and 3. What is preventing you from achieving your ideal work–life balance?

_____

_____

_____

_____

_____

What strategies will enable you to overcome the barriers you identified in Step 4 and achieve your idea work–life balance? Name at least five strategies.

1. _____

2. _____

3. _____

4. _____

5. _____

Myth 87

"I can't make a career change once I've committed to something."

Fact

You must be willing to change. There is no point in your career where you arrive at your destination and stay there forever. In career development, as in all areas of life, change is inevitable—our only choice is how we respond to it. By focusing on the career development process and understanding who you are, you can maintain a sense of progress throughout your journey rather than restarting each time you change jobs. It's better to prepare yourself for change and use it to your advantage than fight against it.

Prepare yourself for shifts by understanding their likelihood. Gone are the days when workers found a job and stayed with it until they retired. Americans spend an average of less than three years in any given job and most people have at least twelve throughout their lives (BLS, 2021). Many workers change jobs by choice, but it's also become a necessity with the decrease in job "lifespan." Currently, 36% of jobs last less than a year (Bolles, 2020). Whether you leave a job by choice or necessity, a career path today usually involves moving from organization to organization to fulfill a variety of different roles.

Even in cases where you can choose to stay in the same role, the world of work continues to evolve and jobs change (Bobek et al., 2013). With increased flux and change in the workplace, office culture and coworker relationships constantly shift. For instance, as you age, you might find that all your coworkers are mostly older than you and then gradually shift to younger than you, revealing stark generational differences. Hearing "back in my day…" stories from older coworkers, you'll likely find yourself soon enough sharing your own such tales with younger coworkers. Technology and innovation as well as global competition also shift job expectations. As a result, the nature and requirements of the job change along with increased skill expectations. A worker accustomed to communicating locally by phone a decade ago may now be expected to communicate internationally by email using language translation software, for example.

In any case, career development is a dynamic process. We learned about the career development process in Chapter 2 in the context of career decision making. It's important to revisit the process now that you're settled into the world of work to consider your next steps. The steps involved in career development remain the same throughout your lifespan but, as you'll discover in later myths, they're applied differently for those anticipating work than those already working.

As depicted in Figure 5.7, career development involves a three-step process: 1) learning about yourself, 2) understanding relevant aspects of the world of work, and 3) finding a synergistic fit between the two. Now that you're in a career, we have valuable information to gather about who you are in relation to the world of work. Contrary to first-time job-hunters making predictions, we now have real data about how you are in a work context that we can use to continually enhance your career fit. In this way, the career development process is increasingly enriched by prior knowledge and experience.

Figure 5.7 Career Development Process

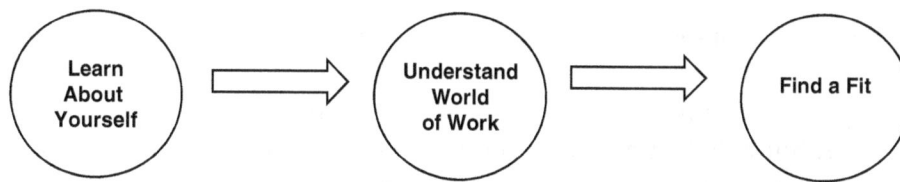

Understandably, as you begin to consider your career future and ways you may or may not fit with your current job, concerns may arise about the possibility of making a career switch. Such a change may be warranted at this point in your career development but that doesn't necessarily require switching careers. Numerous options for change are available, including a job switch, seeking out the same job with a new company, requesting a transfer or pursuing advancement within the same company, reinvigorating your current position with new goals, or simply rediscovering that you already match well with your current job, to name a few. Before you can consider what fit is best for you, take an honest account of yourself in relation to your current job, which can equip you with needed information to make an informed choice. Learning about yourself in the context of work requires a willingness to consider the pros and cons of the fit with your current position. Rest assured that if after gathering and considering all the facts you determine a job change is the best course of action, many of your skills will transfer to other jobs (NACE, 2011).

Action 87 – Career Imagining

It's time to revisit the career development process and learn about yourself in relation to your current job. This way, we can evaluate fit and consider your next steps in your career development process. We'll use a variety of strategies in the coming myths to elicit specific information but let's begin with a general visualization exercise. Visualizations can be helpful in bringing information that may be hidden or unexpressed into our conscious awareness (Mills, 2017).

To do so, follow the audio meditation about career imagining from Two Minute Tidbits (2019), available at bit.ly/careermythlinks, and then answer the following questions about what emerged.

In what ways was your imagining similar to your current job?

_____

_____

_____

_____

_____

In what ways was it different from your current job?

_____

_____

_____

_____

_____

What insights about yourself and your fit with your current job emerged from this exercise?

_____

_____

_____

_____

_____

Myth 88

"As I grow, my personality changes."

Fact

Personality remains surprisingly stable over time. When reassessing yourself in relation to your job, it may be tempting to believe our characteristic pattern of being has fundamentally shifted, but that's unlikely to be the case. As you grow, personality traits become increasingly stable (Roberts & DelVecchio, 2000), meaning that with age, you don't become someone else—you become more of the person you already are.

If our characteristics remain stable, why should we reassess them? The main reason for doing so is that we're interested in learning more about you in the informed context of your job. Doing so requires a reassessment and reconsideration of your personality with the job in mind. In addition, more information about you may come to light now that you have real-world experience. No longer are we working in the realm of the hypothetical or what you believe you *might* be like; we now have comprehensive data about what you're *actually* like in personal and professional settings.

As we learned in Chapter 2, learning about yourself involves five criteria: 1) personality, 2) abilities, 3) likes and dislikes, 4) mission and values, and 5) supplemental factors. You can remember these five criteria using the acronym, PALMS, as shown in Figure 5.8. For detailed information about your PALMS criteria, see Myth 3. Several assessments were presented in Chapter 2 for assessing and reflecting on your PALMS criteria for the purposes of choosing a career to pursue. Now that you're working in an existing job, these same assessments are effective for reassessing your PALMS criteria, so consider revisiting Myths 4 through 14 to utilize those strategies. In the following myths and activities, several new strategies will be introduced for reassessing your PALMS criteria, as well as guided questions for reflection specifically aimed at reconsidering your fit with your current job. Since you can use a variety of strategies to gather information about your PALMS, these activities are intended to offer new methods to add to your repertoire.

Figure 5.8 PALMS

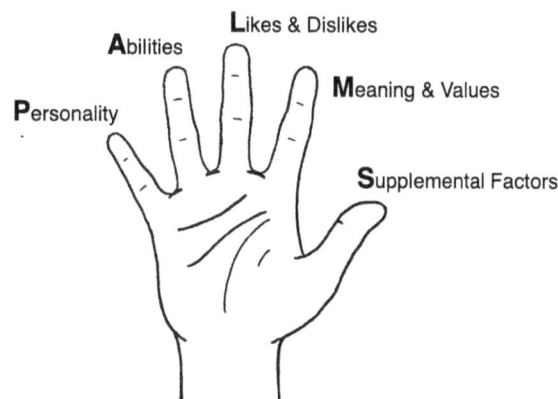

Action 88 – Personality Reassessment

We begin the PALMS criteria by reassessing your personality. Here's a strategy for identifying your personality adapted from career counseling professor, Dr. Mark Savickas (2015):

Identify three role models in your life. These are people, other than your parents, who you admired or considered your heroes. They can be historical or public figures, people you know personally, fantasy characters you made up in your mind, or characters in books or media. If you need some inspiration for admirable personality traits, browse a list of positive traits, available at bit.ly/careermythlinks. For each of your role models, answer the questions below.

Role Model #1 (name): _____

In what ways are you similar to this role model?

_____

_____

_____

_____

_____

In what ways are you different from this role model?

_____

_____

_____

_____

_____

Role Model #2 (name): _____

In what ways are you similar to this role model?

_____

_____

_____

_____

_____

In what ways are you different from this role model?

_____

_____

_____

_____

_____

Role Model #3 (name): _____

In what ways are you similar to this role model?

_____

_____

_____

_____

In what ways are you different from this role model?

_____

_____

_____

_____

_____

Myth 89

"I'll always be the same person."

Fact

While it's false to assume that our characteristics change drastically over time, it's equally false to assume we don't change at all. It's somewhere in the middle; balanced beliefs best represent our enduring tendencies and flexibility to adapt. As we continue to assess our PALMS criteria by focusing on personality, remain open to some possibility of change in your personality characteristics. It's also valuable to remember that although some of your PALMS characteristics such as personality are expected to remain stable over time, other areas are not, such as likes and dislikes (Roberts & DelVecchio, 2000). While an enthusiastic personality may continue to be so, the eagerness may be directed toward different interests; an avid runner may over time become an avid collector of tropical fish. Furthermore, while some areas tend to remain stable for most people, they may still change for you. It is unlikely but still possible your personality has shifted, as it will for a small portion of the population. If that's the case, we want to recognize it and accommodate the new information.

Knowing how our characteristics change is useful for our career development. Recall that the PALMS criteria represent the vital aspects of ourselves that predict career satisfaction and success. When we find a career that matches our PALMS criteria, we're more likely to experience success and satisfaction in our work lives. This positive relationship is strengthened when we're consciously aware of how good a fit our job is for us (Holland, 1997). Thus, if we want to experience ongoing career success and satisfaction, we want to remain in tune with who we are and how it fits with what we do.

Action 89 – Personality Reconsideration

Reflect on your personality and your responses from the previous myth action regarding your heroes and the personality traits you may share. Look closely at your responses and note personality characteristics you described about yourself. Consider your positive personality traits in relation to your current job by answering the following questions.

In what ways is my current position a good fit for my personality?

_____

_____

_____

_____

_____

In what ways is my current position not a good fit for my personality?

_____

_____

_____

_____

_____

What would need to change in my work life to better align with my personality?

_____

_____

_____

_____

_____

Myth 90

"I'll grow most in the areas of my greatest weaknesses."

Fact

As you progress in your career, you'll actually grow the most in your areas of greatest strength. As we continue to reassess our PALMS criteria, we next focus on A, which stands for our abilities, or strengths. While we might like to believe that our weaknesses convert to strengths over time, this is uncommon. With effort, our weaknesses can and should improve, but they're unlikely to surpass our strengths.

As a contributing member of the workforce, it's fascinating to look back and identify the developmental trajectory of our abilities. We might take great pride in the gains made in our areas of weakness, but it's unlikely our skill level went from "bad" to "good." More modest shifts are likely, such as from "bad" to "not as bad," or to "no longer a problem," if we're lucky. For example, in the early days of my career, I struggled with time management. My classes and appointments always ran late, and I often resorted to sprinting across campus to make up time. While helpful for my running endurance, this weakness needed constant effort to change. Through effort, time management is now less of a problem for me, so much so that I haven't had to run to an appointment in years. But I'd still consider time management a weakness, just less so than it was before.

Strengths, alternatively, have tremendous potential for growth. We tend to rely on our natural abilities to accomplish tasks (Snow, 1996), which means our strengths benefit from habitual practice. Furthermore, we tend to like what we're good at and want to spend more effort cultivating and refining our strengths (Lubinski, 2000). Additionally, work offers an environment for previously unidentified strengths to emerge, which necessitates gaining experience in the work world for us to recognize them (Campbell, 2013). For instance, one of my career counseling clients discovered her strength in emergency response skills only after working at a domestic violence shelter. She hadn't encountered such traumas in her life, so her ability hadn't sufficiently expressed itself until her work offered the training and setting to practice. Once in that position, it became clear that she had a special gift for effectively and compassionately handling intense and complicated crises.

The developmental trajectory of abilities may not stop there; interestingly, we can also see strengths pass down through family generations (Metz & Jones, 2013). Biological relatives may pass down genetic characteristics that make certain strengths more likely. For example, thrill-seeking has a high genetic influence, meaning that biological family members are likely to show similarities in their ability to take risks. Social influence also plays a role in how families teach and encourage different abilities. Families who spend time playing sports together, for example, are likelier to cultivate and strengthen athletic abilities in their relatives. Given the genetic and social learning influences on abilities, it's common to see patterns of strengths within families.

Action 90 – Abilities Reassessment

Continuing with your PALMS criteria, learn about your pattern of career abilities by drawing a career family tree in Figure 5.9. This activity is adapted from the Family, Career, and Community Leaders of America (FCCLA, 2019), a national career education program. Fill in each box with information about the listed person. Add more boxes for more aunts, uncles, brothers, sisters, or other family members as needed. Include each person's most memorable career and the top two essential abilities for that career, including yourself. If you need some inspiration for abilities, browse the list available at bit.ly/careermythlinks. Circle any of the skills you listed for your family members that you also possess and answer the question below.

Figure 5.9 Career Family Tree

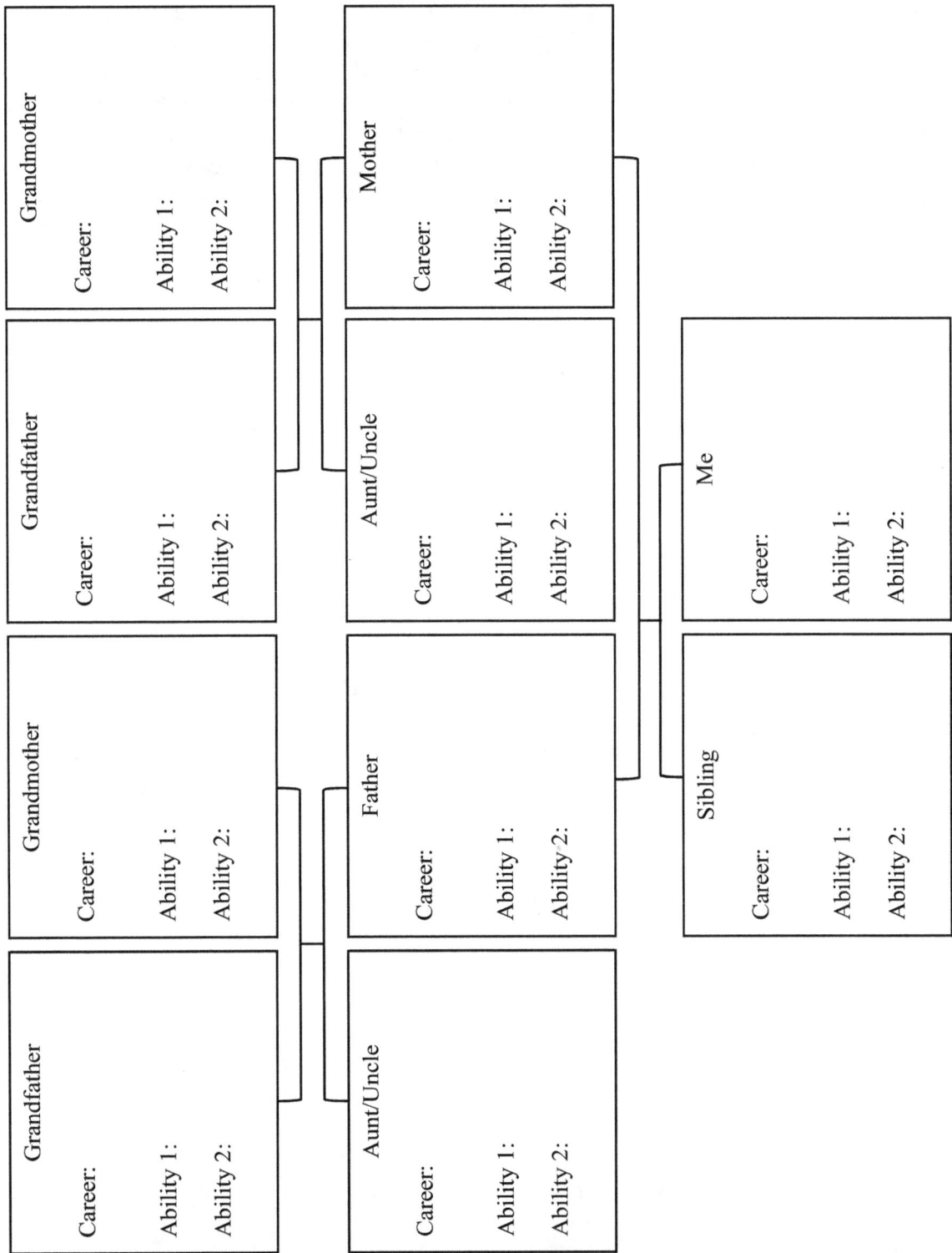

Grandfather	Grandmother		Grandfather	Grandmother
Career:	Career:		Career:	Career:
Ability 1:	Ability 1:		Ability 1:	Ability 1:
Ability 2:	Ability 2:		Ability 2:	Ability 2:

Aunt/Uncle	Father		Aunt/Uncle	Mother
Career:	Career:		Career:	Career:
Ability 1:	Ability 1:		Ability 1:	Ability 1:
Ability 2:	Ability 2:		Ability 2:	Ability 2:

Sibling	Me
Career:	Career:
Ability 1:	Ability 1:
Ability 2:	Ability 2:

What familial patterns do you see in your abilities?

_____

_____

_____

_____

_____

Myth 91

"The job market and economy are too tough to consider a change."

Fact

Choose your next career step based on fit rather than the current job market. Employment opportunities fluctuate constantly. Numerous external factors such as economic conditions, advances in technology, and labor supply can change the job market dramatically. For example, the dot-com boom in the late 1990s spurred a dramatic need for the Internet sector and related fields. When the demand exceeded the supply, opportunities for "good jobs" abounded, but this lasted only a few years before the boom collapsed and thousands of workers were without jobs (Miller, 2010). Since fluctuations with supply and demand can occur with any occupation, job outlook trends should be used cautiously and regarded as a nominal factor in your career choices. There will always be ups and downs that are difficult to predict, but even during the most difficult times, jobs always remain available (Bolles, 2020). Using your PALMS criteria to guide your next steps leads to higher success and satisfaction, even in a volatile job market.

More broadly, as we continue to assess our PALMS criteria by focusing on abilities, I often hear different versions of this myth emerge, like "now isn't the right time to consider a career change." The reason for the inopportune timing is usually contextual circumstances, such as the job market or family demands. While legitimate challenges may exist that would make a change more difficult at a particular time, don't let that stop you in your career development completely. Remember that you get to decide what to do next after learning about yourself and your current fit. After reviewing all the information, you might decide to change nothing at all or make only small changes. Learning about yourself and doing what you can to maintain fit during any circumstances is still beneficial, especially when faced with challenges that limit your options. By taking control of what you can change, you not only improve your likelihood of career success, you also improve your overall mood and well-being through self-empowerment (Campbell, 2020).

Action 91 – Abilities Reconsideration

Reflect on your abilities by considering your responses from the previous myth action regarding your career family tree and patterns of family skills and abilities. Consider your skills and abilities in relation to your current job by answering the following questions.

In what ways is my current position a good fit for my abilities?

_____

_____

_____

_____

_____

In what ways is my current position not a good fit for my abilities?

_____

_____

_____

_____

_____

What would need to change in my work life to better align with my abilities?

_____

_____

_____

_____

_____

Myth 92

"If I ignore career dissatisfaction, it'll eventually disappear."

Fact

As with burnout, ignoring dissatisfaction with your career won't make it go away. In fact, if anything, that will only allow it to grow. You might be able to shrug off the occasional negative thought, but if they're chronic, dissatisfaction will eventually overwhelm you. Ignoring and enduring job dissatisfaction for a long period of time can be extremely harmful in both the workplace and your personal life. Levels of job satisfaction are shown to be a better predictor of life expectancy than tobacco use, hereditary traits, and even a doctor's evaluation of physical functioning (Hansen, 2013). Since job satisfaction is such a powerful influence, it is vital to prioritize finding potential solutions if your job is making you unhappy.

Dissatisfaction is often related to something being uninteresting (Miller, 2010). To optimize your career satisfaction, continue to learn about yourself and the fit with your current position by focusing next on the L of PALMS, which stands for likes and dislikes. Your interests are extremely important for career satisfaction—for both yourself and the organization you work for. Employees who like their job have greater career satisfaction, which also improves the well-being of their coworkers and the organization (Hansen, 2013). Given that interests tend to shift over time and are such an important factor for all, frequent reassessment of your interests is extremely advantageous.

Action 92 – Likes and Dislikes Reassessment

Reassess your likes and dislikes by playing the Career Interests Game, available from the University of Missouri (2021) at bit.ly/careermythlinks. Follow the instructions to think about attending a party with six groups of people and choose the top three groups with whom you'd want to spend your time. Learn about the six groups by repeatedly clicking the hexagon icon at the bottom of the page.

What are your top three choices for which groups you would be most drawn to? List them in ranked order below, starting with the group you're most interested in, and explain why.

Interest Group #1: _____

Why are you drawn to this group?

_____

_____

_____

_____

_____

Interest Group #2: _____

Why are you drawn to this group?

_____

_____

_____

_____

_____

Interest Group #3: _____

Why are you drawn to this group?

_____

_____

_____

_____

_____

Myth 93

"Stay focused on the positive."

Fact

Not only will concentrating strictly on your positive thoughts and emotions not make anxious or negative thoughts go away, refusing to acknowledge fear, anger, or sadness usually amplifies those emotions and makes them even more distressing (Greenberger & Padesky, 2016). These negative emotions aren't pleasant, but they can be incredibly useful and informative. For example, you might experience intense anger when your boss gives you critical feedback on your work. Shoving that anger out of your mind will likely lead to a buildup of anger and increased frustration toward your boss. Alternatively, you could acknowledge the anger and explore some possible explanations for your response. With this increased self-knowledge, you'll experience your anger and recognize the source behind it instead of running from it. This process frees you from holding repressed anger and opens you up to the flexibility and maturity to grow through constructive criticism from others. Thus, facing emotions directly is actually the best way to move through and past them.

Furthermore, acknowledging both positive and negative work experiences is an essential component of addressing career fit. As we continue to assess your PALMS criteria by focusing on your likes and dislikes, it's important to allow yourself to consider the things you like and dislike about your current job. We all experience particularly bad days filled with many things we dislike that leave us questioning whether our job remains the right fit for us. Evolutionarily speaking, humans are designed to focus on what we dislike to help us stay vigilant to threats to our survival (Lyubomirsky, 2008). We dislike experiences that cause even mild pain and discomfort because their ongoing presence threatens our well-being. A consequence of this is hedonic adaptation, in which our brains quickly acclimate to positive experiences and stop noticing their presence to allow our brains to stay focused on negative experiences.

Hedonic adaptation causes us to focus on the negative aspects of work but trying to force yourself to focus on the positive isn't the answer. Allow your brain to continue its job of monitoring negative experiences for your survival while bringing back into your awareness the positive experiences that are overlooked. By allowing ourselves to explore the positive *and* negative reactions to our work, we enable our brain to take advantage of the information contained in both types of experiences. This is a great motivator, reminding us why we still like our jobs and helping us have gratitude for the positive outlet it provides in our lives. If needed, it can even help us identify needed changes to realign our career fit.

Action 93 – Likes and Dislikes Reconsideration

Reflect on your interests by considering your responses from the previous myth action of the Career Interests Game. Consider your likes and dislikes in relation to your current job by answering the following questions.

In what ways is my current position a good fit for my interests?

_____

_____

_____

_____

_____

In what ways is my current position not a good fit for my interests?

_____

_____

_____

_____

_____

What would need to change in my work life to better align with my interests?

_____

_____

_____

_____

_____

Myth 94

"My work should be my passion."

Fact

Your job can be one of your passions but be careful with how you define "passion." Passion is ordinarily defined as an object of deep desire or devotion (Merriam-Webster, 2021), which on the surface would appear to be a lovely way to view your career. As we continue to assess our PALMS by focusing on the next criterion of meaning and values, it seems understandable that you would want to feel devoted to a career that helped you live out your values.

While that's true, we don't want our careers to be our only source of passion or the only place we find meaning in our lives. That's too much pressure to put on one life role and can result in an unhealthy relationship with work (Brooks, 2020). We want to be enthusiastic about our work but stop short of being fanatical. In fact, researchers studied those who identified work as a passion and discovered they could be separated into one of two different categories. One of the categories was the "harmonious passion" group, who experienced positive mood and good concentration when working but also felt fine outside of work. The other group, in contrast, was the "obsessive passion" group, who experienced negative mood and poor concentration when working and felt unhappy outside of work (Vallerand et al., 2003). Valuing work is good but can turn bad when done too intensely.

Obsession leads to additional problems of job idolization and workaholism. Job idolization refers to viewing work as being of ultimate importance over any other life role, to the point that other responsibilities are neglected or abandoned (Dik & Duffy, 2012). Similarly, workaholism is an obsession to work to the point of addiction and results in low self-esteem, dysfunctional relationships, and a host of other life problems. Not only does it lessen satisfaction with work, it interferes with all areas of life.

The take-home message is that our work should be meaningful to us, and that we benefit from valuing what we do, but not to the point of obsession. Unlike other PALMS criteria that benefit from maximizing fit, the criterion of meaning and values needs to be moderated in the context of other life roles. Check yourself to see if you place enough value on work to be meaningful but not so much that it becomes your whole world. Other areas of life such as your family, friends, home, and hobbies can also be great outlets for passionate pursuit and living out your values (Super et al., 1996).

Action 94 – Meaning and Values Reassessment

Reassess your meaning and values using the Work Importance Locator, adapted from the United States Department of Labor Employment and Training Administration (O*NET, 2000). Links to all the materials and instructions are available at bit.ly/careermythlinks. Begin by reading and following the instructions.

Gather the needed materials listed for the activity including the Work Value Cards, Work Value Card Sorting Sheet, and Work Importance Locator Score Report from the link provided.

Copy below your work value scores from Step 4:

Your highest score: _____

Name of work value: _____

What does this work value mean? _____

_____

_____

_____

Your next highest score: _____

Name of work value: _____

What does this work value mean? _____

_____

_____

_____

Myth 95

"Making more money will make me happier."

Fact

After a certain point, more money doesn't bring more happiness. As we continue to assess our PALMS by focusing on the criterion of meaning and values, it's reasonable to focus on the value of money as a primary incentive for our work. Money is a big and necessary part of our lives and it's a hard-wired belief that we'd all be happier if we just had more of it (Brooks, 2021).

But would you be happier if you made more money? That depends on a couple of factors. First, it depends on how much money you make now. A decade ago, a United States poll found that people with higher incomes report being happier up to an annual income of $75,000, which is the equivalent to about $90,000 today (Kahneman & Deaton, 2010). Beyond that, more money wasn't related to higher emotional well-being. This showed that once a person alleviates the problems of poverty and has their basic needs comfortably met, more money didn't make them happier. For you, consider your current salary in light of your current needs (Wu, 2021). If you don't have enough to meet you and your family's needs, you might benefit from a career change that yields a higher salary. If your needs are already reasonably met, other factors also need to be considered.

Second, the question of money increasing your happiness depends on whether you value money over other work values (O*NET, 2000). The answer to this question lies in your results from the previous myth action from the Work Importance Locator. If one of your top two values was "Working Conditions," this value includes pay, as well as job security and good working conditions. For those individuals, pursuing a higher salary would likely increase happiness, since it fits with the meaning they place on their work. Recall that a career that satisfies your meaning and values increases your overall satisfaction, job performance, and organizational commitment (Rounds & Jin, 2013). Alternatively, if your top two values on the Work Importance Locator didn't include working conditions, then prioritizing higher pay might sacrifice other factors that you truly care about, such as needs for independence or supportive relationships, thereby reducing the fit between you and your career. Keep your eye primarily on what you care about; what matters most to you is unique to you.

Action 95 – Meaning and Values Reconsideration

Reflect on your meaning and values by considering your responses from the previous myth action of the Work Importance Locator. Consider your meaning and values in relation to your current job by answering the following questions.

In what ways is my current position a good fit for my meaning and values?

_____

_____

_____

_____

_____

In what ways is my current position not a good fit for my meaning and values?

_____

_____

_____

_____

What would need to change in my work life to better align with my meaning and values?

_____

_____

_____

_____

_____

Myth 96

"If I only had more time..."

Fact

Although all of us, myself included, have found ourselves wishing we had more time, we don't need it. The amount of time available to us is the same for every person, every day. We believe that if we could only manage our time better, we'd have more available to us. Perhaps you are a person who would benefit from improving your productivity; however, the term "time management" doesn't really make sense. Time passes at the same rate no matter how we approach it—whether we're wasting it or using it wisely. In this way, obsessing about managing time is like trying to control the weather: it's out of our control.

Focus instead on what is within your control. Instead of worrying about managing time, focus on managing yourself instead, given the restraint that time is finite. Determine your priorities, including taking care of yourself and attending to the areas of life that are most important to you, and then plan your available time accordingly. You won't be able to do it all, but with self-management you can spend the time on the areas you most care about (Burnett & Evans, 2016).

To effectively consider your priorities regarding your career development, it's important that you consider your career in the context of other areas of your life. This is represented in the S of PALMS, which stands for supplemental factors. Supplemental factors are a catch-all category of internal and external factors that influence career decision making. Review Myth 13 for an extended description of supplemental factors. Supplemental factors can include an extremely diverse range of life circumstances, such as relationships, life roles and lifestyle, and identity and culture. Supplemental factors change over time and it's vital that workers review them often (Hartung, 2013). For example, an early-career worker may find a time-intensive job that fits their PALMS criteria completely, until they have children. Work may still fit their first four PALMS criteria, but not the last one since their priorities have shifted and they want more time at home.

Action 96 – Supplemental Factors Reconsideration

Reconsider your current supplemental factors. Consider the factors presented in Myth 13, including relationships, life roles and lifestyle, and identity and culture, as well as any other factors that spontaneously occur to you. Answer the following questions:

What supplemental factors come to mind that impact my current work life?

_____

_____

_____

_____

_____

In what ways is my current position a good fit for my supplemental factors?

_____

_____

_____

_____

_____

In what ways is my current position not a good fit for my supplemental factors?

_____

_____

_____

_____

What would need to change for my work life and supplemental factors to better align?

_____

_____

_____

_____

_____

Myth 97

"I have to work up the ladder of success at all costs."

Fact

Working up the ladder of success is by no means a requirement in your career. It is perfectly acceptable to stay in your position if you feel content with it. As we move forward with everything we've learned about ourselves using the PALMS criteria, you'll be able to make the best choices for your career success, and that may be to choose to stay exactly where you are. Your definition of success is likely different than others' definitions; success is a subjective concept that is shaped by your PALMS criteria.

When people talk about success, they typically include happiness and fulfillment in some form (Wu, 2021), both of which can be by-products of engaging in work that fits your PALMS. A person can be skilled at making career advancements and can obtain increasingly prestigious titles year after year at a company that they are not particularly passionate about. Outwardly, this person might be showing mainstream signs of success with titles and awards, but if they aren't engaged with their work it's unlikely they'll experience the happiness and satisfaction that characterizes genuine success.

Since we know that success is incredibly subjective, it's helpful for you to identify and establish the various rungs that make up your personal ladder of success by knowing yourself through your PALMS criteria. Starting with a firm knowledge of who you are and what you need in a career can offer guidance when you are considering the pros and cons of career decisions (Miller, 2010).

Action 97 – PALMS Review

Now that you've collected information about discrete aspects of yourself, it's time to compile what you've learned about your PALMS. To do so, return to and review your responses for each of the following myths:

Myth 88 Action – Personality Reassessment
Myth 90 Action – Abilities Reassessment
Myth 92 Action – Likes and Dislikes Reassessment
Myth 94 Action – Meaning and Values Reassessment
Myth 96 Action – Supplemental Factors Reconsideration (first question)

Before you move to assessing the fit between you and your current job, focus first on developing a cohesive understanding of yourself. Consider your answer to the previous myths listed above by looking for similarities and differences across your responses. What patterns emerge? What seems inconsistent? For example, you identify that you have a unique ability for building relationships and hold relationships as a work value, but your interests may have shifted to tasks performed alone. Attempt to explain or reconcile these differences. Perhaps you prefer a balance of time working with others and working alone, or you like working around other people while performing independent tasks. If you can't reconcile them, try reevaluating. Perhaps this reveals that other people are more important to your career than you thought, for example. Note your conclusions by answering the questions below.

What patterns emerged from your responses? In your answer, summarize what you learned about yourself through your PALMS criteria.

_____

_____

_____

_____

_____

What inconsistencies did you discover between your responses? How do you make sense of these patterns and inconsistencies?

_____

_____

_____

_____

_____

What can you take from this information that might be helpful for you?

_____

_____

_____

_____

_____

Myth 98

"I'm either a success or a total failure."

Fact

Success is not confined to a single event; it is a process of changing and growing more into the person we hope to be. As you learn more about yourself in your career development process, it can be threatening to acknowledge unknown or disowned parts of yourself. You will certainly experience both success and failure in your professional life. Those that you consider successful in their field have experienced numerous failures throughout their journeys. Making a poor choice or failing in some way is rarely fatal and does not have the power to negatively define your entire future. In fact, failures can work to your benefit. Mistakes can be catalysts for growth that lead to higher levels of success, or even the teacher of lessons you would not have learned otherwise. In this way, they're not failures at all but rather feedback to help make adjustments (Greenberger & Padesky, 2015).

Be brave, honest, and compassionate with yourself as you engage in self-review. Now that you have a more cohesive understanding of yourself from the previous myth action, we return to the career development process of 1) learning about yourself, 2) understanding relevant aspects of the world of work, and 3) finding a synergistic fit between the two, as depicted in Figure 5.10. If you're already working, Step 2 is represented by your current job. With the information you gathered about yourself and considering your current job, it's now time to assess the level of fit between the two.

Figure 5.10 Career Development Process

Action 98 – Career Patterns Review

Assess for fit between yourself and your job by compiling what you've learned about how each of your PALMS criteria fit with your current position. To do so, return to and review your responses for each of the following myths:

Myth 87 Action – Career Imagining
Myth 89 Action – Personality Reconsideration
Myth 91 Action – Abilities Reconsideration
Myth 93 Action – Likes and Dislikes Reconsideration
Myth 95 Action – Meaning and Values Reconsideration
Myth 96 Action – Supplemental Factors Reconsideration

Note patterns and inconsistencies between your different responses; for instance, your job might be an excellent fit for your likes and dislikes, but not your personality. Summarize in your answers to the questions below what you notice about fit.

Overall, in what ways is my current position a good fit for me?

_____

_____

_____

_____

_____

In what ways is my current position not a good fit for me?

_____

_____

_____

_____

What would need to change for me and my current position to better align?

_____

_____

_____

_____

_____

Myth 99

"I must make a drastic career change."

Fact

Career changes don't necessarily need to be drastic to restore your work satisfaction. Sometimes small adjustments are all that are needed to realign fit between you and your job, including simply reminding yourself that the positive aspects continue to outweigh the negative ones (Lent & Brown, 2013). Confirmation of a good fit elicits gratitude and positive feelings that reinvigorate your work. If dissatisfaction and lack of fit endure, consideration may also highlight additional alterations that are needed.

In the previous myth activity, you determined your current level of fit between yourself and your job. As we continue to work through the career development process, we now focus on realigning and maximizing fit between you and your work. The next few myths present ways you can make changes, which can vary from slight alterations to a complete job shift, depending on need. For complete career shifts in which you want to consider an entirely new industry or career path, return to Chapter 2 for decision making. If instead you already know what career you want to pursue and require retraining or education to do so, return to Chapter 3 for education. If you'd like to stay in the same industry but want to change jobs, return to Chapter 4 for job hunting. For those who still love their current job and career industry, more modest shifts might be appropriate. These possibilities include reinvigorating your current job or seeking advancement.

We'll first look at reinvigorating work here and explore career advancement in the next myth. Reinvigorating work involves making changes to yourself and your job environment to better align the two (Lent & Brown, 2013). Remember that career satisfaction and success, and ultimately fit, rests on your PALMS criteria. Note also that there is a great deal of overlap between the PALMS criteria. For instance, personality and likes and dislikes are often interrelated, such that a more introverted personality style might also like less interpersonal interaction. When you discover a misfit with any of these criteria and your job, you can change yourself and/or your job environment to restore fit. With PALMS, consider what changes are possible and practical for each area of conflict. Utilize creative problem-solving and elicit help from your job supervisor and support network to identify solutions.

For example, when a career counseling client and I discovered that his career dissatisfaction was the result of a misfit between his personality and his job, we resolved it through a combination of self-change strategies and job shifts. He had a personality style of being spontaneous and unstructured, which was a misfit with his fixed work schedule. We addressed the lack of fit through self-change by developing better self-management skills and working on increased communication with coworkers about his needs. He also pursued job environment modifications by requesting a flexible work schedule and commission-based rather than hourly pay, allowing him to work at his own pace. Through these changes, my client realigned his fit with his job and increased his work satisfaction and performance. Both he and his boss were much happier with his work!

Action 99 – Reinvigorating Work

Reinvigorate your work to improve fit by discovering changes you can make to yourself and your job environment. Review your responses to the previous myth activity about your career patterns, specifically ways your current position is not a good fit for you and what would need to change. Brainstorm ways you could address these areas of conflict between you and your job. Consider self-changes as well as requests for job environment alterations, and list them below. If you need some inspiration for self-changes, common ones to boost job satisfaction are available at bit.ly/careermythlinks. For examples of job environment changes, a list of common job satisfaction-boosters to consider is also available at bit.ly/careermythlinks.

What self-changes could you make to help you and your current position to better align?

_____

_____

_____

_____

_____

What job environment alterations could you make or request to help you and your current position to better align?

_____

_____

_____

_____

_____

Myth 100

"I'll be given a promotion when I've earned one."

Fact

Don't passively rely on others to give you what you want, since people won't know your career aspirations unless you tell them. If you seek career advancement, it's up to you to put yourself out there. As we continue to focus on realigning and maximizing fit between you and your work, career advancement can be an effective way to shift toward a better alignment. Career advancement, also called a promotion, is any upward progression in your job rank or position. It typically involves more challenging work duties and higher pay and can involve staying within the same company or switching to a new one (McKay, 2018).

Once you determine career advancement is your next career development aspiration, you need to learn how to pursue advancement. While hard work and quality job performance are crucial aspects of climbing to your next promotion, they usually don't prove to be enough on their own to make significant progress. You must not assume progress is based on your work results alone. To advance in your career, it may take displaying special skills that match the required skills needed for your desired position (Bolles, 2020). Showcasing these skills within your current position and taking on responsibilities that show your aptitude for promotion can greatly improve your chances. It's also important that you display the right skills to the right people (McKay, 2018). Different employers may desire different skills, so pay close attention to who oversees advancement. Whether they're looking for a team player or a go-getter, be sure to fulfill that specific role and show them why you are the best choice for the job.

Action 100 – Promotion

Learn about how to pursue career advancement by watching a video and answering questions about what you learned. Watch an instructional video about promotion from Dale Carnegie Training Australia (2017), available at bit.ly/careermythlinks.

What did you learn from this video?

_____

_____

_____

_____

_____

How will you implement what you learned?

_____

_____

_____

_____

_____

Myth 101

"The goal is the destination."

Fact

It's the journey, not the destination. One of the biggest mistakes people make is treating their career as a means to an end. Perceiving success as a far-off destination that you hope to reach through years of sacrifice leads to unhappiness (Brooks, 2021). Your life isn't a career ladder that you spend your life climbing to reach a singular point of success at the top: it's more like a jungle gym with multiple different paths, challenges to climb, and enjoyment to be had along the way.

When you view work as its own reward, happiness and success are always available to you. Your work won't provide joy and fulfillment every day, of course, but with continued commitment to your career development, you can maximize your success and satisfaction to the fullest.

The truth is that there isn't a destination—you're never done, have never learned it all. Career development is a lifelong process of understanding yourself and the ways you can serve others, and fulfilling those goals through many different roles (Super et al., 1996). You're always developing, beginning at birth and continuing throughout life. You've taken many steps already and you're always on the brink of your next step.

As we come to the end of this book, your career development story is still being written. By completing this workbook, you've demonstrated that you have the foundational knowledge and skills to be successful moving forward. Keep using the career development process and revisit chapters and exercises from this book whenever you need a reminder.

Thank you for bringing me along on your journey through this workbook. It's an honor to get to walk this process with you and I hope that you found this resource helpful. I wish you every success!

Action 101 – Final Reflections

One final time, note your reflections about your career development process. Consider revisiting previous myth actions to recall what you learned and leave notes here for yourself about reminders for the future by answering the questions below.

What have you learned from completing this workbook? What, if anything, has changed?

_____

_____

_____

_____

_____

What is your next step in your career development? What reminders do you want to give yourself for your career development future?

_____

_____

_____

_____

_____

References

Beck, J. S. (2011). *Cognitive therapy: Basics and beyond* (2nd ed.). Guilford Press.

Blair, G. R. (2009). *Everything counts: 52 remarkable ways to inspire excellence and drive results.* Wiley.

Bobek, B. L., Hanson, M. A., & Robbins, S. B. (2013). Counseling adults for career transitions. In S. Brown & R. Lent (Eds.), *Career development and counseling: Putting theory and research to work* (2nd ed., pp. 653–682). Wiley.

Bolles, R. N. (2020). *What color is your parachute? A practical manual for job-hunters and career-changers* (2020 ed.). Ten Speed Press.

Brooks, A. C. (2021, April 15). How to buy happiness. *The Atlantic.* www.theatlantic.com/family/archive/2021/04/money-income-buy-happiness/618601/

Brooks, A. C. (Host). (2018–present). *The art of happiness with Arthur Brooks* [Audio podcast]. The Ricochet Audio Network.

Bureau of Labor Statistics (BLS). (2021, August 31). *Number of jobs, labor market experience, and earnings growth: Results from a national longitudinal survey* [Press release]. www.bls.gov/news.release/pdf/nlsoy.pdf

Burnett, B., & Evans, D. (2016). *Designing your fife: How to build a well-lived, joyful life.* Knopf.

Campbell, E. L. (2013). Anticipating work & family: Experience, conflict, & planning in the transition to adulthood. *Dissertation Abstracts International: Section B. Sciences & Engineering, 73*(8).

Campbell, E. L. (2020). *Helping skills training for nonprofessional counselors: The LifeRAFT model—providing relief through actions, feelings, and thoughts.* Routledge. https://doi.org/10.4324/9780429031380

Campbell, E. L., & Burrows, M. A. (2020). LGBT college student career development: Goals and recommendations for faculty members. *International Journal of Innovative Teaching and Learning in Higher Education, 1*(2), 29–40. https://doi.org/10.4018/ijitlhe.2020040103

Campbell, E. L., Campbell, V. L., & Watkins, E. (2015). Construct validity of anticipated work-family conflict & barriers measures. *Journal of Career Development, 42*(5), 370–380. https://doi.org/10.1177/0894845315571413

Colman, A. M. (2015). *A dictionary of psychology* (4th ed.). Oxford University Press.

Dale Carnegie Training Australia. (2017, February 15). *How to ask for a promotion in the right way* [Video]. YouTube. www.youtube.com/watch?v=aqF9Wo3NEoc

Dik, B. J., & Duffy, R. D. (2012). *Make your job a calling: How the psychology of vocation can change your life at work.* Templeton Press.

Family, Career and Community Leaders of America (FCCLA). (2019). *Career family tree worksheet.* Career Connection. http://breitlinks.com/careers/career_pdfs/familytreews.pdf

Fouad, N. A., & Kantamneni, N. (2013). The role of race and ethnicity in career choice, development, and adjustment. In S. Brown & R. Lent (Eds.), *Career development and counseling: Putting theory and research to work* (2nd ed., pp. 215–243). Wiley.

Greenberger, D., & Padesky, C. A. (2016). *Mind over mood: Change how you feel by changing the way you think* (2nd ed.). The Guilford Press.

Groysberg, B., & Abrahams, R. (2014, March). Manage your work, manage your life. *Harvard Business Review.* https://hbr.org/2014/03/manage-your-work-manage-your-life

Hansen, J. C. (2013). Nature, importance, and assessment of interests. In S. D. Brown & R. W. Lent (Eds.), *Career development and counseling: Putting theory and research to work* (2nd ed., pp. 387–416). Wiley.

Harris, D. (Host). (2016–present). *Ten percent happier podcast with Dan Harris* [Audio podcast]. ABC News.

Hartung, P. J. (2013). The life-span, life-space theory of careers. In S. D. Brown & R. W. Lent (Eds.), *Career development and counseling: Putting theory and research to work* (2nd ed., pp. 83–113). Wiley.

Holland, J. L. (1997). *Making vocational choices: A theory of vocational personalities and work environments* (3rd ed.). Psychological Assessment Resources.

How to Adult. (2017, May 3). *A self-care action plan* [Video]. YouTube. www.youtube.com/watch?v=w0iVTQS8ftg

Jome, L. M., & Phillips, S. D. (2013). Interventions to aid job finding and choice implementation. In S. D. Brown & R. W. Lent (Eds.), *Career development and counseling: Putting theory and research to work* (2nd ed., pp. 595–620). Wiley.

Jordan, L. A., & Marinaccio, J. N. (Eds.). (2017). *Facilitating career development: Student manual* (4th ed.). National Career Development Association.

Kahneman, D., & Deaton, A. (2010). High income improves evaluation of life but not emotional well-being. *Proceedings of the National Academy of Sciences, 107*(38), 16489–16493. https://doi.org/10.1073/pnas.1011492107

Lent, R. W., & Brown, S. D. (2013). Promoting work satisfaction and performance. In S. D. Brown & R. W. Lent (Eds.), *Career development and counseling: Putting theory and research to work* (2nd ed., pp. 621–651). Wiley.

Lore, N. (2011). *The Pathfinder: How to choose or change your career for a lifetime of satisfaction and success.* Touchstone.

Lubinski, D. (2000). Scientific and social significance of assessing individual differences: "Sinking shafts at a few critical points". *Annual Review of Psychology, 51,* 405–444. https://doi.org/10.1146/annurev.psych.51.1.405

Lyubomirsky, S. (2008). *The how of happiness: A new approach to getting the life you want.* Penguin Books.

Maslach, C., Jackson, S. E., & Leiter, M. P. (1996). *Maslach Burnout Inventory manual* (3rd ed.). CPP, Inc.

Maslow, A. H. (1968). *Toward a psychology of being* (2nd ed.). Harper and Row.

Mayo Clinic Staff. (2021, June 5). *Job burnout: How to spot it and take action.* Mayo Clinic. www.mayoclinic.org/healthy-lifestyle/adult-health/in-depth/burnout/art-20046642

McKay, D. R. (2018, September 26). *A simple guide to career advancement.* The Balance Careers. www.thebalancecareers.com/advancement-525653

Merriam-Webster. (2021). Passion. *Merriam-Webster dictionary.* www.merriam-webster.com/dictionary/passion

Metz, A. J., & Jones, J. E. (2013). Ability and aptitude assessment in career counseling. In S. D. Brown & R.W. Lent (Eds.), *Career development and counseling: Putting theory and research to work* (2nd ed., pp. 449–476). Wiley.

Miller, D. (2010). *48 days to the work you love* (2nd ed.). B&H Publishing.

Mills, C. (2017). *Career coach: How to plan your career and land your perfect job* (2nd ed.). Crimson Publishing.

Mind Tools. (2021). *The life career rainbow.* www.mindtools.com/pages/article/newCDV_95.htm

National Association of Colleges and Employers (NACE). (2019). *Starting salary by academic major*. www.cpp.edu/career/nace_salary_survey_winter_2019.pdf

Neff, K., & Germer, C. (2018). *The mindful self-compassion workbook: A proven way to accept yourself, build inner strength, and thrive*. The Guilford Press.

O*NET. (2000). *Work Importance Locator* [Measurement instrument]. www.onetcenter.org/dl_tools/WIL_zips/WIL-Instr-deskv.pdf

Raynier, L. (2019, April 17). *How to succeed in life (in your new job)* [Video]. YouTube. www.youtube.com/watch?v=1CuYbSNbEio

Roberts, B. W., & DelVecchio, W. F. (2000). The rank-order consistency of personality traits from childhood to old age: A quantitative review of longitudinal studies. *Psychological Bulletin, 126*(1), 3–25. https://doi.org/10.1037/0033-2909.126.1.3

Rounds, J., & Jin, J. (2013). Nature, importance, and assessment of needs and values. In S. Brown & R. Lent (Eds.), *Career development and counseling: Putting theory and research to work* (2nd ed., pp. 417–447). Wiley.

Savickas, M. L. (2015). *Life-design counseling manual*. http://vocopher.com/LifeDesign/LifeDesign.pdf

Snow, R. E. (1996). Aptitude development and education. *Psychology, Public Policy, and Law, 2*(3–4), 536–560. https://doi.org/10.1037/1076-8971.2.3-4.536

Sue, D. W., & Sue, D. (2008). *Counseling the culturally diverse: Theory and practice* (5th ed.). John Wiley & Sons, Inc.

Super, D. E., Savickas, M. L., & Super, C. M. (1996). The life-span, life-space approach to careers. In D. Brown & L. Brooks (Eds.), *Career choice and development: Applying contemporary theories to practice* (3rd ed., pp. 121–178). Jossey-Bass.

Toppinen-Tanner, S., Ojajarvi, A., Vaananen, A, Kalimo, R., & Jappinen, P. (2005). Burnout as a predictor of medically certified sick-leave absences and their diagnosed causes. *Behavioral Medicine, 31*(1), 18–27. https://doi.org/10.3200/bmed.31.1

Two Minute Tidbits. (2019). *Narrative forest* [Audio file]. https://soundcloud.com/user-843947917/narrative-forest

University of Missouri. (2021). *Career interests game* [Measurement instrument]. https://career.missouri.edu/career-interest-game/

Vallerand, R. J., Blanchard, C., Mageau, G. A., Koestner, R., Ratelle, C., Leonard, M., Gagne, M., & Marsolais, J. (2003). Les passions de l'ame: On obsessive and harmonious passion. *Journal of Personality and Social Psychology, 85*(4), 756–767. https://doi.org/10.1037/0022-3514.85.4.756

Wu, J. (Host). (2021, June 11). Does money buy happiness? (No. 347) [Audio podcast episode]. In *Savvy Psychologist*. Quick and Dirty Tips.

Index

For Product Safety Concerns and Information please contact our EU
representative GPSR@taylorandfrancis.com
Taylor & Francis Verlag GmbH, Kaufingerstraße 24, 80331 München, Germany

www.ingramcontent.com/pod-product-compliance
Lightning Source LLC
Chambersburg PA
CBHW081736270326
41932CB00020B/3290

9 780367 195120